Taking It to the Hill

**The Complete Guide
to Appearing before
Parliamentary
Committees**

David McInnes

University of
Ottawa Press

The University of Ottawa Press gratefully acknowledges the
support extended to its publishing programme by the Canada
Council for the Arts and the University of Ottawa.

We also acknowledge with gratitude the support of the
Government of Canada through its Book Publishing
Industry Development Program for our publishing activities.

Library and Archives Canada Cataloguing in Publication

McInnes, David, 1961-
   Taking it to the Hill : the complete guide to appearing before
parliamentary committees / David McInnes. -- 2nd ed.

(Governance series)
Includes bibliographical references and index.
ISBN-13: 978-0-7766-0607-1   ISBN-10: 0-7766-0607-7

1. Canada. Parliament--Committees. 2. Parliamentary practice--Canada.
I. Title. II. Series: Governance series (Ottawa, Ont.)

JL148.5.M33 2005   328.71'0765   C2005-905670-3

Cover design: Kevin Matthews
Interior design and typesetting: Laura Brady
Developmental editor: Jeremy Dias
Copy editor: Julie Murray
Proof reader: Dallas Harrison

ISSN 1487-3052

Published by the University of Ottawa Press, 2005
542 King Edward Avenue, Ottawa, Ontario K1N 6N5
press@uottawa.ca / www.uopress.uottawa.ca

Printed and bound in Canada

As my work proceeded on this second edition, it became quickly evident that lobbying starts in the home. Along with my three children, we were all jostling to use our home computer; thank you Kesha, Kerry and Griffin for allowing me to complete my writing task. Now, the computer is yours. To Julie, I am grateful for your unwavering support over the course of this entire book project; I dedicate this book to you.

David McInnes
June 27, 2005

ACKNOWLEDGEMENTS

The author gratefully thanks the many people who helped to make the first and second editions of this book a reality, including a number of current and former members of Parliament, senators, political staff, departmental officials, House of Commons and Senate committee staff, parliamentary research officers, interest group and association representatives, reporters, academics, public affairs advisors, and neighbours in the Park who interact so frequently with those on the Hill.

Collectively, your advice, assistance, and input enabled this book to be written, and refreshed. Your enthusiasm for the subject at hand was motivating. Your suggestions contributed immensely to this book.

Finally, a special thank you to all those at the University of Ottawa Press who made this project a reality.

TABLE OF CONTENTS

"From here to there and there to here, funny things are everywhere." With those words, I concluded the first edition of this book published in 1999. And, while apologizing to Dr. Seuss for borrowing the phrase from his book *One fish, two fish, red fish, blue fish*, it nevertheless offered a not-too-subtle metaphor for politics. *Politics are everywhere* on Parliament Hill. A statement of the obvious, for sure, but it allowed the point to be made that despite all the rules and conventions governing the role and operations of parliamentary committees, politics lurks in every nook and cranny – behind every act and decision.

For witnesses who appear before the standing committees of the House of Commons and the Senate, knowing parliamentary procedure, understanding personalities and being good communicators are critical. Keeping an eye on how things can go astray is essential.

Much has happened since the original publication: changes in parliament, a minority government, changes in leaders, parties and plans, a push to address the democratic deficit, a drive to make politicians more accountable, public servants more forthcoming and governing more transparent. All this has presented opportunities for committees to gain additional profile, exploit some new authorities and do what they do best: publicly engage the issues and draw out what witnesses are thinking.

On the other hand, much remains the same. Our system of government is evolutionary, not revolutionary. Many processes and procedures remain firmly established. The pursuit of effective communication never ceases; party politics and partisanship are ever-present; the debate about the ultimate contribution of standing committees is perpetual.

Since its publication, I have been struck by the number of people who have approached me to suggest their best tip on appearing before a committee, or a noteworthy committee hearing that illuminated some issue or experience. With so many people spending so much time before so many committees, it's clear that there is so much material to draw from.

The second edition of *Taking It to the Hill* incorporates key developments and retains what is relevant. It is not an academic assessment on whether recent changes to parliamentary committees have been positive or negative. As a witness, the changes are just a reality to deal with. Whatever form of government—minority or majority—appearing before a parliamentary committee is an essential part of our country's policy process.

This book remains the complete guide to appearing before (and surviving) parliamentary committees.

Appearing before a parliamentary committee is like meeting your in-laws for the first time. Now is not the time to make a bad impression. What you say, how you say it and even how you look counts.

By targeting parliamentary committees, this guide assists you to make a positive impression and achieve your public policy objectives on the Hill.

The many standing committees of the House of Commons and Senate are where the parliamentary debate truly involves Canadians. This is the place where backbenchers have virtually an exclusive domain: the standing committees of the House of the Commons. To be complete, Senate committees are included as well. (See appendix for a list of standing committees.)

Taking your message to Parliament Hill (and getting heard) means, increasingly, getting in front of one or more of them.

Thousands do. About 5,000 witnesses a year parade through a parliamentary committee.[1]

THE TASK AT HAND

"Witnesses, without distinction, are quite simply at the mercy of the committee."

– Diane Davidson, General Legal Counsel for the House of Commons
before the Standing Joint Committee for the Scrutiny of Regulations,
November 17, 1994

If you appear before such a parliamentary committee, do you know the rules? Is your presentation up to standard? Do you really know why you are going before the committee? Are you really at its mercy?

Your challenge is knowing the agenda, the players, the process and rules of engagement. That is only the beginning. This only positions you for the real task at hand: using this knowledge to deliver your story, to get it understood and, hopefully, to influence decisions in Ottawa.

You've got competition. Combined, MPs and Senators are exposed to a couple of thousand of hours of committee testimony each year![2] Your 60 minutes have to stand out. Here is where wins and losses are possible.

CAN COMMITTEES HELP ME OR HURT ME?

> "We made a report to the House of Commons, which was considered by the finance minister in his budget, and probably 90% of what we had in our report was in that budget last year."
>
> – Jim Peterson (L), Chair, Standing Committee on Finance,
> November 30, 1995

Parliamentary committees can advance your cause depending, of course, on what side of the issue you are on. Consider this sampling of committee activity:

- *Tax:* Responding to disgruntled retailers, the Standing Senate Committee on Banking, Trade and Commerce prompted the government to amend the controversial harmonized sales tax legislation after hearing from nearly 200 groups in Atlantic Canada. Said the Retail Council of Canada: "The committee has saved the retail industry $100 million in adjustment costs."[3]

- *Environment:* After the House of Commons Standing Committee on Environment and Sustainable Development tabled 75 amendments to the Endangered Species Act, a *Globe and Mail* business columnist declared that its chair "managed to adopt just about every change pushed by environmentalists and ignore every proposal put forward by people with an interest in human economic development."[4]

- *Human Rights:* The House Standing Committee on Justice recommended to the justice minister to drop electronic monitoring of high-risk offenders. The minister agreed. The issue, and the decision, pitted civil libertarians and defence lawyers against police officers and victims' groups.[5]

- *Natural Resources:* The Standing Committee on Fisheries was unanimous in their pursuit of senior scientists at the Department of Fisheries—those who were seen to be responsible for destroying the Atlantic fishery. Members were making national headlines to get officials fired.[6]

- *Social Issues:* Cutting a last-minute deal with the Senate Standing Committee on Social Affairs, Science and Technology, the government pulled a child support bill from the brink of being lost by agreeing to amend its guidelines after one "renegade" senator lined up vigorous opposition from groups wanting changes to shared custody rules.[7]

- *Human Resources:* A recommendation from the House Standing Committee on Citizenship and Immigration urged that certain technology jobs be exempted from the usual rigorous application process to attract these high-skilled workers. The work of this committee expedited getting foreign high-tech workers to Canada to fill vacant technology jobs here.[8]

"Committees play a far more important role than the public perceives."
– The Rt. Hon. Joe Clark (PC), former Prime Minister,
Interview, July 23, 1997

Committees can be thought-provoking. They can take the initiative and get out ahead on issues.[9] Bills are tackled here. It can be ground zero for policy development. They open the book on departmental spending. They scrutinize public appointee resumés. They can do it all while being televised coast to coast.

Committees make an impact. But they are certainly not always successful in triggering action—a frustration for members, too.

"This is the fourth time in 12 years that we have seen such a crisis.
By the time crisis number five hits, it may be too late to act."
– Tom Wappel (L), Chair, Standing Committee on Fisheries and Oceans,
in "Saving the sockeye", *The National Post*, March 24, 2005[10]

As members, themselves, well know, committees can end up doing a lot of wheel-spinning.

> "I hesitate to say, in some instances, as make-work projects for committees that did not have enough legislation or Estimates to look at, we started having special studies on areas in which certain senators had a particular interest. Unfortunately, that has occurred in some instances and it has become the *raison d'être* of a number of our committees and subcommittees ..."
>
> – Senator John Bryden (L), Standing Committee on Rules,
> Procedures and the Rights of Parliament, May 30, 2001

Like a ball of string, policy making is a tangled affair. The work of standing committees is essentially visible but much of what goes on in Ottawa is buried within the many circles of power and influence, from departmental activity to cabinet committees. Within this swirl of policy activity, parliamentary committees are highly active and are generally busier: they're wading through more meetings, pegging more hours of testimony, and coping with more bills.[11]

This guide's objective is not to critique the committees' contribution to the policy process. It is devoted to unravelling the complex world of parliamentary committees. This guide assists witnesses in enhancing their performance before one of the formal access points to government.

FOCUS: Standing Committees

> "Our goal is clear. To make Parliament what it is supposed to be—a national forum in which citizens of Canada from every region of our vast land make their views known and their interests heard."
>
> – Rt. Hon. Paul Martin, Prime Minister, *Reply to the Speech
> from the Throne*, February 3, 2004

Much has been done in recent years to empower parliamentarians and boost the role of committees. In part, its about giving you—the witness— a more meaningful opportunity to get heard.

This guide focuses on parliamentary standing committees because they formally connect Canadians to the policy process. There are other contact points, such as being engaged in departmental consultations where many ideas germinate. However, so much is done in committee.

> "Maybe because of my being new to this place, I see the House of Commons as very complex and very rigid and a place… that can be quite manipulated by the people who know the rules very well… [The standing committee] is a place where we could sit down at a more relaxed pace and really do what has to be done and debate things without the formality that exists in the House."
>
> – Mark Muise (PC), Standing Committee on Canadian Heritage,
> October 21, 1997

In fact, the House of Commons devotes only about eight hours of debate for bills.[12] Yet committees can spend many dozens of hours examining a bill, hearing from witnesses and considering amendments.

For most Canadians, committees are where the action is. But there should be no doubt left that committee is only one part of a much larger and convoluted policy-making process.

The bottom line as one company executive put it: "You've got to sow the seeds of an idea at the top, with cabinet, and at the same time fill out the solution with the bureaucracy and within committee."

ARE YOU READY TO TAKE THE PLUNGE?

> "In my opinion, there is no limitation in law constraining the House of Commons or a standing committee of the House of Commons in the exercise of their powers."
>
> – Rob Walsh, Law Clerk and Parliamentary Counsel, House of Commons,
> Standing Committee on Public Accounts, February 17, 2004

But are you truly ready to engage them head-on?

Appearing before a committee for the first time or as a seasoned witness, do you truly understand committees? Take this quick test:

Do You Know How They Work?

1. House standing committees must get consent from the House of Commons before undertaking any study or inquiry.
   TRUE or FALSE?

2. Standing committees receive bills for consideration only after second reading stage.
   TRUE or FALSE?

3. Witnesses must submit written submissions to committees in both of Canada's official languages.
   TRUE or FALSE?

4. Standing committees can enforce a summons issued to an individual in order to require that he or she will testify.
   TRUE or FALSE?

5. Live stream audio and visual feeds of committee hearings and witness testimonies are restricted to those who work on Parliament Hill.
   TRUE or FALSE?

6. Public servants appearing before committee are expected to explain and justify government policy decisions.
   TRUE or FALSE?

If you answered "true" to any of the above, then you may be ill-prepared. Each one of these statements is false (although the answers are not necessarily black or white).

Getting your message across is also essential to any appearance. Are you effective? Compare yourself against what others do based on a survey of those researchers who staff parliamentary committees.[13]

Are You Effective?

1. Are you putting politicians to sleep?
   4 out of 10 witnesses take too long to read their *opening remarks*.
2. Are you your own worst enemy?
   Nearly 1 in 3 witnesses sometimes contradict their own written submission during their oral testimony at committee.
3. Can your research be called into question?
   Nearly 80% of witnesses don't footnote their research, or only sometimes do so.
4. Does your written submission discourage busy politicians from reading your masterpiece?
   Nearly 90% of briefs rarely or occasionally include an *executive summary*.

It's up to you to make a positive impact with your remarks and submission. Doing well also requires a knack for handling the curves that can be thrown your way during the testimony.

COULD THIS REALLY HAPPEN TO YOU?

No matter how well prepared you may be, appearing before a parliamentary committee can be an unpredictable exercise. You are subject to the vagaries of a political forum. Be advised.

Expecting the Unexpected

"You must understand that a committee investigation is largely a political exercise, and not primarily an exercise in pure reason."

> – Advice for committee contract staff, in *So You're Going to Work for a Committee?, A Booklet for Contract Staff of the House of Commons Standing Committees*, 1989[14]

Each of these scenarios has actually happened:

1. Your president flies to Ottawa to appear before a committee only to have MPs get up and leave the room for a vote in the House.

2.   Your "perfect" opening statement is abruptly cut short by the chair. It's taking too long to read.

3.   You've urged members to consider a matter of great importance. The first question probes your political affiliation and your personal credibility.

4.   After a compelling testimony, a reporter picks up on a careless remark made privately to your staff. That becomes the next day's headline.

Appearing before a committee might not be a pleasant experience. Knowing how to cope with the tricky situations can make the visit more palatable.

WHAT THIS BOOK IS ABOUT

By taking the mystery out the parliamentary process and flagging some of the political pitfalls, this guide assists you to concentrate on the task at hand: how to get the most out of your committee visit. At the end of the day, it's about understanding process and delivering your message as effectively as possible so you can advance or defend your public policy interests.

CHAPTER OUTLINE

CHAPTER 1: THE PARLIAMENTARY BACKDROP (KNOWING THE CONTEXT)

Committees work in the shadow of a parliamentary system shaped by cabinet supremacy, party discipline and reform.

CHAPTER 2: TECHNIQUES (SEEING HOW IT IS DONE)

Scenarios and techniques demonstrate how witnesses can advance their interests on Parliament Hill.

CHAPTER 3: COMMITTEES 101 (KNOWING COMMITTEES)

The basics: committee types, mandates and authorities.

CHAPTER 4: PROCESS AND OPPORTUNITIES (KNOWING THE PROCESS)

Opportunities are presented when considering how committees intersect the legislative and policy process.

CHAPTER 5: THE COMMITTEE DYNAMIC: THE KEY PLAYERS (KNOWING THE PLAYERS)

Committees are all about the dynamic of key individuals on committees and some of those behind the scenes.

CHAPTER 6: "ON YOUR MARK…" (GETTING PREPARED)

Checklists and pointers get you ready to testify.

CHAPTER 7: THE HEARING (HANDLING THE COMMITTEE HEARING)

A committee performance requires a convincing testimony, parrying tough questions, dealing with the media and doing the necessary follow-up.

CHAPTER 8: FROM HERE TO THERE (FINAL THOUGHTS)

The conclusion wraps up and offers some thoughts about the future of parliamentary committees and implications for witnesses.

HOW TO USE THIS GUIDE

WHAT TO DO

This identifies specific action you should consider taking.

TIP

Read this tip for some special advice.

A POLITICAL VIEW!

This offers a political perspective about what can happen.

QUOTATIONS:

Unless otherwise indicated, quotations are taken directly from committee *Evidence*, or the verbatim transcript of parliamentary committees (as found on the House and Senate committees' websites). Quotations generally identify the name of the member, his or her political party affiliation, the committee in which the comment was made and the date of the statement. Note that, over time, some members have changed political parties (e.g., Belinda Stronach, Anne Cools, etc.), and new political parties have been formed (e.g., Reform, Conservative), but all quotations refer to the party affiliation at the time of the actual quote.

Political Party Abbreviations:

BQ	Bloc Québécois
CA	Canadian Alliance
CPC	Conservative Party of Canada
L	Liberal Party of Canada
NDP	New Democratic Party
PC	Progressive Conservative
R	Reform Party

Other Abbreviations:

Rt. Hon.	stands for "Right Honourable" and applies to prime ministers.
Hon.	stands for "Honourable" and precedes the names of ministers among others.
MP	member of Parliament (in reference to elected members).

Key Terms:

Chair	refers to the chairperson of the committee. It seems easier to use than "chairperson."
Committee	generally refers to a standing committee of either the House of Commons or the Senate, although this can include a standing committee's subcommittee, a legislative, joint or special committee.
Member	refers to MPs and senators who sit on these committees; it's preferable to always using "parliamentarians."

ENDNOTES

1. During only a portion of Jean Chrétien's tenure as prime minister, well over 24,000 Canadians pitched their views before House of Commons and Senate committees. This number includes standing, special, sub- and joint parliamentary committees as determined by the Committees and Legislative Services Directorate of the House of Commons and the Senate Committees and Parliamentary Associations Directorate during the 35th Parliament (1994 to 1997) and the 36th Parliament (September 1997 to April 1998). More recently, House of Commons committees heard from 3,719 witnesses over the course of one year. (Committees Directorate, House of Commons, *2003-2004 Annual Report on Committees Activities and Expenditures*, 1.) The Senate indicates that its committees hear (over a five-year period) on average over 1,200 witnesses annually. (Committees Directorate, The Senate of Canada, *Activities and Expenditures, Annual Report*, reference: table on Committee Operations.)

2. MPs were exposed to over 2,000 hours of committee testimony in 1996-97 (Committees and Legislative Services Directorate, House of Commons, *Activities and Expenditures, Annual Report* (September 1996-97), 6.) In 2003-2004, MPs held over 900 meetings taking up over 1,500 hours of time (*2003-2004 Annual Report on Committees Activities and Expenditures*, 5). Senators have spent over 770 hours in committee over a five-year average (*Activities and Expenditures, Annual Report*, Committees Directorate, The Senate of Canada; reference: table on Committee Operations).

3. April Lindgren, "Liberals Abandon Plan to Hide Tax," *The Ottawa Citizen*, March 12, 1997, A3.

4. Terence Corcoran, "Endangered Economy Acts," *The Globe and Mail*, March 15, 1997, B2.

5. Stephen Bindman, "Rock's High-Tech Shackles Dropped," *The Ottawa Citizen*, March 5, 1997, A1.

6. Stephen Thorne, "MPs Seek Firing of Bosses in Fish Stocks Fiasco," *The Toronto Star*, March 2, 1998, A1.

7 Anne McIlroy, "Child Support Bill [C-41] May Be Killed," *The Globe and Mail*, January 30, 1997, A1.

8. Amanda Lang, "Ottawa OKs Foreign Technology Hirings," *The Financial Post*, April 30, 1997, 10.

9. Commentators still point to Conservative maverick Don Blenkarn, a Mulroney-era Finance committee chair, who garnered respect for many unanimous and quality reports on complex issues. Independent-thinking is rewarded by the media. To this day, they love seeing the government squirm a bit because of the work of a committee chaired by a government member. Under the Chrétien government, the work of the environment committee, under the chairmanship of Liberal Charles Caccia, stirred up some attention for its critical work on the environment

department's enforcement activity. See Hugh Winsor, "MP Holds Grits' Feet to Environmental Fire," *The Globe and Mail*, May 27, 1998, A3.

10. Tom Wappel authored the article "Saving the sockeye" which was based on the committee's report on the disaster of the Fraser River salmon spawning run; the committee's report also prompted a supportive editorial in this same edition. *The National Post*, March 24, 2005, A16.

11. A five-year report on Senate committees notes that, among several measures, over the period of 1999-2000 to 2003-04, committee activity increased significantly in the number of meetings held, the number of witnesses to testify, the number of bills, the number of hours in committee, etc. (*Activities and Expenditures, Annual Report, 2003-2004*; reference: table on Committee Operations). On the House side, over that same five-year period, the number of meetings increased (although comparatively somewhat lower than in the mid-1990s) from 921 to 1,013 while the number of reports has gone up from 114 in 1999-2000 to 163 in 2003-2004 (*2003-2004 Annual Report on Committees Activities and Expenditures*, 3). Numbers vary over time. In the 1990s, the number of House committee meetings grew from 774 in 1992-93 to 1,151 in 1996-97, although over this period the number reached 1,389 meetings in 1994-95 (*Activities and Expenditures, Annual Report 1996-97*, Committees and Legislative Services Directorate, the House of Commons, September 1997, 4). In the Senate, the number of witnesses per bill considered – another indication of volume of work – generally went up year by year for the same period, although 1994-95 also marked a big year for the number of actual witnesses appearing before Senate committees. (Committees and Private Legislation Directorate, The Senate of Canada, *Senate Committees Activities and Expenditures Annual Report 1996-1997*, 4).

12. Chris Charlton, "Obstruction in Ontario and the House of Commons," *Canadian Parliamentary Review* (Autumn 1997): 28. From 1974 to 1993, the average number of hours for bills to become law was 7 hours and 45 minutes. Standing committee time was not included in this timeframe.

13. The following statistics are from the author's survey of Parliamentary Research staff, May 1996.

14. The Committees Directorate of the House of Commons, *So You're Going to Work for a Committee? A Booklet for Contract Staff of the House of Commons Standing Committees* (March 1989).

CHAPTER ONE

The Parliamentary Backdrop

"The House has the power. It has to be that way. It has the final say on committee matters and findings. But, once given a mandate by the House, committees have full authority to fulfill that mandate as they please."

– Camille Montpetit, former Deputy Clerk of the House of Commons,
and co-editor of *House of Commons Procedure and Practice*, Interview,
June 17, 2005

Standing committees are basically *masters of their domain*.[1] But, whoever controls the House essentially rules the Hill, including its standing committees.

Put another way, committees lean against a backdrop where the parliamentary agenda is largely prescribed, party discipline rules members' lives, the bureaucracy's guiding hand on policy development is everywhere, and the shifting sands of public opinion overshadow the bigger political decisions of the day. With all this in mind, committees do have considerable scope to organize their affairs, pursue issues and witnesses.

"It's often said that committees are *masters of their own destiny*. Well they are not. The chairs are appointed by the prime minister. Party discipline is tight. The whip keeps things in line."

– Ron Macdonald (L), former Committee Chair and
Parliamentary Secretary, Interview, August 19, 1997

In recent decades, parliamentary reform has resulted in some big changes for standing committees. Although they are not in quite the same operational straightjacket as only a handful of years ago (chairs can now be elected) and individual members have greater latitude to manoeuvre (such as with improvements to navigating a private member's bill through the legislative process), at the end of the day, the executive is, or wants to be, supreme.

Getting the most out of your committee experience involves knowing how government works. You need to be aware of the *rules of engagement.*

SECTION ONE The Battle of the Benches

MOVE OVER, SIR JOHN A.

After nearly 100 years of Confederation, Canada's first prime minister might have been amazed at the state of standing committees.[2] Up until the 1960s, little had changed.[3] Only recently have substantive committee reforms taken place.[4]

As government grew more complex, its standing committees became the legislative workhorses. Committees now largely do the work previously undertaken by the whole House itself.[5] Twentieth-century government just could not cope with a process designed in Sir John A. Macdonald's time.

PRIME MINISTERIAL PLEDGES & PROGRESS

1963 "… how we can make the committee system of the House operate more effectively … [is] one of the most serious problems of Parliament—the more effective discharge of work through committees [is] a way that will give the committees authority and power to make decisions, and when the decisions are referred to the House of Commons we will not have to go through the same debate over and over again that has taken place in the committees."

– Rt. Hon. L. B. Pearson (L), Prime Minister,

May 18, 1963[6]

Committees have the capacity to do more. Since the 1960s, and especially more recently, committee authorities have been steadily upgraded. In 1985, committees were empowered to initiate their own inquiries—no longer requiring a direct order of reference from the House being a big step forward. House committees have practically unfettered capacity to review any matter falling under the department assigned to them.[7]

Electioneering brings out the desire to make Parliament work better. Tinkering with standing committees becomes a visible and tangible way to enhance Parliament's performance and demonstrate it to Canadians.

> **1993** "A Liberal government will take a series of initiatives to restore confidence in the institutions of government… A Liberal government will give MPs a greater role in drafting legislation, through House of Commons committees. These committees will also be given greater influence over government expenditures."
>
> – *Creating Opportunity: The Liberal Plan for Canada*
> ("The Red Book"), September 1993

By the mid-1990s, committees could consider bills prior to second reading, before the government commits to its principles (and offering backbenchers a greater opportunity to mould legislation).[8]

When moving things on the Hill, packaging matters. By the mid-2000s, parliamentary rule changes were wrapped under "democratic reform," which directly and indirectly influenced the operations of House standing committees.

> **2003** "The Prime Minister has made democratic reform a top priority… The reforms are geared toward changing how the House functions, and ensuring that Parliament is an effective forum for expressing Canadians' interests. They will strengthen the roles of individual parliamentarians and committees…"
>
> – "Democratic Reform," Office of the Prime Minister, Website,
> December 22, 2003

DEMOCRACY IS ARRIVING IN CANADA

> "Are there any other nominations? We will now proceed to a secret
> ballot election."
>
> — Marc Bosc, Procedural Clerk, Subcommittee on Committee
> Budgets of the Liaison Committee, December 2, 2004

These few words signal one dramatic change in House committee operations: secret ballot elections of the chair and vice-chair positions. However,
the rules put some notable parameters around this notion of being "democratic." While the official opposition is allowed to chair three specific standing committees, elections of chairs are restricted to members of the
government party and only if more than one candidate is nominated. As one
parliamentary observer puts it, "It's not an open election; the opposition cannot theoretically chair all committees." (It was not too long ago that chairs
were only "elected" or appointed from a list nominated (that is, approved) by
the Prime Minister's Office.[9]) Still, the ability to hold "genuine" committee
elections became one of the more visible democratic reform initiatives.[10]

> "One of the significant moves for committees was the shift to their
> choosing their own chairs and vice-chairs; in the minority situation,
> the government whip can no longer control that process. Another
> was giving committee chairs and vice-chairs extra pay for their posi-
> tions thus giving them extra stature."
>
> — Hugh Winsor, National Affairs Columnist, *The Globe and
> Mail*, Interview, June 8, 2005[11]

But as is the case so often, there is the political reality.

> "Election of chairs is not as big a change as people might have antic-
> ipated. Elected chairs are not more independent. The fact is, parlia-
> ment is a partisan chamber and the policy-oriented committees are
> generally chaired by government members."
>
> — The Hon. Don Boudria (L), Chair, Standing Committee on
> Procedure and House Affairs, Interview, September 9, 2005

Changes involving parliamentary secretaries deserve mention. They sit on committees, provide a connection to the minister and her department, and, for some, unduly tether the committee to ministerial influence. (The role of parliamentary secretaries and implications for committees are further addressed in Chapter Five.) As part of strengthening the role of parliamentary secretaries under democratic reform, they are now sworn in as privy councillors who can sit at the cabinet table. Some see this as actually undermining the democratic imperative.[12]

The rules affecting private members' bills are relevant. Members have long been able to prepare and table bills, once selected to do so, but now they can force committees to respond to bills' subject matter. (This is addressed in Chapter Four.) As one member put it, "Under a minority government, this is a way for the opposition to enact legislation and set an agenda that the government must deal with."

OF WHIPS AND DISCIPLINE

> "Democratic reform really can't last beyond a minority government. It's created expectations that can't be sustained. I expect we'll see more discipline in a future majority because the government will need to govern."
> – The Hon. John Manley (L), former Deputy Prime Minister,
> Interview, June 27, 2005

Over time, standing committees have wrestled away tasks previously the exclusive domain of the government or the House (and many of these changes were seen to take aim at loosening party discipline).[13] Still, party discipline has been perpetuated (although recent reforms have tried to untie some of the disciplinary strings).[14] This hallmark of the Canadian system deserves some focus.

The pressure imposed by party discipline on members can be subtle or ham-fisted. Not getting promoted (such as to parliamentary secretary), denying trips abroad, and, in the extreme, refusing to sign a member's nomination papers for the next election can be dangled in front of difficult members.

A POLITICAL VIEW!

"Don Boudria, the Liberal Party whip, is very angry with you for even calling this meeting. Now, when you called this meeting, did you check with
the people upstairs in the Liberal Party?"
> – Jason Moscovitz, Host, "The House," CBC Radio, to Patrick Gagnon on
> whether his committee would examine the lack of bilingual signs
> in the National Capital, August 31, 1996

"… it is true that the party whip has the power, if you will, to fire us all…"
> – Patrick Gagnon (L), Chair of the Standing Joint
> Committee on Official Languages

"I voted for the government 6,000 times in my long political career and
against the government twice. When I voted against the gun control
bill, I was taken off the standing committee and placed on another
one. No one has any idea how tough it is to go against the grain."
> – Member of Parliament (L), Interview, Spring 1997

Government members can be reined in if a committee's work threatens to
disrupt the government's plans. The constraint is clear. Government controls the agenda (especially in a majority) because it must be able to govern.

"While the relationship between the cabinet and a parliamentary committee varies from government to government, committees are generally used to support cabinet decisions. So, in a majority government,
committee efforts are somewhat emasculated."
> – The Hon. Donald Johnston (L), former Minister of Justice
> and past President of the Liberal Party of Canada, Interview,
> August 24, 1998

The "frontbenchers"—the prime minister and his or her ministers—are
zealous guardians of the legislative agenda. Power rests largely with them,
the executive. A majority assures this. The levers of party discipline and
cabinet supremacy reinforce it.

However, by working smartly within the system, backbenchers (and committees) can advance the markers.

> "The committee chair will have to go to the minister to see if he will
> accept the recommendations prior to reporting them to the House. He
> better persuade the minister to agree. After all, the minister sits at the
> cabinet table. Amendments don't become government amendments
> until the government agrees."
>
> – The Hon. Doug Peters (L), Secretary of State, International
> Financial Institutions, Interview, June 9, 1997

The prime minister relies on his or her backbenchers for ideas and support to help sell policy decisions, but Ottawa teems with studies and consultations. It's policy thinking by a thousand initiatives. Ultimately, decisions are made by relatively few.

Still, parliamentary life is not static. Democratic reform in the mid-2000s has rustled the leaves.

> "Discipline is looser now. With changes to handling private members'
> business and the freedom to vote on most bills, government members
> don't have the same sense of team. It's democracy. But this makes the
> whip's job harder."
>
> – Derek Lee (L), Interview, May 10, 2005

The desire to make individual members more relevant, and change the established order, has been achieved in spades largely because of minority government. Here, opposition members run committees, and every single government member's vote in the House is depended upon to prevent the government from collapsing. Party discipline has not been side-lined completely. On essential votes, it's front and centre as every party nimbly positions itself to survive in this high-stakes environment. The whip's job is harder, indeed. A missing member might mean a lost vote.

> "In the general public's mind, democratic reform is basically about
> being free to vote, but the whips of all parties are forcefully ensuring

the votes are there—especially in a minority situation. Democratic reform is not there yet."

> – Camille Montpetit, former Deputy Clerk of the House of Commons,
> and co-editor of *House of Commons Procedure and Practice*, Interview,
> June 17, 2005

Witnesses must realize that how committees operate and the leverage that individual members have within this system change with the shape of each Parliament itself.

SECTION TWO The Body Count

> "The only time government has problems with Senate committees is when it doesn't have the majority in the [Senate] chamber."
>
> – Senator John Lynch-Staunton (PC), Leader of the Opposition,
> Interview, May 22, 1997

Clearly, the makeup of the House of Commons and Senate is important. A majority means control, if not a near monopoly, over what is done. A minority situation loosens that grip on power and requires sharing it. Numbers count.

MAJORITY GOVERNMENTS

> "The problem with committees is that they do not work on the basis of consensus but of majority. The government must implement their views. It's hard to argue that government can't rule by majority. It can win. I understand this. It's the conundrum of majority government."
>
> – The Hon. Audrey McLaughlin (NDP), former Leader,
> Interview, October 31, 1997

The allocation of seats in standing committees will largely mirror the allotment of seats among official political parties in the House. An impregnable majority where the government dominates the standing committees virtually assures the passage of the government's agenda.

In a majority government situation, witnesses tend to gravitate toward keeping government members on side and perhaps the odd opposition member. Witnesses do the math. The majority of committee seats are held by government members, so those tend to be the focus. (A theme of this book, however, is that working with all members is recommended.)

PIZZA PARLIAMENTS: THE SLIM MAJORITY

"One big difference in the backbench rumble in this Parliament is the slim Liberal majority. Let's say a few more independently minded [Liberal members] risk losing favour within caucus, and speak their minds. Then the Liberal back bench will be flexing muscle that the Liberal front bench can't ignore."

– Jennifer Fry, Parliamentary Reporter, CBC Radio,
"The House", October 18, 1997

A slimmer majority can increase the uncertainty. It might only take a handful of disgruntled government backbenchers in the House to upset the government's legislative plans. Or deaths, departures, and by-elections could tip the balance perilously close to achieving a minority government. A tighter majority and several opposition parties mean greater relevance of individual parliamentarians—each vote is important.[15]

This situation makes committee life more complex. Each party wants time to question witnesses; each wants a say. There could be several dissenting opinions during report writing and headaches for committee chairs who seek consensus. Many MPs can have double, even triple, committee duty.

"Everyone will have to adjust to the new reality in the House of Commons with its five recognized parties. This reality could indeed make the work of committees considerably more cumbersome."

– Yves Rocheleau (BQ), Standing Committee on Fisheries
and Oceans, October 7, 1997

For witnesses, this situation means more work: more time spent briefing committee members and tracking party positions and greater need for forging stronger links with opposition members.

MINORITY GOVERNMENTS

> "… this minority Parliament [the 38th] will cause the rules and prac-
> tices of the House to be tested in ways they haven't been for a very
> long time, and in the case of some standing orders—ones that have
> changed significantly since the last minority government in
> 1979…"
>
> – William Corbett, Clerk, Standing Committee on
> Procedure and House Affairs, October 21, 2004

Minority governments rely on a tenuous balance of power in the House of
Commons. A minority government needs the support of a certain number
of opposition members to get legislation passed. A minority situation is
not necessarily an unproductive one for committees.[16] Depending on the
situation, members can always find ways of leveraging their circumstances
to make policy gains.

> "I can also attest that, as a private member, committees on which I
> served were able to change government policy with respect to envi-
> ronmental legislation and election expenses law. It is worth noting that
> those committees were most effective in a Parliament (1972-74) where
> the government was in a minority position."
>
> – The Rt. Hon. Joe Clark (PC), former Prime Minister,
> Interview, July 23, 1997

An enduring lesson for minority governments is that members must
remain sharp. In the opening days of 2005, a ministerial assistant put it
this way: "Minority government imposes a burden of responsibility on all
members. Taking positions has consequences." Each vote is mission critical. Positioning and procedure become even greater tactical tools. As one
committee insider has observed, "Government members tend to become
lackadaisical about procedure when in a majority. Doing so in a minority
could be fatal."

> "It's like night and day. The government doesn't control committees in
> this minority government. No more can you just rely on going to the

minister's staff and a couple of influential committee members. You have to deal with all MPs."

– The Hon. John Manley (L), former Deputy Prime Minister,
Interview, June 27, 2005

A minority government means the opposition holds the majority of seats in a standing committee. Combined, they can outvote government members. For witnesses, a committee strategy must involve closely working with the opposition. Having a majority mindset (only working with government members) in a minority government will stop you dead in your tracks.

THE SENATE-HOUSE AXIS

"People have to understand the relationship between the Senate committee and the Senate and, then, the Senate to the government. If the committee has the muscle in the Senate—a majority opposition—then you can get the government to acquiesce. We can remind the government about their spending bills that need to go through."

– Senator (L), Committee Chair, Interview, Summer 1997

Different parties can be in a majority in the House of Commons and Senate at the same time—giving senators a means to pry out greater influence over policy or bills (although unelected senators are usually reluctant to unduly disrupt the passage of legislation). Interest groups should remain aware of the numbers in the Upper Chamber.

SECTION THREE Other Forces at Play

BUREAUCRATS: OUTLIVING MINISTERS

"By the time the deputy minister presents a matter for decision to cabinet, he or she tends to present three options: 'the unacceptable,' 'the politically courageous,' and 'the bureaucrat-preferred' option. As such, it is usually best to get down into the department to the person doing the first drafts of any policy."

– The Hon. Donald Johnston (L), former Minister of Justice and past
President of the Liberal Party of Canada, Interview, August 24, 1998

The role and influence of the bureaucracy should not be underestimated. Cabinets come and go, elections churn out the members, but the bureaucracy remains intact. Departments run many parallel consultations with Canadians, such as through task forces and national forums.[17] These efforts feed the policy-making process. Ministers may establish the broad policy framework, but departmental officials design, implement, and manage the programs. Determining *who holds the pen* is always important.

> ✓ **TIP** Take a dual-track approach: political and bureaucratic. For instance, one national charitable organization carries its message (on tax policy) to the Finance Committee's pre-budget hearings, and it works closely with Finance Department officials to scope out the details and justification of any proposals.

THE SWING OF PUBLIC OPINION

"Governments pay attention to polls. I know this from having worked for government for a short period of time. [. . .] Sometimes they pay too much attention, though, to the detriment of what could be effective laws or policy, and it may be unpopular, yet governments will look at a poll and say that is a poll; therefore, I will not make a decision and just go with what Canadians are telling me."

– Senator Jim Munson (L), Standing Senate Committee on
National Security and Defence, December 6, 2004

You should pay attention, too. No discussion of policy making would be complete without recognizing the importance of public opinion. How does picking up your issue stand in the public's mind?

SECTION FOUR The Rules of Engagement

"What a joke it is being on a committee in this Parliament. It is an absolute embarrassment to me as an MP."

– Mike Scott (R), House of Commons, April 21, 1998

It's beyond the scope of this book to analyze committee performance (even though there is no shortage of fodder).[18] For witnesses, the reality is that when you appear you want to do it right. Part of this is knowing how committees fit into the broader scheme and how the rules work.

> "What sort of Hill are you facing? As a result of the pressure to change, things on the Hill are in a state of flux, with old and new practices and attitudes co-existing. Either way, given the degree of uncertainty, you would be well-advised to size up each situation and test your assumptions before you leap into action."
>
> – Dr. John Chenier, Editor, *The Lobby Monitor*, Interview,
> September 9, 2005

Committees are tethered to the parliamentary schedule and its outputs, both largely dictated by the executive (and, in the case of a minority government, subject to the multitude of compromises made by the executive to ensure passage of its agenda).

All members work within an environment set by the speech from the throne, the budget, the legislative timetable, and countless ministerial announcements supported by the departmental machine. Committees are buffeted by other sorts of activity, including cabinet shuffles, backbencher promotions, and even the death of a senator. Committee agendas are influenced by *Red Books*, and green and white papers. (Little is black and white in Ottawa!)

To simplify it, there are certain *rules of engagement* when dealing with parliamentary committees:

1. Whoever controls the House controls the agenda. (In a majority government, this is largely assured; the parliamentary agenda and legislative decisions are prescribed mostly by the prime minister and the cabinet. In a minority, the agenda is constrained, and control over the agenda depends on compromise.)
2. Standing committees have the capacity to handle a broad range of parliamentary business, organize their internal affairs, and determine how they will proceed with witnesses. (Committee authorities are discussed in detail in Chapter Three.)

3. Rule Two directly impacts witnesses (and is the subject of this book), but don't lose sight of Rule One.

PROSPECTS

"Parliamentary procedure is always changing and certainly has accelerated in the last few years and even prior to the current minority Parliament."

– Stephen Knowles, former committee clerk, Interview, April 5, 2005

Parliaments change. Rules evolve. Over time, new authorities have been added to the committees' quiver. While parliamentary procedure is unlikely *Book Club* material, it should be assigned reading for witnesses who frequent parliamentary committees. As Chapter Three will reveal, the implications of a committee exercising its formal authorities is serious business for witnesses. (Check out what happened to Mr. Miller and more recent forays into summoning witnesses.)

Assessing the evolution of Parliament is best left to academics, but it is worth offering a quick point. If the objective of committee reforms was to give committees complete independence from the executive, then the reforms only worked at the fringes. If the purpose was to enhance committee participation in policymaking, then indeed the reforms have given committees considerable scope—and this has been one enduring premise of reform over the years.

"Over time there has been a significant evolution of committees and in the ways groups respond to them: committees are taken more seriously. But committees must continue to work at making a contribution."

– Peter Dobell, Founding Director, Parliamentary Centre,

Interview, April 24, 1998

There has been, and will continue to be, plenty of commentary about what committees must do to remain truly relevant in a changing Parliament (and society).

"If the country continues to decentralize, then MPs will have to better reflect riding concerns and regional interests. Standing committees will be the vehicles to do so."

> – The Rt. Hon. John Turner (L), former Prime Minister,
> Interview, September 15, 1997

The challenge for witnesses is to gauge how incremental rule changes truly affect how things are done on Parliament Hill and in committee. The question is whether the increased policy role of individual members will be sustainable in future Parliaments (and under majority governments). If such a cultural shift occurs, this may start to recalibrate the rules of engagement for all.

"In a minority government, everything is negotiable, less predictable—Parliament is more alive. But it will take time, and may take consecutive minority governments, to institutionalize the gains and truly change the culture."

> – Gary Levy, Editor, *Canadian Parliamentary Review*,
> Interview, May 31, 2005[19]

MOVING FORWARD

As later chapters will show, committees have the procedural tools to dissect really any issue (falling under their purview). However, it is *how* a committee exercises its powers which often makes the difference. Much depends on the motivation of a determined chair and a focused committee.

Chapters Three and Four highlight the rules, the committee powers, and the legislative steps involving committees. It is useful to understand what committees are all about and how they fit into the overall process.

But, before looking at these matters, the next chapter diverges somewhat to reveal how a number of groups have pulled it all together (or have tried to). Their techniques emphasize the importance of communication, style, and strategy when dealing with committees. Knowing parliamentary procedure helps, yet, at the end of the day, a committee appearance is all about how you communicate.

ENDNOTES

1. While working within the relevant rules of the House, committees are, says one authority, "free to organize their work," and, as reiterated by many speakers, "committees are said to be 'masters of their own proceedings'." Robert Marleau and Camille Montpetit, eds., *House of Commons Procedure and Practice* (Montréal: Chenelière/McGraw-Hill, 2000), 804 and 809.
2. For a good overview of the history and evolution of parliamentary committees, reaching back to British parliamentary tradition and practice and to Canadian developments, see ibid., chap. 2, 798-804.
3. Report of the Special Committee on Reform of the House of Commons, June 1985, 12.
4. Senator John Stewart, "Procedure in the Trudeau Era," in ed. John Courtney, *Canadian House of Commons: Essays in Honour of Norman Ward* (Calgary: University of Calgary Press, 1985), 12.
5. Ibid., 24.
6. Michael Rush, "The Development of the Committee System in the Canadian House of Commons," *The Parliamentarian* LV, no. 3 (July 1974).
7. Table Research Branch, House of Commons, *Précis of Procedure*, 5th ed., 1996, 106. Note that Senate standing committees must get orders of reference to proceed with inquiries.
8. There have been frequent standing committee reforms since the 1960s and especially since the mid-1980s. For instance, procedural changes in 1968 included authorizing committees to review departmental spending or estimates. In 1982, the "Lefebvre Reforms" granted committees the capacity to require the government to respond to their reports within 150 days (which has since been changed to 120 days). The substantive "McGrath Reforms" of 1985 allowed committees to initiate studies, among other changes. In 1987, committees were given the power to review non-judicial Order-in-Council appointments, and in 1994, among other changes in other years, committees were granted the capacity to essentially draft legislation under reference from the House. Chapter Three discusses more fully what committees can do.
9. Elections of chairs are restricted to members of the government party and the vice-chairs by one member of the official opposition and another from the opposition. The three pre-designated standing committees which are chaired by the official opposition are Public Accounts, Access to Information, Privacy and Ethics, and Government Operations. For these latter committees, the first vice-chair is a government member, and the second vice-chair is a member of the opposition. A secret ballot election is only held if there is more than one candidate nominated for the office in question (Standing Order 106(2), (3)). In previous Parliaments, and before the recent development of such elections, sometimes a "spontaneous" democratic initiative just took over as committees actually elected a chair of their

choosing, thus outflanking the wishes of the executive. See Ann Sullivan, "House Fisheries Committee elects Baker, not PMO's choice," *The Hill Times*, October 20, 1997, 11; see also Editorial, "Old-style carrot and stick politics," *The Hill Times*, March 18, 1996. Senate chairs are not chosen by secret ballot.) Standing Senate Committee on Foreign Affairs, *Proceedings*, October 19, 2004.)

10. Other reform initiatives include allowing members greater choice in the committees they wish to sit on; referral of bills to committee after first reading (for bills subject to One-line and Two-line votes); a general call for greater engagement of parliamentarians and committees in the legislative process; enhanced opportunities for committees to review government appointments; and greater resources for committees to undertake their work. How members vote has been a *cause célèbre* of democratic reform. Under a scheme whereby each bill is designated as either a One-, Two- or Three-line vote, government members are now freer to vote on One-, and Two-line bills in the House, although on essential votes of confidence (Three-line votes) they are expected to fall into line and support the government's position. This is seen as loosening the grip of cabinet supremacy at the edges and giving individual members greater relevance. Only Liberal members are bound to this system; it is not a parliamentary initiative. Moreover, voting in a minority government causes members to rally around—or be rallied around—the party line as every single vote counts. For a fuller discussion, see the website of the Office of the Prime Minister, "Democratic Reform," http://www.pm.gc.ca/eng/dem_reform. asp, accessed May 14, 2004.

11. Note that Senate committee chairs and deputy chair positions also get paid now.

12. "I have always thought of backbenchers, however, as a kind of fourth order of governance and that anything that restricts their ability freely to speak or freely to act is dangerous to the health of our democracy. That is why I was concerned to see so many additional privy councillors created when the Martin government decided to make all parliamentary secretaries members of the Privy Council. This means fewer free and independent voices in the House of Commons. It enlarges the executive at the expense of Parliament." John Bryden (former Liberal MP), "The Primacy of Parliament and the Duty of a Parliamentarian," *Canadian Parliamentary Review*, 28, no. 1 (Spring 2005).

13. F. Leslie Seidle, "Interest Advocacy through Parliamentary Channels: Representation and Accommodation," in ed. F. Leslie Seidle, *Equity and Community: The Charter, Interest Advocacy, and Representation* (Montreal: The Institute for Research on Public Policy, 1993), 206.

14. One commentator has said that "The reforms [of the 1980s] never worked because of a reluctance to lift the whip and change party discipline." Hugh Winsor (national political columnist, *The Globe and Mail*), interview, September 3, 1997.

15. The term "pizza Parliament" was initially used in the media to describe the Liberal majority of the late 1990s and the presence of several opposition parties; the term continues to be used; see Abbas Rana and Kate Malloy, "Next election the '$64,000' question" on Parliament Hill," *The Hill Times*, May 9, 2005, 1.

16. Minority governments in the 1960s led to procedural reforms. The government of the day was open to making the House more efficient, such as delegating more work to committees. See House of Commons, *Report of the Special Committee on Reform of the House of Commons*, 3rd report (June 1985), 12. However, not wanting to risk losing control of the government's agenda, the Liberal minority government in the early 1970s reduced the committee's capacity to review departmental budgets. See Mike Scandiffio, "MPs want 'Super House Accounting Committee' on government spending," *The Hill Times*, March 10, 1997, 11. The election of a minority government in 2004 implemented democratic reform—discussed earlier in this chapter.

17. Indicative of the scope of departmental activity, by one account some years ago it was noted that there were some 300 consultative exercises under way by federal departments. See Jocelyne Bourgon (clerk of the Privy Council Office), quoted in Kathryn May, "Top bureaucrats discuss shift in thinking," *The Ottawa Citizen*, May 28, 1998, A12.

18. Committee performance is often a subject of debate both on and off the Hill. Not surprisingly, performance gets mixed reviews as there are many examples of influential committees and ones that fall flat in each Parliament. Commentators still point to Conservative maverick Don Blenkarn, a Mulroney-era Finance Committee chair, who garnered respect for many unanimous and quality reports on complex issues. Independent thinking is rewarded by the media. To this day, they love seeing the government squirm a bit because of the work of a committee chaired by a government member. Under the Chrétien government, the work of the environment committee, under the chairmanship of Liberal Charles Caccia, stirred up some attention for its critical work on the environment department's enforcement activity. See Hugh Winsor, "MP holds Grits' feet to environmental fire," *The Globe and Mail*, May 27, 1998, A3. Members themselves formally review the role of the standing committees and their contribution to the policy process. See, for example, House of Commons, *Report of the Liaison Committee* (February 1997). Members recognize the importance of better publicizing their work, and of getting media coverage, such as better informing Canadians of their influence over the expenditure process. See Standing Committee on Procedure and House Affairs, *The Business of Supply: Completing the Circle of Control*, 65th report (1997), 53.

19. This notion of a change in culture was commented on by a minister responsible for democratic reform: "… full implementation of democratic reform requires a fundamental change in our political culture. As MPs elected to represent our constituents, we must also embrace the three pillars of our reform: ethics, responsibility, and accountability.", Hon. Jacques Saada (L), Standing Committee on Procedure and House Affairs, February 19, 2004.

CHAPTER TWO

Techniques

"My view of props is 'go for it.' Your appearance is a public affairs exercise. Whatever you can do to draw attention to the cause the better."
— Michael Makin, President, Canadian Printing Industries
Association, Interview, July 3, 1997

SECTION ONE See How It's Done

Every committee appearance is unique. The issue. The mix of witnesses and members. The parliamentary agenda. Public opinion. The media's interest.

Each appearance requires a tailored response. Props help, too. These techniques shed light on some enduring lessons about taking your message to the Hill.

SCENARIO ONE: *Airing Concerns at the Right Time*

"Senior Canada Customs and Revenue Agency (CCRA) officials, concerned about the prospect of critical testimony before the Senate committee from Canada's largest airport, returned to cabinet to seek explicit approval for a new amendment that met the airport authority's objectives. In a rare move, cabinet agreed."[1]
— Tony Stikeman, President, Tactix Government Consulting Inc.,
Interview, June 28, 2005

When the Customs Act was being amended in the spring of 2001, the Greater Toronto Airports Authority (GTAA) and other Canadian airport authorities aired concerns about the possibility of increased incidents of smuggling and drug trafficking. The issue revolved around the expansion of in-transit pre-clearance facilities, which would allow arriving international passengers transiting through Canadian airports to come into direct contact with departing Canadian passengers. The airport authorities wanted additional powers to enable customs officers to search departing passengers, provided there was a clear definition of "reasonable grounds." Although the government supported the proposed changes in principle, it was reluctant to introduce them because of legal concerns that questioning international passengers in the arrivals hall or in-transit areas could be found to violate the Charter of Rights and Freedoms.

CCRA recognized the airports' security arguments might be publicly raised at the Senate National Finance Committee, which might paint the picture of a missing vital security measure that threatened Canada's border security. Accordingly, the government shortly thereafter tabled a new and key amendment in committee. It was immediately adopted and came into force a few short months before the terrorist attacks on 9/11, which dramatically reinforced the need for this very amendment.

➤ GTAA landed a victory because:

1. Going before a committee has to be timed right. While not the first choice, reaching deadlock with the department sometimes requires groups to go public and force, or threaten to force, a decision in public. If departments are comfortable with the policy direction of the proposed amendment, they are willing to use the leverage of a key stakeholder to persuade ministers to correct the government's bill.

2. Success is not about shooting down bad policy; it requires searching for win-wins by floating workable alternatives.

SCENARIO TWO: *Play It Again, Sam*

"The bill just didn't make sense. MPs didn't know what the problem was, so we changed the name of the legal concept, and we grabbed their attention with the booklet."

– Michael McCabe, President and CEO, Canadian Association of
Broadcasters, Interview, May 27, 1997

The Canadian Association of Broadcasters (CAB) wanted to persuade committee members that the proposed revisions to the Copyright Act (1997) would have hindered replays of taped music and broadcasts. To catch their attention, CAB distributed a booklet with a length of actual black magnetic tape crumpled up inside. They added a catchy cover page that declared that this time the problem wasn't "red tape" but "magnetic tape." CAB also explained the technical language. In its booklet, CAB replaced the technical term found in the legislation with a more user-friendly phrase. Their booklet was well received.

➤ CAB's play on words shows that:

1. Grabbing members' attention with a sense of humour helps get your message across.

2. Educating members is critical to helping them understand the cost or implications of legislation and includes putting complex, legal language in terms people can understand.

SCENARIO THREE: *Santa Claus Came to Town*

> "For us, the Santa Claus Parade offered a timely example to make our point. It gave the committee a reason to respond to our concern. But it also worked against us. The anecdote defined the problem very specifically, which limited the solution."
>
> – Jay Thompson, Vice-President, Legal and Regulatory Affairs, Canadian Cable Television Association, Interview, May 5, 1997

The Canadian Cable Television Association (CCTA) also had to effectively communicate its concerns with the Copyright Act. The Santa Claus Parade set the backdrop. In the association's view, the legislation would have required community television channel operators, for instance, to get the authorization of each participant in a marching band, such as those in a Santa Claus Parade, in order to later broadcast the event—impractical to say the least. Company spokespeople and association staff pumped this example in pre-meetings with individual members and at the hearing. The anecdote became a focus of discussion during the CCTA's testimony. Members of the Heritage Committee agreed that this was a problem but then tailored a solution to address this situation by developing a limited exemption from the act.

➤In parading its messages before committee, this group reveals that:

1. Anecdotes allow committee members to immediately grasp the implications of a complex problem. (You know it is working when members use the case as a basis for discussion.)

2. Anecdotes can become a straightjacket if members interpret your problem in only one way. Think through the anecdote; does it get you where you want?

3. The message sinks in when delivered by people actually confronting the problem (as opposed to association staff) both inside and outside the committee room.

SCENARIO FOUR: *The Eagle Has Landed*

"You know some of those members hadn't even seen a clear-cut, and here they were dealing with legislation about it. We had a great photo to share with them. It was a lone fir tree with an eagle's nest on top. In the background as far as the eye could see was a clear-cut; not a tree was standing except for that one. It was the visual we needed."

– Elizabeth May, Executive Director, Sierra Club,
Interview, June 13, 1997

When the Endangered Species Act was being discussed at a Natural Resources Committee hearing in Vancouver, the Sierra Club had to get across to "pro-clear-cut members" how logging practices affect the flora and fauna. An enlarged photo of a clear-cut did it. When the committee was in Toronto, this group showed slides of recent clear-cuts. This hearing was televised on CPAC (Canadian Public Affairs Channel), and the slides also came across clearly on television. In the end, while the committee reported that clear-cutting was a legitimate silviculture tool, it acknowledged that clear-cuts shouldn't be excessive. The Sierra Club felt that its efforts to visualize the issue changed the way the committee members thought about this logging practice.

➤The Sierra Club's efforts clearly demonstrate that:

1. Photographs can crystallize an issue in a way that written briefs and testimony cannot. If a visual prop is used, will a picture show up well on television?

2. Repetition reinforces the message, particularly at separate hearings.

SCENARIO FIVE: *Held Together by Steel*

"An all-party caucus—an interest group of sorts—provided a dimension of congeniality which might have been highly partisan. And when it came down to specific points [in the act], we were able to achieve certain objectives because of who was on the committee."

– Donald Belch, Director, Government Relations, Stelco Inc.,

Interview, June 2, 1997

The steel companies pulled together an all-party group of MPs who had steel plants in their ridings or had a significant number of constituents who worked in that sector. The "steel caucus" succeeded because it was non-partisan. Its aim was, over time, to educate members about the challenges facing the industry. It also broadened its focus to include suppliers and other businesses dependent on this sector. The group became a bridgehead for dealing with standing committees. For instance, in responding to Special Import Measures Act amendments in 1996, the steel industry worked with the chairs of the Finance and International Trade Committees to create a more effective joint subcommittee to handle the tax legislation. Some members on this subcommittee were also part of the steel caucus.

▶ The steel industry reinforces the point that:

1. Members of Parliament and organizations can work together and better understand each other (after all, employers and employees are constituents); putting a check on partisanship facilitates this.
2. Developing a rapport takes time, but it can facilitate thoughtful consideration of the issues, such as in committee.

SCENARIO SIX: *The Product of One's Labour*

"People met for many evenings to thrash out these contentious issues. Our joint statement on unemployment insurance was a watershed for us. We reached consensus. But the government wasn't prepared to listen. It was a major disappointment."

– Arlene Wortsman, Director, Labour, Canadian Labour Market Productivity Centre, Interview, August 12, 1998

In 1994, the Canadian Labour Market Productivity Centre (CLMPC), a national business-labour organization, was asked by the minister of human resources to develop a position on the impending unemployment insurance reform. The CLMPC took up the challenge. By overcoming entrenched biases on both sides, the CLMPC negotiated a joint statement with 12 recommendations. Generating a common position on such a contentious issue was unprecedented. Labour and business interests seemed, initially, too divergent, an agreement unreachable. However, the minister's request came at a time when many acknowledged the need to revamp the UI system, and the prospect of tabling a common position during the standing committee review pushed the CLMPC members. "Unfortunately, while the Human Resources Committee embraced some of our ideas, the government chose a different course in the end." Ms. Wortsman adds, "We learned that we could overcome our differences. But it raises the question about the value of such consultative exercises if groups and the committee aren't listened to."

➤ The CLMPC's work indicates that:

1. When taking your message to a standing committee, you are not necessarily communicating to "government."
2. A committee visit (and the formulation of a position on a tough public policy issue) can become a healthy learning experience for an organization.
3. Groups also have to carefully assess the value of devoting resources and time to preparing for and participating in any government consultation.

SCENARIO SEVEN: *"A" for Effort; "A" for Results*

"Getting people listening and understanding what you are saying takes persistence. It pays off when others start reinforcing what you want. We needed and got champions in committee, in caucus, among backbenchers, the departments and ministers."

– Robert Best, Director of Government Relations and Public
Affairs, Association of Universities and Colleges of Canada,
Interview, July 3, 1997

The Association of Universities and Colleges of Canada (AUCC) scored an $800 million success with its persistence. But it took four years to do so. This association looked to the Finance Committee's 1996 pre-budget consultations to tailor a special roundtable to discuss funding "university research infrastructure," such as the importance of upgrading lab facilities. A key challenge was getting all the players to buy into the need to enhance university infrastructure as a way to lead to sustainable research jobs. There were many ingredients to the success of the roundtable. Noteworthy, the AUCC had a rapport with the standing committee chair and a caucus chair who were both receptive to the idea. As well, the AUCC and several partner organizations had a set of concrete proposals to announce and used the committee as the platform to do so.

"The committee members became for us a very supportive voice in caucus. In turn, they encouraged us to get our act together and rally the disparate higher education community around some common positions," noted Best. The AUCC also worked with bureaucrats and had a sense as to what proposals would work. On the basis of recommendations from caucus members, the Departments of Finance and Industry, key ministers and the Finance Committee pre-budget report, the 1997 budget announced the Canada Foundation for Innovation, an $800 million core commitment to fund university research.

➤ The AUCC's straight "A" performance reveals that:
1. Success requires getting buy-in from as many policy leaders as possible. They must understand and embrace your message. This involves developing a long-term strategy.
2. The AUCC, and its allies, pushed for new funding while the political environment was ripe. It is important to do quality research to support your proposals and get others to champion your cause, too.
3. Working closely with others means being receptive to advice on how to proceed.

SCENARIO EIGHT: *Feeding off False Hopes*

"You have to understand the dynamic between the minister and his department. If a tight relationship exists, the committee is pure window dressing. It's possible and probable for the department to circum-

vent the committee and for the minister to have the committee act on
his instruction. It's happened, I tell you. They short-circuit the committee's contribution."

— George Fleischmann, President and CEO, Food and Consumer
Products Manufacturers of Canada, Interview, June 5, 1997

The Food and Consumer Products Manufacturers of Canada (FCPMC)
had some concerns with the government's proposed Canadian Food
Inspection Agency. Being unable to persuade the Department of
Agriculture that this agency needed major restructuring, the association
looked to the Standing Committee on Agriculture. The FCPMC, an association of some 180 companies, presented a constructive alternative to
having a government-appointed and directed agency. The FCPMC tabled
ideas about creating a board of directors from the business community that
would report to the minister; it would adhere to internationally recognized
quality standards; it would operate at reduced costs; and it would establish
a neutral third-party arbitrator for complaints. It also explained that there
were international precedents as models. The FCPMC was invited to the
committee for one hour, it stayed for two, and it left the room feeling that
the committee was genuinely interested in this proposal. In the end, when
the bill was promulgated, there was not a single mention of this idea.
Moreover, the government imposed just the opposite of what FCPMC
wanted and exactly what the department had in mind.

▶ For the FCPMC the essential ingredients of approaching a committee
are:

1. Go to the committee prescribing a well-developed solution (not just
   reeling off complaints).
2. A positive reception at the hearing may not mean that the committee
   will actually have an appetite for your solution (and recommend it to
   the minister) in the end. Unpredictable outcomes can occur in committee.
3. The committee should not be your only stop in the lobbying process.
   After the committee stage, you must do the necessary follow-up to press
   your case.

SCENARIO NINE: *Quick, out of the (Housing) Blocks*

"We had to move quickly along all fronts and bring forward the right amendment. Within two weeks of the budget, we got a $250 million saving for the industry. If we had waited only until the bill got to committee, it would have been too late."

— Richard Bertrand, formerly of Executive Consultants Limited,
Interview, November 18, 1997

Virtually overnight, the MacEachen budget of the early 1980s caused havoc in the construction and housing supply sectors by suddenly cancelling the Multiple Unit Residential Buildings program. "MURB" was initially developed to increase the pool of affordable rental units but largely resulted in granting tax credits to "wealthy dentists and doctors" (and many higher-end housing blocks were built). The abrupt policy change had lumber companies, rug manufacturers, appliance suppliers, and the like scrambling to adjust their production runs in anticipation of lower housing demand. These industries wanted either to rollback the announcement (unlikely) or to win some transition time (possible). An integrated and rapid response was in order. "We had to draft the right amendment that not only benefited our clients but also had to be in the *common good*," comments Mr. Bertrand.

Through a government relations firm, the affected industries worked with the bureaucracy to develop an amendment allowing for such a transition period. As the government began to feel the heat for shutting down MURB, the consultant worked with the opposition to tailor a series of pointed questions for Question Period to needle the government. But it also kept the ministers informed that questions would be coming their way. The firm worked both sides to ensure that the impact of the budget change was known. Work then shifted to a House committee. In considering the budget bill, an amendment to get a six-month transition period was vetted and embraced. In the end, MURB was still snuffed out, but industry won its transition period and, overall, saved some $250 million in forgone housing revenue.

► This housing sector case hammers home the point that:

1. Committee work is only one part of a much broader and integrated lobbying effort.
2. A speedy response requires lining up all the key players involved in an issue, having good information at hand on the cost/impact of a government policy, and tabling a workable solution.

SCENARIO TEN: *Taking a Holistic Approach*

"One doesn't automatically equate nurses with lobbyists, but the views of 110,000 registered nurses send a powerful message. By taking a multifaceted approach, we appear before committees and lobby at the political and bureaucratic levels."

– Carole Pressault, Government Relations Senior Advisor,
Canadian Nurses Association, Interview, May 27, 1998

Pursuing public policy objectives can involve a two-pronged effort: an association must pull back the curtain in Ottawa so members of Parliament can see whom the group represents and what they stand for, as well, efforts taken in Ottawa get a boost when a group engages politicians at the riding level. As the Canadian Nurses Association (CNA) states, "Political action has become a way of life for many nurses in Canada ... nurses who, every day on the front lines, are working toward making Canada a healthier place."

Effective *grass-roots lobbying* often depends on nurturing a group's vital parts—its own members. To encourage and support nurses across the country, the Canadian Nurses Association prepared a handy booklet on lobbying. It helps nurses get a better feel for the political and policy-making process; it also includes tips on developing key messages, appearing before parliamentary committees, and dealing with the media. To this association, political action is not a one-time contact with MPs but an ongoing commitment. "Standing committees do valuable work," adds Ms. Pressault (author of the CNA's guide), "but a thirty-minute visit may not be enough."

▶ The care given by the Canadian Nurses Association to its own members reveals that:

1. Communicating with government in Ottawa, including its committees, can be complemented by developing links with MPs at a local level.

2. Local representatives, who have "day jobs" after all, may need some assistance or support when assuming government relations and public affairs responsibilities.

SCENARIO ELEVEN: *Show Me the Money*

"We had to find a time and place to give a real world example. We set up a model clothing store adjacent to the committee room. Items were priced with and without taxes; there were also sale prices. The senators were amazed. They could see that it was impossible to compare prices."

– Peter Woolford, Senior Vice-President, Policy, The Retail Council
of Canada, Interview, July 3, 1998

The Retail Council of Canada's members not only faced tens of millions of dollars in adjustment costs to accommodate a proposed blended or harmonized sales tax in Atlantic Canada but also would have swallowed some $75 million in annual costs. (Coping with differential tax structures across the country would have upset the factory pricing and just-in-time inventory system now so critical to control costs). No small change, indeed. The challenge was communicating this to government.

The Retail Council pursued the usual approaches: submission preparation, coalition building, and a testimony before a House committee without success. "We had sympathy but no support from the department, and the House Finance Committee had predictably voted along party lines," commented Woolford. "Tactically, we went to the Senate Banking Committee because we felt that they were prepared to do some independent thinking." Mark's Work Wearhouse, a council member, created a mock clothing store in a meeting room of the Halifax hotel where the committee was holding hearings. A confusing array of price tags on pants and shirts had the desired effect. The senators agreed that mandatory hidden or tax-in pricing was not doable. Even people passing through the room picked up on the confusion! With the committee's recommendation in hand, and consensus among Liberal and Conservative senators, the government later agreed not to push for mandatory harmonization of prices and taxes.

➤ The Retail Council of Canada shows that:

1. Real examples demonstrate how policy makes an impact.
2. Time, place, and the target audience are critical to maximizing the effect. This requires a careful assessment of the right conditions.
3. "It isn't over until it's over." Organizations may give up on a bill after it goes through the House stage. The Senate can play a critical role, and organizations should not forgo an opportunity to tell their story to both House and Senate committees.

GETTING YOUR FIX

"People don't understand that they can influence parliamentary committees. But they can't expect to do so just by saying 'fix that' or 'fix this.' It's a far more difficult process than people realize."

– Senator Anne Cools (L), Interview, June 23, 1997

Fixing public policy problems is not easy nor always successful. There are countless ways to respond to government and its parliamentary committees. Each situation should be treated differently. Your message is critical. There is room for creativity in terms of how you deliver it.

"You've got to capture their attention so you can get MPs to buy into your idea."

– Jayson Myers, Senior Vice-President and Chief Economist, Alliance of Canadian Manufacturers and Exporters, Interview, May 8, 1997

Designing the best approach also requires understanding what is driving the committee's work.

SECTION TWO From Paper to Practice

GRASP THE OBJECTIVE

"… I've said this before, that we as the legislative branch need to hold the executive branch accountable, and we do that through this committee."

– Gary Carr (L), Standing Committee on Public Accounts, December 14, 2004

As a witness, getting prepared (and managing your own expectations of what you can accomplish) means trying to get a sense for what is really driving a committee; it may or may not be completely evident.

Committees float trial balloons. By testing ideas, ministers gauge public reception. They can also be a communications pipeline for ministers and their announcements.

Committees can play an ombudsman-like role, such as examining pricing practices within the marketplace. (Calling senior executives to account and pressing for affirmative service quality spur headlines.)

Committees are political heat deflectors. Directing hot issues to committee gives the public (and MPs) a place to vent some steam. The government is seen to be doing something (although little may come of it).

Committees are a forum for political accountability. They want to show Canadians that government spending practices and policy are transparent and that officials can be held to account.

Committees may seek out national thinking on emerging issues and, essentially, be a counterweight to policy development in the bureaucracy.

Senate committees, in particular, strive to be a place for serious second thought, such as by assuming more in-depth studies on issues. (They also want to check any impression that they are merely a rubber-stamping body for House initiatives.)

Committees occupy multiple roles. Witnesses need to assess what's motivating committee members. The lesson for witnesses is "tailor your strategy." Each visit to committee requires a customized approach. Witnesses also need a good grasp of parliamentary rules and process, discussed in the next chapter.

ENDNOTES

1. This is considered a rare move because majority government cabinets rarely introduce amendments to government bills while they are being debated at committee, particularly after second reading.

CHAPTER THREE

Committees 101

"Committees are free to set their own priorities, establish work plans and schedule their business."

– The Hon. Gilbert Parent (L), The Speaker,
House of Commons, March 20, 1997[1]

"THEY ARE WHAT THEY DO"

House of Commons and Senate committees have considerable operating scope. In a sense, and adapting a line from the movie *Forrest Gump*, *committees are what committees do* because their sphere of activity is so broad.

While the latitude is there, standing committees are still creatures of Parliament. This is the reality check. Even despite recent committee reforms, they are neither independent from nor more powerful than the House or Senate. (This has significance later in the chapter when considering committee powers to summon witnesses.) This chapter offers a primer on committee basics: what committees are and what they do.

SECTION ONE Committee Types

There are several general types of parliamentary committees: standing committees, legislative committees, special committees, joint committees, and the Committee of the Whole (see Appendix for list). Variations occur, such as the creation of a joint special committee or a subcommittee. Except for the Committee of the Whole, such committees can be referred to collectively as "select committees," although this is not a widely used term off the Hill. (Parliamentary committees do not include caucus committees, although they are briefly mentioned below because of their particular role.)[2]

STANDING COMMITTEES

The number of House of Commons and Senate standing committees (and joint committees) fluctuates as new committees are formed or merged.[3] Standing committees are referred legislation, or other matters, from the chamber for review; they also consider departmental spending or estimates (House committees only) or may initiate a study on a subject, according to its specific authorities. The powers of House and Senate committees are essentially the same, except that Senate standing committees require a specific reference from the Senate to conduct their activity.

STEERING COMMITTEES

"It is a very well-established principle that [Senate] committees obey the Senate, as steering committees and subcommittees obey the larger committees. We have here a very thinly veiled instruction from the steering committee, which is trying to impose its will."

– Senator Anne Cools (L), Standing Senate Committee on Social
Affairs, Science and Technology, April 24, 1997

The Subcommittee on Agenda and Procedure, or the steering committee, is a smaller planning group for the full committee.[4] Sometimes a "steering committee meeting" may be little more than a private conversation between the chair and opposition vice-chair about future business. Or it could involve broader participation of committee members during in camera, or closed, discussions. (And whether it is a House or Senate committee, sometimes members may not like how it manages the agenda.) Still, steering committee decisions, or their reports, have to be concurred by the full committee.

SUBCOMMITTEES

Subcommittees are used as a tool to manage issues and are appointed to deal with subject matter or a piece of legislation. Standing committee chairs will direct the energies of a small group of members to study or handle a particular issue. Or a standing committee can split into two subcommittees and, for example, hold hearings in different parts of the country.

LEGISLATIVE COMMITTEES

Legislative committees are established on an ad hoc basis and are designed to look at specific bills. After reporting the bill back to the House, they cease to exist. There has been little use of these committees in recent years. Standing committees, or subcommittees, can do the work previously done by legislative committees, although legislative committees have some unique authorities.[5]

STANDING JOINT COMMITTEES

"I have an even more fundamental preoccupation with [the Joint Committee on the Library of Parliament]. Has it even met in the last twenty years?"

– Senator Eymard Corbin (L), Standing Senate
Committee of Selection, March 26, 1996

There are a small number of permanent standing joint committees. These are made up of members from the Senate and House of Commons and are co-chaired by a member from each chamber.

While the Joint Committee on the Library of Parliament is highly unlikely to be on the radar screens of interest groups (and it does actually meet), the Standing Joint Committee on the Scrutiny of Regulations might be. It reviews all government regulations and can help to revoke them (this is discussed more fully in Chapter Four).

At times, special, or ad hoc, joint committees are set up in order to allow the government to expedite an issue. Joint committees combine the efforts of both chambers and avoid duplicating studies, or they might help to broaden support for controversial issues.[6] Such committees are also used to build internal consensus on administrative issues primarily of concern to parliamentarians.

SPECIAL COMMITTEES

A special committee is assigned specific tasks or research and, sometimes, legislation. It ceases to exist once it tables its final report. It does not have the power to send for papers or records unless authorized by the House.[7] Its powers are specified in the orders of reference. Sometimes they are dubbed "task forces."

CAUCUS AND ITS COMMITTEES

> "Successful [standing] committees work with the government to pursue matters. In turn, ministers need the support of caucus colleagues. This is an invisible circle and explains why witnesses can feel frustrated at times."
>
> — David Zussman, President, Public Policy Forum,
> Interview, September 8, 1997

Caucus committees are distinct from parliamentary committees and deserve mentioning. What goes on in caucus affects events in House and Senate standing committees.

> "We saw the committee as a forcing point to get a decision. We went to caucus. Caucus members pressed the committee members, and the committee recommended changes to the department. When we appeared, we got on the public record what the committee needed to go forward."
>
> — Association President, Interview, May 27, 1997

Composed only of members from the same political party, caucus plays a central but largely behind-the-scenes role. The legislative and political agenda is discussed and debated in caucus. Also, members have the capacity to voice concerns to the party leadership. Obviously, government members have easier access to ministers and the prime minister because they meet every week in National Caucus and at other party events.

Party caucus can also be subdivided into groups representing special interests. They can conduct their own public inquiries and issue reports with an eye to influencing caucus colleagues and the legislative process. Or caucus presentations and background briefings given by interest groups can influence how members position themselves for issues to be aired in a standing committee. Parallelling parliamentary committees doesn't escape criticism.

> "All parties have internal committees in their caucuses. I notice the Liberal Party has had many in the last few years: a task force on the cities, on rural affairs, a bank merger committee, an EI committee, and so on. [. . .] All too often, I think, a lot of work has been done in the Liberal caucus itself that maybe should have been done by all-party committees."
>
> – The Hon. Lorne Nystrom (NDP), Standing Committee on Procedure and House Affairs, February 19, 2004

"Caucus" can assume a broader context. Members of different political parties will often form a "caucus" and actively promote the interests of, say, a specific industry. The Sugar Caucus, for example, has represented the interests of sugar refiners and producers in ridings across the country.

 WHAT TO DO

- Depending on the issue, your standing committee efforts might include broader contact with caucus members.
- Consider this: by meeting with members of a standing committee, you are interacting with only about 5% of all MPs. Conducting a caucus presentation means, potentially, communicating with a bulk of party members, and perhaps 100% of them.
- Meeting with MPs in their ridings, doing caucus presentations, and keeping influential caucus members informed set the stage for getting your messages heard beyond the standing committee door.

COMMITTEE OF THE WHOLE

> "This is not the first occasion on which I have seen representatives of labour unions appear before this chamber. I would remind the witnesses that, in the past, a number of unions saw improvements to the legislation as a result of amendments originating in this chamber... This afternoon, I listened to two ministers. This evening, I listened to representatives of the post office. I was not impressed with any of them."
>
> – Senator Orville Phillips (PC), Consideration in Committee
> of the Whole, the Senate, December 3, 1997

The Committee of the Whole is not a standing committee but represents the full membership of the House of Commons or Senate, although not all members may actually be present in the chamber during this phase. The Committee of the Whole is used to expedite legislation through the chamber, such as at one sitting. Witnesses can be called before the Committee of the Whole (although it is not usually a practice in the House) and will actually sit in the chamber to take questions. The calling of private-sector witnesses is not that common; for instance, it occurred in December 1997 during consideration of the back-to-work legislation to end the postal strike (and questioning here can be just as trying as in a standing committee).[8]

SECTION TWO Operations of House of Commons Standing Committees

> "Being the good and studious new little member of Parliament that I am, I read all of the Standing Orders."
>
> – Françoise Boivin (L), Standing Committee on
> Procedure and House Affairs, October 21, 2004

If you're so motivated, go for it. The Standing Orders cover all aspects of running the House. Spanning dozens of Standing Orders, the key rules relating to standing committees are highlighted below[9]; parallel rules relating to the Senate committees are also noted.

KICK-STARTING COMMITTEES

House and Senate committees cease to exist when Parliament is dissolved (i.e., when an election is called).[10] In a new Parliament, they must be reconstituted, and a new list of members must be drawn up.

To get the committees up and running, the House Standing Committee on Procedure and House Affairs acts as a striking committee. It gets the standing committee member lists in order within the first 10 sitting days of the start of each session[11] and makes its recommendations in a report to the House. Once this report is adopted (there can be delays), individual committees have another 10 days to hold their organizational meetings and internal elections (for the chair and vice-chair positions).

COMMITTEES' GENERAL POWERS (STANDING ORDER 108, ETC.)

"In terms of press coverage, what is starting to become apparent in the press is that committees actually have powers."

– Roger Gallaway (L), Standing Committee on Procedure and House Affairs, February 19, 2004

Of the many written rules relating to committees, the "wellspring of authority" is Standing Order 108.[12] It grants House standing committees broad powers and specific mandates.

House Standing Order 108(1-2): "Powers of Committees"

Committee powers are "severally empowered" to:
- examine and inquire into any matter referred to them by the House—essentially the House can instruct a committee to undertake any action it pleases;[13]
- issue reports expressing opinions or recommendations—it allows dissenting opinions, too;
- send for persons, papers, and records—this reference is significant for witnesses and is considered in greater detail toward the end of this chapter, in Section Four;
- sit during periods when the House is sitting and when it stands adjourned;

- delegate work to subcommittees and allow them to do anything that the full committee can do except report directly to the House; and,
- among some other matters, study and report on all matters relating to government departments assigned to each committee, including their mandate, management, and operation. This broad authority includes assessing the statute law relating to that department, its programs and policy objectives, and its effectiveness in their implementation and expenditure plans (the estimates), etc. (The estimates process is considered in more detail in Chapter Four.)

Committees also have the authority to:

- request from the government "a comprehensive response" to its reports within 120 days (Standing Order 109, discussed further in Chapter Four); and
- retain services of "expert, professional and clerical staff" as is necessary (Standing Order 120).
- when the House is not in session, a committee can meet with five days' notice as long as four members agree (Standing Order 106(4)).[14]

SPECIAL MANDATES

"Having opposition members chair the Standing Committee on Public Accounts and the Joint Committee on Scrutiny of Regulations sort of counterbalances the immense power of the government and its team."

– Michel Gauthier (BQ), Leader, House of Commons,
April 21, 1998

The Standing Orders also tailor mandates and features of certain standing committees, some of which are noted below.[15]

Not included in this discussion is the fact that there are often certain statutory requirements placed on committees to regularly review acts of Parliament. Such "mandatory reviews" by committees are becoming increasingly common.[16]

The **Standing Committee on Finance** considers the government's budgetary policy (Standing Order 83.1). Its pre-budget consultations in the fall are now a "permanent feature of citizen participation in budget-making."[17]

The **Standing Committee on Procedure and House Affairs** has responsibilities relating to the administration and operation of the House (Standing Order 108(3)(a)). It may also, on instruction from the speaker, review issues relating to breaches of parliamentary privilege or contempt.

Three committees have been granted specific advocacy roles.

The **Standing Committee on Canadian Heritage** monitors federal multiculturalism policy. It encourages departments and agencies "to reflect the multicultural diversity of the nation" and "encourage sensitivity to multicultural concerns..." (Standing Order 108(3)(b)).

The mandate of the **Standing Committee on Human Resources, Skills Development, Social Development and the Status of Disabled Persons** includes "proposing, promoting, monitoring and assessing initiatives aimed at the integration and equality of disabled persons in all sectors of Canadian society" (Standing Order 108(3)(d)).

The **Standing Committee on Justice, Human Rights, Public Safety and Emergency Preparedness** reviews and reports upon the activities of the Canadian Human Rights Commission (Standing Order 108(3)(e)). This is seen as applying to both domestic and international human rights issues.[18]

The **Standing Committee on Public Accounts** reviews and reports on the Public Accounts of Canada and all reports of the auditor general of Canada (Standing Order 108(3)(g)). This committee is traditionally chaired by a member of the official opposition.

> "Just so people here understand our role, it's basically to examine the function of government and to see if services are delivered in the most economical fashion... But [Public Accounts] does not decide how the rules are set..."
>
> – Andrew Telegdi (L), Standing Committee on Public Accounts,
> November 29, 1995

Within the broad mandate of the **Standing Committee on Access to Information, Privacy and Ethics**, its scope includes reviewing legislation and other government initiatives that impact "upon the access to information or privacy of Canadians or the ethical standards of public office holders" (Standing Order 108(3)(h).

Regulations are permanently referred to the **Standing Joint Committee for the Scrutiny of Regulations** (Standing Order 108(4)(b) and Senate Rule 86(1)(d)). The operation of this committee, and its power of disallowance, are discussed in Chapter Four. This committee is co-chaired by a senator and the official opposition.[19]

REVIEWING PUBLIC APPOINTEES

> "Certainly, as a very successful businessman, you don't need this job. I would like to ask you, though, a couple of personal questions."
> – Senator Finlay MacDonald (PC), Special Senate Committee on
> the Cape Breton Development Corporation, May 27, 1996

Parliamentary committees have the power to call most Order-in-Council appointees and nominees within 30 sitting days of notice being placed in the *Canada Gazette* with the purpose of reviewing the "qualifications and competence" of the individual (Standing Order 111(2)). Unlike U.S. committees, Canadian standing committees cannot confirm or revoke the appointment; they can only report their views in the form of recommendations.

The appointee or nominee's curriculum vitae must be supplied to the committee and is subject to scrutiny.[20] However, appointed or nominated career civil servants are not able to comment on policy matters with which they have been associated in previous positions.[21]

> "I just wanted to add that, when I look down this list, my personal view is that I don't think it's realistic for us to say that over the next year we're going to look at 159 appointments."
> – Bev Oda (CPC), Standing Committee on Canadian Heritage,
> December 13, 2004

Committees have to be choosey. There simply isn't the time to review all appointments. Chances are that only the highest-profile appointees will have the pleasure of being invited to committee. The review can become highly partisan with the appointee becoming a bit of a political football.

> "… right after Treasury Board puts in place some new guidelines, we have the minister showing a blatant disregard for all the rules, and for all the world, for all intents and purposes, using some old buddy system, some good old boy secret handshake connection to put one of his old buddies in place here in complete disregard of all the rules."
>
> – Pat Martin (NDP), Standing Committee on Government Operations and Estimates, October 26, 2004[22]

UNWRITTEN RULES AND POWERS

> "Making the system work requires the ability to negotiate. This is our informal power. It's much more micro-managing the process than I would have guessed."
>
> – David Walker (L), former Chair, Standing Committee on Industry, Interview, June 25, 1997

Important for both House and Senate committees are the unwritten rules. Likely the most important of these is the power of the majority. Without the support of the majority in committee, little can be accomplished.

Parliamentary committees give members a platform for publicity. The power of speech is the politicians' greatest tool. They can say what they want, and the media can cover it. Witnesses can have their say, too, but members will always get the last word.

> "You know as well as I do that the procedural rules of committees are determined by the committees themselves. It is not the government that sets those rules, but rather the committees themselves."
>
> – The Hon. Jacques Saada (L), Standing Committee on Procedure and House Affairs, February 19, 2004

So long as they do not exceed the basic powers delegated by the chamber,[23] committees develop their own operational rules, such as agreeing among themselves how to deal with witnesses, considering motions, and handling day-to-day business. Each committee is different.

In the end, committees draw upon their power to negotiate to achieve their objectives. Much depends on the chair's negotiating skill and his or her rapport with the relevant minister.

 A POLITICAL VIEW!

Question: *"Can you find out whether a committee can actually examine issue "x?"*
— An association president's inquiry to her government relations advisor

Reply: Committees are masters of their own agendas and have the authority to study seemingly any matter within a department's purview, as defined under Standing Order 108(2). However, as issues straddle departments, there is often the scope for an enterprising chair to justify studying a broad array of issues. This explains why two or more committees can embark upon similar inquiries.

Example: In the 35th Parliament, the Standing Committee on Procedure and House Affairs pursued the small-business issue despite its mandate of being focused on internal administration matters. Its chair hooked the popular small-business issue (largely in the Industry Committee's domain) by exploring how entrepreneurs could enhance their access to government procurement contracts. For witnesses, this is like a second front opening up on an issue: possibly another committee to monitor, new members to brief, and another testimony to prepare for to advance or defend your interests.

MEMBERSHIP

"Okay, we'll call the meeting to order. [The chair] is ill. I understand she's suffering from pneumonia. I understand we have some substitutes on the Liberal side, which has some ill people as well. We have two survivors. Only two survivors on the health committee—that doesn't look good."

— Rob Merrifield (CPC), Vice-Chair, Standing Committee on Health, February 3, 2005

On any day, it's unpredictable who will show up. But official committee membership is prescribed. Membership is based generally on the proportional standings of the political parties in the House. The number of members on each committee can also vary somewhat among committees and from one Parliament to the next.[24]

Each House committee has a chair and two vice-chairs. The government does not chair every committee. Two committees are habitually chaired by the opposition—the House Public Accounts Committee and the Scrutiny of Regulations Joint Committee, although in a minority government the opposition can negotiate to chair more committees. Vice-chair positions are usually held by a government and an opposition member. The rules do not require the latter to be occupied by the official opposition, but it usually is.[25]

There are also "associate members." On the House side, individual voting members of a committee can be substituted by over a dozen members of his or her respective party. (One House committee had 35 associate members, although this was in relation to a specific policy review and report.) The whip usually ensures that an absent member is replaced, particularly on the government side.

Whatever the configuration, whoever controls the majority of members largely dictates how the committee functions—for better or worse.

"You know, I fear this is becoming a charade because of the activities of the Liberal members. They have a majority on this committee."

— Vic Toews (CPC), Standing Committee on Public Accounts, March 31, 2004

MUSICAL CHAIRS

> "Point of order, Madam Chair, I want the minutes to recognize that there is no opposition member present while we are hearing the witness."
>
> – Senator Serge Joyal (L), Standing Committee on Rules,
> Procedures and the Rights of Parliament, October 30, 2003

House committee member lists are drawn up by the Procedure and House Affairs Committee. Whips also have a say in who goes where, although members can indicate their preferences. Some members spend up to 50% of the available time on committee detail, so where they go is a major decision.[26]

Committee memberships remain largely intact during a session and even between sessions, such as over a summer recess, although Standing Order 104(1) formally allows committee memberships to be changed within a certain period of time after the commencement of each session and after Labour Day.

Adding to the confusion, any member is allowed to attend a committee's public proceedings. Non-members cannot vote or move any motion or participate in quorum. All this contributes to the "musical chairs atmosphere" at committee, as one MP put it.[27] Predicting which members may be present on any one day of proceedings can be a challenge, although a core group of members usually shows up.

 A POLITICAL VIEW!

Memberships can be changed at any time, subject to approval by the party whip. For instance, to keep a controversial bill from being held up, certain dependable or knowledgeable members may be shifted to the committee.

Very rarely, non-members have been made *ex officio* members of special committees who can participate in the questioning of witnesses and in the drafting of the report.[28] A representative of the Assembly of First Nations, for example, sat on one subcommittee relating to self-government.[29]

SECTION THREE Operations of Senate Standing Committees

"… the publicity the Senate gets is 95% from its committee work and about 5% from the chamber."

> – Senator Michael Kirby (L), Standing Senate Committee on
> Privileges, Standing Rules and Orders, October 3, 1996

SENATE COMMITTEES AND ORDERS OF REFERENCES

"[The orders of reference look] at everything except operating a railroad and a bank, and allow us to do the things that are correctly and clearly described by the name of our committee, that is to say, matters having to do with energy, natural resources and the environment . . . pipelines, hydro, oil, coal, gas, effluent, particulates, wind, the lot, and the environment, in all respects, and those things that affect the environment, including all the things we have talked about. It is our menu. It is like a big menu from a Chinese restaurant. We can take one from column A and one from column B."

> – Senator Tommy Banks (L), Chair, Standing Senate Committee on
> Energy, the Environment and Natural Resources, October 7, 2004

Unlike House committees, Senate standing committees must receive a specific reference from the Senate chamber to conduct each new piece of business (with the exception of certain internal or administrative committees). An order of reference allows a committee to proceed. It defines the scope of any study and its authority to issue a report, permits the hiring of staff, approves travel, etc. When a Senate committee receives a bill, the bill itself is the order of reference needed to commence its consideration.[30]

The prerequisite of Senate authority can sometimes restrict a committee's plans. One Senate chair, for instance, was denied the authority to do a study on the Constitution (presumably so as not to attract unwanted political attention to this sensitive issue).

Once the committee has reported, its order of reference expires. This can frustrate senators, for instance, who may want to revisit a matter. Senators are a crafty lot, though. They usually ensure that mandates are broad enough not to hold them back. Also, rather than going to the chamber for a specific order, committees can conduct informal briefings or hearings, but these are not official meetings.

RULE 90

Similar to House committees, Senate committees have the authority to send for persons, papers and records, subject to its order of reference (this authority is discussed later in the chapter).

> **Senate Rule 90: "Powers of Committees"** – "A standing committee shall be empowered to inquire into and report upon such matters as are referred to it from time to time by the Senate, and shall be authorized to send for persons, papers and records, whenever required, and to print from day to day such papers and evidence as may be ordered by it."

SPECIAL MANDATES

> "If the mandate is broad enough, you could go to Great Britain and look at mad cow disease."
>
> – Senator Arthur Bernston (PC), Standing Senate Committee on Energy, the Environment and Natural Resources, March 26, 1996

Senate committees, too, have the capacity to chase just about any issue they want, subject to an order of reference. Mandates of Senate standing committees are set out in the Senate Rules.[31] Due to the length of some of these mandates, they are not reprinted here. However, there are some noteworthy observations to make.

Mandates can be obvious: the **Senate Standing Committee on Fisheries** deals with fish. Others may be less so. The **Standing Committee on Transport and Communications** considers tourist traffic, among other matters.

Mandates evolve. Recently, the **Standing Committee on Foreign Affairs** was given the authority to monitor and report on trade agreements, such as NAFTA.

In practice, certain issues can be heard in more than one committee. The extensive mandate of the **Standing Committee on Social Affairs,**

Science and Technology, for instance, includes consumer affairs, yet the **Standing Committee on Banking, Trade and Commerce** handles consumer issues in financial services.

Some Senate subcommittees tend to have near-permanent status, such as the **Subcommittee on Veterans Affairs**, which has been around since 1984. Subcommittees must be reestablished in each session by their parent standing committees to remain operational.

Senate committees face some unique requirements. Its committees are to invite provincial or territorial governments to make representations where a matter or bill has a special interest in that region.[32]

Unlike the House, Senate committees cannot sit if the Senate itself is sitting (unless the committee is granted special permission to do so).

A POLITICAL VIEW!

"There is generally no hard and fast rule about what committees get which bills. It's a negotiating process. But sometimes the government will threaten to put its foot down, and could use its majority, and direct a bill to one Senate committee over another. It can depend on the committee, the chair, and the issue."
– Bruce Carson, Senior Advisor to the Deputy Leader of the Opposition (PC), Interview, August 13, 1998

Overlapping committee mandates give the government flexibility to manage the legislative agenda. On the controversial tobacco bill in 1997, for example, the government directed the bill to the Legal and Constitutional Affairs Committee for consideration,[33] not the Social Affairs Committee, although the latter conceivably could have had a stake in this type of issue.

Bills can be stickhandled to one committee over another for any number of reasons, such as ensuring a better chance of speedy passage. Interest groups will put their oar in, too. They can pull for certain committees. For witnesses, being left in the dark about which committee has jurisdiction over an issue until, perhaps, the last minute means not knowing which senators will consider the bill. This makes the organizing of pre-meetings (consultations before the hearing) a challenge.

SENATE COMMITTEE MEMBERSHIP

> "In the short time that I have been in the Senate, I have come to the conclusion that the strength of the Senate is in its committees."
> – Senator William Rompkey (L), Standing Senate Committee on Privileges, Standing Rules and Orders, October 3, 1996

Most Senate committees generally have 12 members. The political parties are represented proportionately. The Senate leader of the government and opposition are *ex officio* members of all committees.

Senate chairs are held by Liberals or Conservatives and are allocated by agreement according to party numbers. Independent senators can chair committees.

Any senator can sit in on a committee proceeding, but only official committee members can vote or be included in the quorum. Unlike in the House, Senate committees do not have associate members. Committee memberships can change at any time provided a notice is filed with the clerk of the Senate by the respective party leader in the chamber.[34]

A POLITICAL VIEW! **House vs. Senate Committees**

> "I am asking that either today or sometime very soon some time frames be put on the House committee. Will they start where we left off, or are they going to start all over again consulting with the same groups, meeting, and filing a report that the minister and the department will study further? I think that we will be into another election before that will happen. We need to give some hope to Aboriginal women and children."
> – Senator Raynell Andreychuk (CPC), Chair, Standing Senate Committee on Human Rights, November 22, 2004

Witnesses can get caught in a consultation loop. House and Senate committees do their own thing, often are not co-ordinated, and members, themselves, become frustrated at their own process. Witnesses are subject to these whims, as are Canadians who are ultimately at the receiving end of government programs.

SECTION FOUR Understanding the Authority "to Send"

"What do you mean no powers? We can subpoena witnesses, we can hear them under oath, we can report, assign responsibility or blame if we like. We have arguably more powers than the Royal Commission."
    – Senator Lowell Murray (PC), Radio Interview, March 21, 1997[35]

"PERSONS, PAPERS, AND RECORDS"

"It has been a year since I was elected. This is the first time I have been told exactly what my powers as part of a parliamentary committee are in this regard."
    – Gilbert Fillion (BQ), Standing Joint Committee for the
    Scrutiny of Regulations, November 17, 1994

As noted earlier in this chapter, parliamentary committees have the authority "to send for persons, papers, and records."[36] Members and prospective witnesses may not be fully aware of the breadth and implications of this rather simple phrase. This section outlines this authority.

"Perhaps this very simple wording is misleading in that it does not describe the very, very broad nature of the committees' powers."
    – Diane Davidson, General Legal Counsel, House of Commons,
    Standing Joint Committee for the Scrutiny of Regulations,
    November 17, 1994

LONG ON HISTORY, SHORT ON EXPERIENCE

"I recognize that this concept of parliamentary privilege is not readily comprehensible in general public discussion, although I would argue that, as soon as a member of the public were presented with appearing before a parliamentary committee, that person would fast understand what parliamentary privilege is about, and for understandable reasons."
    – Rob Walsh, Law Clerk and Parliamentary Counsel, House of
    Commons, Subcommittee on Parliamentary Privilege of the Standing
    Committee on Procedure and House Affairs, November 16, 2004

In the long history of British parliamentary government, upon which Canadian parliamentary tradition is based, charges of contempt have been levied against witnesses for failing to answer questions and for appearing before a committee in a state of intoxication, among other reasons.[37] Neither is advisable.

But in the relatively short history of Canadian Parliaments, committees have *rarely* triggered such formal powers. In the past, there seems to have been a relatively small number of experiences with issuing a summons and particularly in enforcing them. (More often than not, Canadians are lobbying to get on witness lists! Committees turning groups away is more often the norm. As well, committees pursue witnesses through effective questioning, among other techniques, not summoning.) Still, the authority is definitely there, and you should understand it.

OFF YOU GO, MR. MILLER

The last time the chamber took a recalcitrant witness into custody was in 1913.[38]

Mr. Miller, Go to Jail... In 1913, only poor Mr. R. C. Miller had ever been sent to jail for refusing to answer questions before a Canadian parliamentary committee. After being summoned to the House, he remained intransigent and he was promptly escorted to the Carleton County jail.[39] (Yes, he was later released).

The Senate has used its power of summons only sparingly (in 1995 during the Pearson Airport Inquiry and in 1982 when a committee adopted a motion summoning a reluctant official to appear).[40] House committees have been more active and have wielded their formal power, or seriously contemplated doing so, several times in the past 25 years alone.[41] Interestingly, most cases have seemed to involve public servants and ministers, including even an attempt to summon the prime minister in 1990![42] More recently, though, emboldened members, testy Parliaments, and scandals have prompted committees to lean on witnesses. More on this to come.

SYMBOLISM MATTERS – IT JUST DOES

"Former privacy commissioner George Radwanski should be found guilty of contempt and put in jail to reassert the authority of Parliament in the 21ˢᵗ century..."
– Paul Forseth (CA) as quoted in *The Ottawa Citizen*, October 28, 2003[43]

Perceived power is as important as real power. While calling for a symbolic day in jail is highly uncommon, lately members have developed a keen political sense of accountability. (This has been especially true in a minority government situation where opposition members can outvote controversy-shy government members.)[44]

Committees can't actually put someone in jail or actually reduce a department's budget. Final decisions rest with the House of Commons. With majority support on the committee, it can force matters to the floor of the House for tackling (and into the headlines). With such symbolic gestures, backed by real authorities, members are signalling a broader message—committees are to be reckoned with.

"Sometimes you want a witness in committee, just to call them—call them so they know you're looking, since the threat of scrutiny can be as good as actual scrutiny. Committees have plenty of power, but I feel that they have to use it or fear being perceived to have lost it."
– Derek Lee (L), Interview, May 10, 2005

A POLITICAL VIEW!

"Committees? They're not working! We recommended against confirming a Governor in Council appointment, but it went ahead anyway. We were rolled over by the centre."
– MP (L), Interview, July 26, 2005

While the authority is there to review public appointees and make recommendations, the government can often do as it pleases and override committee wishes. Real power also remains with the PMO, the Prime Minister's Office.[45]

While not to be considered as legal advice, this section highlights the authority to send for persons, papers, and records, the summons process and its enforcement, and other related matters.

The 10 Things You Need to Know about Committee Powers

"If someone asked us the question about the breadth of committee powers, we'd probably have to get our general counsel in and get him to look it up."

– President of a national association, Interview, May 27, 1997

Keep in mind these 10 points:

1. *Appear and Answer*
   Witnesses are expected to appear before committees when invited and answer all members' questions.

2. *Authority to Send*
   Witnesses can be formally summoned to appear and produce relevant information.

3. *Moral Suasion*
   Committees usually get what they want through questioning or by moral suasion, compromise, public criticism and embarrassment, media attention, and, infrequently, just threatening to issue a summons or place a witness under oath.

4. *Pursuit of Accommodation*
   Consequently, committees are more inclined to work it out with witnesses about what information is truly necessary to disclose (particularly if witnesses demonstrate a willingness to assist the committee).

5. *Oath*
   Witnesses can be placed under oath, or affirmation.

6. *Immunity*
   Witnesses are granted immunity, under protection of the House, when testifying before its committees.

7. *Enforcement*

While committees can send for persons, papers, and records, they cannot enforce this. Only Parliament (i.e., the House or Senate) can do so after the committee reports the matter to the chamber. Parliament retains the power to reprimand (and even imprison!) recalcitrant witnesses if the House or Senate finds the person in contempt of Parliament.

8. *Process*

Committees must embark on a certain process to activate their formal authority to send.

9. *Public Servants*

By respecting the committee's desire for information and by upholding their responsibilities to their minister, public servants face a unique situation when dealing with parliamentary committees.

10. *Political Forum*

Committees, members, and witnesses interact in a political forum. Political considerations seem to be an implicit part of exercising and enforcing these authorities.

These and other key points are addressed below.

APPEAR AND ANSWER
Am I Being Invited or Summoned?

"[Committee] powers include the right not only to invite witnesses to appear but to summon them to appear, if necessary."

– Speaker, House of Commons, March 17, 1987

Being invited does not mean you have been summoned. The overwhelming number of testimonies given to committee are done on the basis of invitation.

Answering Questions

> "Okay. In a parliamentary committee, can a witness refuse to respond to a direct question?"
>
> – The Hon. Judi Longfield (L), Chair, Subcommittee on Parliamentary
> Privilege of the Standing Committee on Procedure and House Affairs,
> November 16, 2004

While witnesses must answer all questions,[46] reasonable considerations and practices often influence how this is done.

For instance, a parliamentary authority declares that witnesses are to be "given the opportunity to be heard."[47] Questions may be objected to, but a witness is obliged to answer if the committee agrees so.[48] The witness's capacity to explain is critical to fulfilling this obligation—assisting committees in carrying out parliamentary business (and in protecting his or her interests at the same time). One consequence is that hearsay becomes a mainstay of a parliamentary evidence.[49]

There are no rules dictating the nature of member questions, although they should be relevant to the issue at hand, and members are expected to undertake questioning that shows "appropriate courtesy and fairness."[50] A witness cannot refuse to answer a question on the basis of self-incrimination, of risk of civil or criminal action, of client-solicitor privilege, of any oath, or of a lack of client consent, among other situations.[51]

AUTHORITY TO SEND

> "I would like you to table all your documents on child care programs and expenditures, public health programs, day care programs, disease prevention programs, diabetes programs, substance abuse programs, women's programs, water quality programs, and housing improvement programs. You talked about special needs students. I want to see those documents, and I want to see your community wellness program documents too, please, Mr. Minister."
>
> – Carol Skelton (CPC), Standing Committee on Aboriginal
> Affairs and Northern Development, October 28, 2004

Committees can require the production of papers "provided that such papers are relevant to the committee's work as defined by its order of reference."[52]

While committee authority to send for papers is seen as "unlimited" or "unrestricted"[53]—and members won't hesitate to ask—the House is also guided by the reasonable principle that there is "a general rule that papers should only be ordered on subjects which are of a public or official character."[54] As one source notes, "it may not be appropriate to insist on the production of papers in all cases."[55] Convention is an integral part of understanding such powers.[56]

These authorities are also subject to member points of order. For instance, individual members themselves can appeal to the chair and to committee colleagues about a fellow member's inappropriate line of questioning.[57] Ultimately, the chair plays a role in determining such matters.

MORAL SUASION

"The committee went out of its way to accommodate us. They made it hard for us to say 'no' to their invitation."

– Association executive, Interview, June 5, 1997

Committees are adept at getting witnesses to appear.

They will use the media. Few individuals want to be slammed in the press for shunning a parliamentary committee. Taking the matter public opens a second front—the court of public opinion.

"When [a senior official] refused to appear before the committee, we went after him. We said, 'If you refuse, we'll bring in the media.' He came."

– Len Hopkins (L), Interview, May 28, 1997

Going public raises the stakes for the committee, too. It may attract scrutiny of its own actions.[58]

"Committee powers and its limits comes down to what is in the public interest. This should dictate how far the committee can pursue a matter."

– Hugh Winsor, National Political Columnist, *The Globe and Mail,*
Interview, September 3, 1997

Infrequently, committees pass motions ordering a person to testify or threaten a witness with a summons if the witness still refuses.[59] This shot-across-the-bow approach was employed at the Pearson Airport Agreements Inquiry in 1995.[60] In another case, a committee passed a motion declaring departmental officials to be in "virtual contempt," signalling the committee's willingness to give the officials another chance to respond before escalating the matter.[61]

More often than not, it is through effective questioning and the give and take of discussion that committee members can refine their thinking and determine what is truly relevant. Is the witness truly refusing to comply? Is the information sought by the committee clearly articulated? While refusing a committee's request risks souring political relations with members, a reluctance to answer may also be nothing more than not having "the right witness." For example, the minister may be required to appear before the committee instead of her departmental officials.[62]

What is interesting is that committees function without really having to tap into their formal authority to send.

GOING IN CAMERA

"Going in camera is fine as long as everybody can be trusted to keep it in camera. There's no guarantee that people will keep it in confidence."

– Beth Phinney (L), Standing Committee on Public Accounts,
February 17, 2004

In camera is not "off the record." What's said here is recorded, but access to that information is protected. Access to evidence given in camera is possible but with "restrictions" if the House and witness give their consent.[63] Still, there is always the possibility of a leak.[64]

ACCOMMODATION AND THE RESPONSIBLE EXERCISE OF POWER

"In my opinion the issue is not whether Parliament has the right to require the appearance of witnesses or the production of papers, including papers relating to legal advice. I believe it is clear that Parliament has such rights. The real question on which I think we need to reflect is the extent to which Parliament should exercise those powers."

— The Hon. David Anderson (L), Minister of National Revenue,
Standing Committee on Public Accounts, December 13, 1994

The exercise of formal authority (summons) could have profound implications for any witness. Having power requires sensibly drawing upon it. The Senate, for example, could kill every bill that reaches it. But it doesn't. The Senate judiciously applies its influence. Discretion rules the day. The same applies to parliamentary committees.

"I would not want to suggest that, just because we have the right to insist that all questions be answered, that right be exercised in a flagrant or abusive way."

— Peter Milliken (L), Standing Joint Committee for the Scrutiny
of Regulations, December 1, 1994

Holding an in-camera meeting to receive sensitive information is one way committees can accommodate witnesses. Another approach might involve working with the chair (and delivering the information to the chair only) or talking to the member off-line to clarify exactly what is needed. *Working it out* can minimize member frustration about getting information and witness reluctance in sharing it.

"… [C]ommittees will often endeavour to strike a compromise whereby the desired information is obtained in a manner that still respects the concerns of the witness."

— Report of the Chairman and the Deputy Chairman, Special
Senate Committee on the Pearson Airport Agreements, 1995[65]

The chair will know that it is not an individual member's right to get an answer to the question. It is the committee's. Says one authority: "In the final analysis, witnesses must rely on the collective common sense of the members of the committee and their good graces."[66] The witness's tone and behaviour can be instrumental to working out a situation. Members may be more inclined to be accommodating in return for a show of good faith that a witness is trying to satisfy, not stymie, the committee.

> "We have an expression in French. We call it *noyer le poisson*. You drown the fish. You put so much water in the tank, so much information is coming from all sorts, that the information you really need you don't get."
>
> – Phil Edmonston (NDP), Standing Committee on Consumer and
> Corporate Affairs and Government Operations, November 6, 1991

(Chapter Seven more fully advises witnesses how to respond to member questions.)

FREE SPEECH, YES ... BUT NOT (OF COURSE) A LICENSE TO LIE

> "I believe that the privilege of free speech is fundamental to the workings of the House and parliamentary committees. A member must feel entirely free to express his views, without fear of prosecution, without fear of being intimidated in any way because of what he says. [...] The same protection was granted witnesses in order to create an environment of trust between them and parliamentarians during questioning."
>
> – Robert Marleau, former Clerk of the House of Commons,
> Subcommittee on Parliamentary Privilege of the Standing
> Committee on Procedure and House Affairs, November 17, 2004[67]

Delving into the land of parliamentary privilege is for true aficionados of procedure. Suffice it to say that it exists to allow parliamentarians to do their jobs, which includes getting the information they need out of witnesses.[68] In return for receiving information in committee, a witness's evidence is protected by *privilege*. It is the same protection granted to members themselves.[69] Being granted parliamentary immunity means that committee evidence cannot be used against the witness, basically, in any subsequent civil or criminal action.[70] This is to encourage witnesses to answer member questions—truthfully. Immunity is extended to any witness whether someone has been summoned or not.[71]

ANOTHER VIEW OF PRIVILEGE...

"I'll give you a hypothetical example. A witness appears before the Finance Committee, which is investigating banking fees. The witness complains about his bank and mentions a series of problems. Several weeks later, he asks for a mortgage, which isn't granted to him because he made some negative comments about the bank. Parliament would react strongly to such a situation, and rightfully so. If Parliament were not to react, even though in this case we're not dealing with a crime or perjury, but rather the intimidation of a witness, all future witnesses would raise this situation where that previous witness had not been defended."

— Robert Marleau, former Clerk of the House of Commons,
Subcommittee on Parliamentary Privilege of the Standing Committee on
Procedure and House Affairs, November 17, 2004

"Parliamentary privilege, and all the protections it affords, is not a protection to persons who mislead committees, who misrepresent the facts to committees, who, in short, lie to committees. It is not a licence to lie."

— Rob Walsh, Law Clerk and Parliamentary Counsel, House of Commons,
Standing Committee on Public Accounts, October 26, 2004

THE OATH

"When the oath is used, the witness is put on notice that the committee is upset."

— Senior official, Interview, February 14, 1997

Committees have the authority to place witnesses under oath.[72] Of course, witnesses must tell the truth. The oath has been rarely employed (although it has been used somewhat more frequently in recent years). When done, it is so seemingly for effect. Mainly, it impresses upon the witness that what he or she is about to say to the committee is important. Lying under oath may cause the witness to be prosecuted for perjury and for contempt of Parliament.[73]

"… a witness once summoned by a parliamentary committee would be ill-advised to walk out because of an unwillingness to be sworn."

> – The Speaker, House of Commons, March 17, 1987

THE BOTTOM LINE ON ENFORCEMENT

"When thinking of committee powers, their only real power is to embark on a process of initiating contempt proceedings. This is the bottom line. For this, you are in the hands of the committee."

> – Joseph Maingot, former Law Clerk and Parliamentary Counsel,
> House of Commons, Interview, July 9, 1997

Before anyone starts envisaging certain witnesses behind iron bars, it is important to keep in mind that a committee cannot enforce its summons on its own. It can't punish. Nor does it conclusively or finally determine if the recalcitrant witness is in contempt of Parliament. Refusing to appear or testify once summoned "could be regarded as a contempt,"[74] and the committee's "only recourse is to report the matter to the House."[75] Only the House or Senate can decide on the matter after receiving a report from the committee.[76]

"The willingness of private individuals to respect the threat of a parliamentary summons was a bit surprising since committees themselves have no power of enforcement."

> – Gary Levy, Editor, *Canadian Parliamentary Review*, Spring 1996[77]

THE "SENDING" PROCESS

"As you know, a parliamentary committee has the power to call anybody to appear before the committee. It will be the decision of the committee as to who will appear before the committee."

> – John Williams (CPC), Chair, Standing Committee on Public
> Accounts, February 12, 2004

At the end of the day, sending for persons, papers, and records is largely an unfettered power. The decision to do so rests with the committee itself (although the politics of doing so would seem to encumber that authority somewhat). Also worth noting is the relatively limited experience with exercising this authority. Sending for persons, papers, and records is not taken without adhering to certain measured steps. This would seem to allow for thoughtful consideration and debate within committee.

> "In a sense, witnesses have an advantage. Members are going to think twice before going to the House in order to go after a witness. From a practical point of view, getting a matter to the House is awkward. For the House to pick it up, it has to drop everything else. Yet it has been done [i.e., in 1913]."
>
> – Joseph Maingot, former Law Clerk and Parliamentary Counsel,
> House of Commons, Interview, July 9, 1997

A committee can only send for persons within the bounds of its orders of reference.[78] The evidence given by such a person is deemed by the committee as "material and important."[79] The rules require a "certificate" to be filed by a member stating this and that the chair only has to "apprise" the committee of its existence.[80]

With a hand on the helm, it is the committee chair who decides what course to steer after receiving this certificate. The chair's role appears pivotal; a parliamentary authority notes that "… the chairman of a committee *may* entertain a motion that certain events that occurred in the committee *may* constitute a breach of privilege or contempt and that the matter be reported to the House."[81] The chair may determine if the motion is in order and how it will be handled (e.g., whether unanimous consent is required, whether a notice of motion is required before voting, and whether other matters are "in order").[82]

If the committee desires to pursue the recalcitrant witness, a motion (sometimes referred to as a resolution) explaining the problem is then adopted by the committee and reported to the House.[83] Taking a vote in committee also requires quorum.[84]

Upon receiving the committee's motion, it is now up to the chamber (House or Senate) to consider how to proceed with the matter. The chamber "would have to decide whether the matter is sufficiently serious for it to take the time to debate and adopt the committee report, then to debate a motion to order the attendance of the person."[85]

A POLITICAL VIEW! *"A Perfect Summons"*

"That the House of Commons find that [the witnesses] remain in contempt of the House of Commons. If after a further delay to produce documents ... the said production of documents is not complied with, each of these companies shall pay a fine of $250,000.00 for each day ... until they comply with the request stated in the Committee's letter..."

– Standing Committee on Agriculture and Agri-Food, request to the House of Commons to compel the production of documents, May 6, 2004[86]

For the first time in many decades, a committee pursued a witness to the fullest extent of its authority.

Following the high-profile BSE crisis, this committee probed into the differential between significantly declining cattle prices and the largely "unresponsive" wholesale and retail pricing of beef. It raised questions about competition practices within the industry, among other matters.[87] This triggered a process to pull commercially confidential financial information out of certain meat packer companies (some complied) and led to witnesses being declared in contempt for failure to comply with requests and summons.

The situation demonstrated how a standing committee engaged its authority (and faced its limitations) against a reluctant witness. The entire exercise also revealed the methodical nature of the pursuit. The issue basically came down to making it clear to the witness that it was serious about the information it wanted to get but that it was also prepared to be accommodating in doing so. Over the course of this episode, the committee refined its information request and developed specific assurances and mechanisms to protect commercially sensitive information. At the same time, some of the witnesses embarked on a bold strategy to press the committee about its authority to ask for commercial information and the means with which it would receive and protect it.[88]

While, at the time of writing this book, this matter continues to unfold, the saga reveals certain observations about committee behaviour.

Persistence: After three reports and many parliamentary motions and witness letters later, it's clear that a unanimous committee can doggedly chase down its request for information.

Adherence to process: After attempting to get the information in the normal course of inquiry, the committee formally summoned witnesses to appear before it and to supply specific information. Upon reaching deadlock with the witnesses, the committee was forced to appeal to the House of Commons to confirm that the witnesses were in contempt, and to compel them to supply the requested documents to the committee.

Embracing the principle of "working it out": Certain witnesses expressed serious reservations about the committee's lack of statutory obligation to request financial information and its legal obligation to protect its confidentiality (as delivering information in camera was seen as inadequate).[89] The sticking point was how the committee could actually protect commerical confidential information without jeopardizing the witnesses' competitive situation. This resulted in the crafting of an elaborate mechanism to receive, use, and protect the data. Indeed, the committee pledged not to have the information directly provided to members themselves—a previously unheard of approach. Instead, the clerk was directed to channel sealed envelopes to an auditor appointed by the Office of the Law Clerk. Independent of the committtee, a report was to be prepared in a way that protected sensitive business information. The committee also pledged to destroy the information should a successor committee following a general election not pick up the issue again (although this never transpired as the committee resumed its work in the subsequet minority government).

> "The committee gave all the protection it could in exchange for the witnesses' collaboration."
> – Jean-Denis Fréchette, Principal, Economics Division, Parliamentary Information and Research Services, Library of Parliament, Interview, June 6, 2005

A ripe environment: Conditions appeared ripe for all this to happen. The subject involved a critical billion-dollar domestic industry (and export success story), a government support program (where government money flowed out), a highly visible issue to the public (consumer prices and a closed border due to BSE), and controversy (questions about conspiracy and anti-competitive conduct and the levelling of contempt charges). Moreover, committee members were highly motivated and persistent; their inquiry occurred at a time when the Standing Committee on Public Accounts was successfully pursuing the sponsorship scandal and the pursuit of accountability was front of mind for many members. As one insider observed, conditions were set for "the perfect summons."

UNCHARTED TERRITORY

"Parliament's historic privileges and immunities are now confronted with
the rights and freedoms guaranteed to individuals in the Charter."
— Senator Brenda Robertson (PC), Chair, Standing Senate
Committee on Privileges, Standing Rules and Orders[90]

Largely unknown is the impact of the Canadian Charter of Rights and
Freedoms on this matter of enforcement.[91] However, a former law clerk of
the House of Commons has since concluded that, where the liberty of the
individual is affected (by enforcing a summons), the charter must be reckoned with.[92]

PUBLIC SERVANTS AS WITNESSES ("THE CONFLICT WITHIN")

"It's been a long-standing principle that we don't hold public employees
up to criticism for carrying out the jobs they have been given under
legislation by Parliament..."
— Marlene Catterall (L), Standing Committee on Procedure and
House Affairs, November 19, 1996

Public servants face a unique situation. They, too, can be summoned
except that the principle of ministerial responsibility complicates the situation. Public servants appear on behalf of their minister and not in their
personal capacity.[93]

Ministers are accountable to the House of Commons; officials are
not.[94] The principle of responsible government is a central consideration.[95] Still, officials are expected to produce information (thus upholding
the powers of the House or Senate as the case may be) and, at the same
time, respect their obligations to the minister (thus upholding the notion
of ministerial responsibility).[96] Another obstacle for committees to compel
officials to supply information is *Crown privilege*; this enables officials to
refuse answering a question "because the disclosure of certain information
would not be in the public interest."[97]

"In my opinion, it is the duty of the responsible minister, or his representative, to answer questions put by a committee of the House. A committee could abuse its power by forcing an official to testify if the official has not received authorization to do so by the minister on behalf of the minister, since this would go against the principle of responsible government, whereby only the minister responsible can be held accountable to Parliament."
– Rob Walsh, Law Clerk and Parliamentary Counsel, House of Commons, Standing Committee on Public Accounts, November 17, 2004[98]

Invariably, this entire situation can create some friction between members and bureaucrats. Importantly, "political compromise" is the solution.[99]

"Committees can ask public servants for privileged information; however, there are limits to what can be provided. Still, committees have a task, and we should help them. We shouldn't blindly or wilfully say 'no' every time. There are ways to disclose certain information or narrow down what is necessary to disclose."
– George Thomson, former Deputy Minister of Justice, Interview, December 15, 1997

To help officials sort through all of this, quite a string of memoranda, guidelines, and opinions (that tend to be somewhat repetitive) has been prepared in recent years.[100] These documents advise officials on a range of issues, including how to "enable Members of Parliament to secure factual information about the operations of government to carry out their parliamentary duties ... consistent with... the protection of the security of the state, rights to privacy and other such matters ..."[101] Public servants, generally, are advised to answer parliamentary committees.[102] Justice lawyers are encouraged to "do their utmost to assist the committee" and are also encouraged to "work out ways of disclosing the information in the least damaging manner for the client [i.e., the government department], keeping in mind the interest of the government as a whole," such as suggesting that evidence be heard in camera. If disclosure of information is of "paramount importance to the government," one memorandum suggests that the committee refer the matter to the House for determination.[103]

Should a public servant be asked to take the oath, officials are encouraged by the Privy Council Office (PCO) to make certain "observations" at committee. Before being sworn (and like inserting the *verbal small print*), officials are to advise that they are appearing on behalf of their ministers, that they are obliged to support ministerial accountability, and that, if members have any doubt about the truthfulness of the answers about to be provided to the committee, then it may be best just to have the minister appear.[104]

Such guidelines attract criticism.

> "I have run across [the 1990] document at the Al-Mashat enquiry in the last Parliament [the 34th], where it was used extensively to hide from the committee inquiries."
>
> — Tom Wappel (L), Standing Joint Committee for the Scrutiny of Regulations, November 17, 1994

When scandal is in the air, testifying before committee becomes a tense business indeed.

> "I'm wondering if public servants today aren't feeling so vulnerable, given some of the statements made around the sponsorship scandal and other announcements pertaining to restraint in the public service, that there will be a reluctance to come forward no matter what whistle-blower protections are now put in place."
>
> — Judy Wasylycia-Leis (NDP), Standing Committee on Public Accounts, February 17, 2004[105]

At the best of times, officials can face blunt questioning. Being administrators of public programs, senior public servants are held to account.

> "That's a fine speech, sir, and I agree with the sentiment, but we've heard it all before. This is the place of accountability. This is where we want to know why things aren't being done that should be done, or things we're committed to. What gives?"
>
> — David Christopherson (NDP), Standing Committee on Public Accounts, January 31, 2005 [a question posed to a ceputy minister]

CROWN CORPORATIONS AS WITNESSES

"Although considered at arm's length, Crown corporations have a designated minister and are subject to the same responsibilities to testify
before committees. Since the employees and officers of Crown corporations are not public servants, they do not come under the control
and directives of ministers. As such, the same deference to the minister by employees of Crown corporations may not apply, though the
employee may need authorization from the CEO of the Crown corporation."

– Rob Walsh, Law Clerk and Parliamentary Counsel, House of Commons,
Standing Committee on Public Accounts, November 17, 2004

PCO provides the following advice to representatives of Crown corporations and agencies when appearing before committee. They are
expected to avoid commenting on matters of policy that could "give
rise to a lack of confidence within the Ministry and within Parliament
concerning the capacity of an agencys [sic] head or board to adminis-
ter its Act impartially."[106]

A POLITICAL FORUM

"… committees are not courts; chairmen are not judges; and electorates
are not juries."

– Gary Levy, Editor, *Canadian Parliamentary Review*, Spring 1996[107]

Understanding committee authorities requires keeping in mind what
committees "are." A parliamentary committee is a political forum.[108] This
couches what they can do and how they operate. (For instance, being "gov-
erned by considerations of public policy" means, in part, accepting hearsay
as evidence.)[109]

Political consideration envelops all. Like an unseen hand, it can guide
committee actions. A chair that insists that information be disclosed by
recalcitrant public servants, for instance, must ultimately consider the con-

sequences of pressing forward. In a system of party discipline, playing hardball now may risk future promotions.[110] While senators are less susceptible to such pressure, their task seems to be no less easy.

> "When a parliamentary committee embarks on an investigation of the actions of the present government, the whole power of government descends upon you. The PCO, the PMO, Justice Department, everybody is out to make things difficult and prevent us from getting information."
>
> — Senator Finlay MacDonald (PC), Interview, May 21, 1997

How committees exercise their authority to send for persons, papers, and records is a complex matter that the parliamentary rule book does not truly reveal (nor is there considerable experience to draw from). Exercising that authority is based on a mix of elements brought together at once. It has to do with the will of the committee to press the witness, the importance of the issue to the committee, the motivation to seek out compromise, and a genuine desire to avoid escalating the matter. As well, much would seem to rest on the judgement of the chair, the support of the members, the sensitivity of the issue, the witness's respect for the committee or the degree to which he or she wishes to co-operate, the triangular relationship of the chair, committee and the minister, and the very importance of the issue to the government itself.

All this explains why, on the one hand, committees deserve respect because of their authorities; on the other, committees must exercise restraint because of their own limitations.

> "It is a matter of balancing competing interests: the interests of the individual in being treated fairly, consistent with the fundamental principles of justice underlying our legal system on the one hand, and the interests of the country and good government."
>
> — Rob Walsh, Law Clerk and Parliamentary Counsel, House of Commons,
> Standing Committee on Public Accounts, February 17, 2004

The upshot? A "simple" read of the parliamentary rules may not be enough to understand how committee authorities work, or could work as the case may be, in practice.

UMBILICAL CORDS

"… I think we have to go on the premise that the business of committee, regardless of the business of the House, really is separate from the business of the House. We have our own agenda and our own issues that we want to deal with. We would hope that what we pass here at committee gets picked up by the House and turned into something legitimate…"

– Gerald Keddy (CPC), Vice-Chair, Standing Committee on
Fisheries and Oceans, December 9, 2004

As noted earlier, Standing Order 108 and Rule 90 grant House and Senate committees, respectively, a full range of authorities. On a day-to-day basis, committees are run by the chair and the members. But committees are not totally free spirits. The whips exert their influence, committee summons are enforced beyond the committee door, and, in the Senate, orders of reference remain as an umbilical cord for its committees. True, the House and Senate remain, ultimately, in charge. However, witnesses should know that parliamentary committees have certain leeway to conduct their legislative and policy reviews—how they do so is the topic of the next chapter.

ENDNOTES

---

1. Canada, *House of Commons Debates* 134, no. 148, 2nd session (20 March 1997), 9282 (Mr. Parent, MP).
2. There are other types of committees; depending on the situation, such committees can have a direct impact on witnesses. The House Liaison Committee is a committee of all House committee chairs. They control standing committee budgets, such as what is allocated to committees for travel, for witnesses, for publication of documents, and for video conferencing, etc. (As one member put it, "The Liaison Committee is the committee where all the chairs of all the various standing committees get together and in many cases plead for money…".) Committees can be really formed for any matter: a National Security Committee of Parliamentarians

was announced as part of democratic reform in 2004 to enable members to be briefed on matters of national security. Note that committees can be described as "fact-finding missions" when travelling outside of Canada.

3. Actually, the number of parliamentary committees is higher if one includes subcommittees and special committees. See the website of the House and Senate, www.parl.gc.ca. House of Commons Standing Order 104(2), (3), and Senate Rule 86(1) prescribe the chamber's respective standing committees.

4. House steering committees can include the chair, two vice-chairs, the parliamentary secretary, and a representative of the opposition parties. Senate steering committees are smaller in number and include at least three senators.

5. Legislative committees have a number of unique features. For example, having the same broad powers as standing committees, legislative committees have the authority to send for "persons whom the committee deems to be competent to appear as witnesses on technical matters, to send for papers and records." Standing Order 113(5). Legislative committees actually take priority over standing committees, and no standing committee can sit at the same time as a legislative committee on a bill affecting the same department or agency. Standing Order 115(1). The committee's members are chosen soon after the committee is announced or the bill is about to be referred to it. Standing Order 113(1).

6. Special joint committees have included such "hot" issues as amendments to the Meech Lake Accord in the 34th Parliament and the Newfoundland School System in the 36th Parliament.

7. Robert Marleau and Camille Montpetit, eds., *House of Commons Procedure and Practice* (Montréal: Chenelière/McGraw-Hill, 2000), 812.

8. Sometimes a committee hearing can become effectively a Committee of the Whole. This occurred during a Senate committee on Meech Lake when Pierre Trudeau appeared and the turnout of senators was so large that the only room large enough to hold everyone was the chamber, effectively making it a Committee of the Whole. If the Committee of the Whole meets, it prevents other committees from sitting. Standing Committee on Rules, *Procedures and the Rights of Parliament* (May 30, 2001).

9. The Standing Orders are negotiated by the political parties and do change. For instance, in 2004, two new standing committees were created.

10. Note that the Senate Internal Economy Committee continues both during dissolution and prorogation; moreover, there have been cases where "task forces" of senators have undertaken committee-like work during a prorogation. Members of the House of Commons undertook a similar initiative and even heard testimony from witnesses on the subject of airline mergers. In doing so, such task forces lack the protection of parliamentary privilege. Gary O'Brien, review of *Taking It to the Hill: The Complete Guide to Appearing before (and Surviving) Parliamentary Committees*, by David McInnes, *Canadian Public Administration* 42, no. 3 (Fall 1999), 393.

11. Standing Order 104(1); Rule 85 applies to getting Senate committees up and running.

12. Department of Justice, *Appearances before Parliamentary Committees* (January 16, 1996), 2.

13. Marleau and Montpetit, *House of Commons Procedure and Practice*, 805-06. The committee may receive certain *instructions*, for instance, from the House to require the committee to give priority to a portion of a bill and report separately on this part. A. Beauchesne, *Beauchesne's Parliamentary Rules and Forms*, 6th ed. (Toronto: Carswell Co. Ltd., 1989), 204, para. 686. As well, individual members have the capacity to formally prompt committee actions. See the discussion of private members' business in Chapter Four. Moreover, any four members of a standing committee may request the chair of the committee to convene a meeting to discuss a particular issue, although additional requirements must be met to proceed. Marleau and Montpetit, *House of Commons Procedure and Practice*, 843.

14. This Standing Order has been viewed as making the government more account-able, such as allowing committees to be more responsive such as when a major issue or crisis comes up; see "Liberals are powerless to stop a united opposition," *The Hill Times*, October 11-17, 2004, 8.

15. The following special mandates fall under the authority of Standing Order 108(3), (4), except the one relating to the Finance Committee, which concerns Standing Order 83.

16. House of Commons, *Committees: A Practical Guide*, 7th ed. (2004), 7.

17. Chairman of the Standing Committee on Finance, foreword to House of Commons, *The Next Steps to Fiscal Health after a Year of Historic Progress: Building the 1996 Budget through Consultation* (1996). Note, the government financial cycle is captured in a fact sheet prepared by the House of Commons and available on its website. See *The Financial Cycle* (Procedural Services of the House of Commons Fact Sheet).

18. Beauchesne, *Parliamentary Rules and Forms*, 234, para. 834.

19. Actually, in the 36th Parliament, the official opposition, the Reform Party, opted not to assume this position.

20. Table Research Branch, House of Commons, *Précis of Procedure*, 5th ed. (1996), 108.

21. House of Commons Liaison Committee, Report of the Liaison Committee (1997), 17.

22. New processes are being considered for parliamentary committee review of Crown appointments; the measures being taken include seeking a "workable" appoint-ment review process that does not "unduly delay" appointments. The Treasury Board notes that, "The Government Leader in the House of Commons has pro-vided parliamentary committees with a list of appointments, including those made to Crown Corporations, and asked the committees to determine which key appointments they wish to review prior to these appointments being finalized. The Procedure and House Affairs Committee has been asked to determine how the reviews would be conducted, and to consult with parliamentarians from both Chambers on how these reviews should be implemented." Treasury Board of Canada Secretariat, *Review of the Governance Framework for Canada's Crown*

Corporations—Meeting the Expectations of Canadians (February 17, 2005). There has been some criticism that appointment vetting by parliamentary committees may also be a disincentive to recruitment. See Dean Beeby, "Crown corps bristle at rules shedding light into their operations: Documents," The Canadian Press, February 5, 2005.

23. *Précis of Procedure*, 98.

24. See Standing Order 104(2). There are variations in committee memberships from one Parliament to the next. In the 36th Parliament, there were generally 16 members of Parliament on House standing committees (and upwards to 18); in the 38th Parliament, there were 12.

25. The rules state that "a Member in opposition" must hold one of these three executive posts on the committee (Standing Order 106(2)).

26. Peter C. Dobell, "Comments on the Survey of Attitudes to Committee Work," *Parliamentary Government* (August 1993), 20-21.

27. "Sharing Power?" *Parliamentary Government* (August 1993), 12.

28. Marleau and Montpetit, *House of Commons Procedure and Practice*, 826.

29. *Parliamentary Government* (June 1993), 27.

30. Erskine May, *A Practical Treatise on the Law, Privileges, Proceedings, and Usage of Parliament*, 21st ed. (London: Butterworths, 1989), 618.

31. See *Rules of the Senate of Canada*, Rule 86(1); the mandates are also reproduced on the Senate website.

32. "Provincial Representations to Senate Committees," *Rules of the Senate of Canada* (March 1996), app. 1, 123.

33. Mike Scandiffio, "Tensions rise in House and Senate," *The Hill Times*, March 10, 1997, 1.

34. Senate Rule 85(4), 85(5).

35. Senator Murray's comment was in response to a reporter's suggestion on CBO-FM radio that the government's decision to have a Senate committee commence its own hearings on the Somalia Affair was "toothless."

36. Standing Order 108(1)(a) and Senate Rule 90.

37. Erskine May, *A Practical Treatise on the Law*, 116.

38. Apparently, being called to the chamber to account has occurred fewer than 20 times since Confederation; the last time being in 1913. House of Commons, *Committees: A Practical Guide*, 7th ed. (2004), 39, 6n.

39. Beauchesne, *Parliamentary Rules and Forms*, 30, para. 125.

40. *Companion to the Rules of the Senate of Canada* (1994), 313-14; the other four occasions listed occurred early in the 1900s and just after Confederation.

41. *Companion to the Rules of the Senate of Canada* (1994), 314.

42. See examples of committees discussing the summons process in Minutes of Proceedings and Evidence of the Standing Joint Committee on Regulations and Other Statutory Instruments, February 25, 1982; the Standing Joint Committee of the Senate and of the House of Commons on Official Languages, May 2, 1990 (which discussed summoning Prime Minister Mulroney); the Standing Committee on Consumer and Corporate Affairs and Government Operations, November

26, 1992; the Standing Committee on National Defence and Veterans Affairs, December 8, 1992, and the Standing Committee on External Affairs and International Trade, May 6, 1993.

43. Kathryn May, "MP wants to lock up ex-privacy czar—Make an example of Radwanski, says Alliance hardliner," *The Ottawa Citizen*, October 28, 2003, A1.

44. While in a majority government, opposition members attempted to reduce the governor general's budget but got outvoted. See Bill Curry, "Liberals catapult into committee to block cuts to Clarkson's budget," *The Ottawa Citizen*, February 27, 2004, A4. However, in the minority government of 2005 (38th Parliament), one committee managed to recommend a reduction in the supplementary estimates of the Department of Foreign Affairs by one dollar as a protest over the government's insistence to split up the Department of Foreign Affairs and International Trade into two entities. A near-negligible reduction for sure, but this was an exercise of demonstrating real and symbolic power. Opposition members had the votes to get the matter reported to the House. See Sarah McGregor, "Petty Cash—Commons Committee Votes to Cut Foreign Affairs' Budget by a Buck," *Embassy: Diplomacy This Week*, March 23-29, 2005, 5.

45. The Standing Committee on Environment and Sustainable Development reviewed the government's proposed appointment of chairperson to the National Round Table on the Environment and the Economy on March 7, 2005. It called on the prime minister to withdraw this appointment; the appointment proceeded. See "MPs want to review DM appointments," *The Hill Times*, March 28-April 3, 2005, 25.

46. Marleau and Montpetit, *House of Commons Procedure and Practice*, 863. Note, in response to the question by the Hon. Judi Longfield, as quoted, the response from Rob Walsh, Law Clerk and Parliamentary Counsel, House of Commons, was "No. Witnesses are obliged to answer all questions put to them by a parliamentary committee. The penalty, if you like, for refusing to answer is that the committee could report the witness to the House for purposes of contempt." Subcommittee on Parliamentary Privilege of the Standing Committee on Procedure and House Affairs, November 16, 2004.

47. Joseph Maingot, *Parliamentary Privilege in Canada*, 1st ed. (Toronto: Butterworths-Heinemann, 1982), 228.

48. Marleau and Montpetit, *House of Commons Procedure and Practice*, 863.

49. Joseph Maingot, *Parliamentary Privilege in Canada*, 2nd ed. (Ottawa: House of Commons and Montreal/Kingston: McGill-Queen's University Press, 1997), 268.

50. Marleau and Montpetit, *House of Commons Procedure and Practice*, 863.

51. Beauchesne, *Parliamentary Rules and Forms*, 239, para. 863.

52. May, *A Practical Treatise*, 630.

53. Beauchesne, *Parliamentary Rules and Forms*, 236, para. 848(1); see also May, *A Practical Treatise*, 630.

54. May, *A Practical Treatise*, 214.

55. Marleau and Montpetit, *House of Commons Procedure and Practice*, 865. This source references a declaration that "The House of Commons recognizes that it

should not require the production of documents in all cases; considerations of public policy, including national security, foreign relations, and so forth, enter into the decision as to when it is appropriate to order the production of such documents."

56. *Companion to the Rules of the Senate of Canada: A Working Document*, 1994, i.

57. Maingot, *Parliamentary Privilege in Canada*, 1st ed., 163.

58. Forcing witnesses to go to the media to defend themselves can illuminate the committee's actions and enable witnesses to get their message across outside the committee room. See Paco Francoli and Kady O'Malley, "O'Leary's lawyer says Public Accounts Committee 'ambushed' and 'misled' her—the House Public Accounts Committee subpoenaed three high-profile Liberal players recently, but the 'circus' show may be over," *The Hill Times*, May 9, 2005, 3.

59. Beauchesne, *Parliamentary Rules and Forms*, 237, para. 856.

60. The Special Senate Committee on the Pearson Airport Agreements, 1995.

61. Standing Committee on External Affairs and International Trade, May 6, 1993.

62. Standing Joint Committee for the Scrutiny of Regulations, November 17, 1994, 13.

63. Giving access to in-camera evidence occurred, for example, in 1978, during the MacDonald Commission inquiry into alleged wrongdoings by members of the RCMP. It was granted access to the in-camera proceedings to testimony given in November to the House Standing Committee on Justice and Legal Affairs under permission from witnesses and "with some quite severe restrictions." This included getting written permission from each witness to allow the testimony to be examined by the commission, and the commission was asked to examine the transcripts in camera and that the transcripts be returned to the committee following its use. Subcommittee on Parliamentary Privilege of the Standing Committee, *Evidence* (November 16-17, 2004). Note that in-camera transcripts can be destroyed at the end of the parliamentary session or archived for a period of 30 years, at the committee's request. Standing Committee on Procedure and House Affairs, *Evidence* (October 7, 2004).

64. One case of apparent leaking of an in-camera testimony was discussed during the Standing Committee on Public Accounts (March 31, 2004); reference was made in committee to a March 30th *Toronto Star* article which said, "The gist of Guité's secret testimony was leaked by opposition MPs after he appeared before the public accounts committee, which was investigating three questionable contracts in 2002."

65. Special Senate Committee on the Pearson Airport Agreements, "The Power to Send for Persons, Papers, and Records: Theory, Practice, and Problems," in *Report of the Chairman and the Deputy Chairman* (1995), part 3, 2.

66. Maingot, *Parliamentary Privilege in Canada*, 2nd ed., 191.

67. Robert Marleau went on to say, at that same hearing, "In a case of a non-co-operative witness or in very serious circumstances, the swearing in of witnesses crystallizes, shall I say, the importance of the process as well as the witness's presence and his testimony. Legal action may be brought against him for perjury under a section of the Parliament of Canada Act if the witness is not being truthful."

68. An interesting discussion among members unfolded in 2004 involving whether parliamentary privilege should be waived to satisfy a request from an external commission of inquiry (i.e., the Commission of Inquiry into the Sponsorship Program and Advertising Activities, under the Honourable Justice John Gomery). In October 2004, the commissioner wanted to use transcripts of the Standing Committee on Public Accounts to cross-examine inquiry witnesses and, effectively, waive parliamentary privilege. Members discussed the implications of doing so—notably that if the House waived privilege it would weaken Parliament's authority and credibility. See a fuller discussion on this matter in the Subcommittee on Parliamentary Privilege of the Standing Committee on Procedure and House Affairs, November 16, 2004. One result: reaffirming its own authority and the notion of parliamentary privilege, the chair of the Standing Committee on Public Accounts noted that a letter had been provided to its witnesses that "All testimony provided to parliamentary committees is protected by privilege. Consequently, you may not be subject to criminal prosecution and no civil action may be instituted against you in respect of any testimony you provide the committee." John Williams (CPC), December 2, 2004.

69. Maingot, *Parliamentary Privilege in Canada*, 2nd ed., 36.

70. Senate of Canada, Committees and Private Legislation, *A Guide for Witnesses Appearing before Senate Committees* (January 1994), 8.

71. Katharine Dunkley and Bruce Carson, *Parliamentary Committees: The Protection of Witnesses, the Role of Counsel, and the Rules of Evidence: Backgrounder* (Library of Parliament Research Branch, February 1986), 15.

72. Marleau and Montpetit, *House of Commons Procedure and Practice*, 861. A witness can make a "solemn affirmation". Beauchesne, *Parliamentary Rules and Forms*, 238, para. 860(1). Note that one recent use of the oath was in 2004; with Bible in hand, a former public servant was sworn to say "I swear to tell the truth, the whole truth, and nothing but the truth in my testimony. So help me God." Standing Committee on Public Accounts (December 7, 2004).

73. House of Commons, *Committees: A Practical Guide*, 5th ed. (1997), 16. Lying under oath might also open the possibility of criminal charges under the Criminal Code says one authority.

74. *Précis of Procedure*, 15. As well, from a separate source, the chair of the Standing Committee on External Affairs and International Trade stated in 1993 that a failure of a witness to appear before a committee is regarded as a contempt only "when the House decides it is." *Minutes of Proceedings and Evidence* (May 6, 1993), 64: 10.

75. *Précis of Procedure*, 105.

76. Maingot, *Parliamentary Privilege in Canada*, 2nd ed., 268. Note, a significant case occurred in 2003 when the former privacy commissioner was nearly summoned to the bar of the House for alleged contempt after the Standing Committee on Government Operations and Estimates found his testimony to be misleading. One government member was prepared to move a motion that would have summoned Mr. George Radwanski to the bar of the House to conclude this proce-

dure—something that the House had not done for some 90 years, it was noted. The speaker concluded that the situation, as reported by the Standing Committee, was "sufficient to support a prima facie finding of a breach of the privileges of this House." It would have been left up to the House to decide how to deal with this question of privilege or a case of contempt. However, a letter of apology was received from Mr. Radwanski and tabled in the House at the last minute, which resulted in the motion being withdrawn. Opposition members were nevertheless dismayed by this action and one member declared, "The House of Commons should find him in contempt with consequences and sanctions up to and including time in prison." Later in the day, the House passed a motion recognizing this letter of apology and declaring that this individual had been in contempt of the House. House of Commons, edited *Hansard*, no. 152, 37th Parliament, 2nd session (November 6, 2003), www.parl.gc.ca/37/2/parlbus/chambus/house/debates/152_2003-11-06/HAN152-E.htm. Mr. Radwanski became the first parliamentary officer to be found in contempt. See also Kathryn May, "MP wants to lock up ex-privacy czar."

77. Gary Levy, "Summoning and Swearing of Witnesses: Experience of the Pearson Airport Committee," *Canadian Parliamentary Review* 19, no. 1 (Spring 1996): 4.

78. Diane Davidson, *Presentation of General Legal Counsel to the Standing Joint Committee for the Scrutiny of Regulations on the Powers of Parliamentary Committees* (November 16, 1994), 2. As well, this authority is also subject to a matter within Parliament's competence.

79. Beauchesne, *Parliamentary Rules and Forms*, 237, para. 857(1).

80. Standing Order 122 reads: "If any Member files a certificate with the Chairman of a committee of the House, stating that the evidence to be obtained from a particular person is, in his or her opinion, material and important, the Chairman shall apprise the committee thereof."

81. *Parliamentary Privilege in Canada*, 1982, 189, emphasis added. If a member feels that he is prevented from doing his job as a member of Parliament, you may hear him declare that there has been a *breach of parliamentary privilege*. Interfering with a witness's testimony or preventing a witness from testifying, for example, can also be punishable as a breach of privilege. Beauchesne, *Parliamentary Rules and Forms*, 239, para. 865. Breach of privilege is a complex matter. A committee chair cannot actually rule on the matter of privilege. This is up to the speaker to decide on how to proceed. Privilege is to be distinguished from *contempt of Parliament*; a refusal to testify, for instance, could be seen as a contempt. *Précis of Procedure*, 15. Given the propensity of members to raise privilege apparently without cause, various speakers have urged members to restrict the use of privilege procedure.

82. See examples of discussions about pursuing a summons in Standing Joint Committee on Regulations and Other Statutory Instruments, February 25, 1982; Standing Joint Committee of the Senate and of the House of Commons on Official Languages, May 2, 1990; and Standing Committee on External Affairs and International Trade, May 6, 1993.

83. Dunkley and Carson, *Parliamentary Committees*, 7.

84. Standing Order 118(2); Senate Rule 89. For House standing committees, the majority of members constitutes quorum. Standing Order 118(1). Four members constitutes quorum on Senate committees. *Overview of Senate Committees*, Senate website, 1997. Note that quorum is not necessarily required to hear evidence from witnesses.

85. *Parliamentary Privilege in Canada*, 2nd ed., 337, 112n. There is a process to determine contempt. Beauchesne, *Parliamentary Rules and Forms*, 27, para. 107. Contempt proceedings are not a *done deal* simply because the committee has initiated the matter and has taken it to the chamber. Other steps can be pursued at this point. The chamber can instruct the individual to appear immediately at the bar of the House for punishment. Beauchesne, *Parliamentary Rules and Forms*, 238, para. 861. Or the matter might be assigned to another committee for consideration. *Précis of Procedure*, 16; and *Parliamentary Privilege in Canada*, 2nd ed., 269. After the committee presents its report, the motion to concur in it is considered. *Précis of Procedure*, 16. If the chamber agrees with the committee's motion about a recalcitrant witness, there is actually little experience to indicate what happens next. Another debate could then be undertaken on whether the speaker would be authorized to issue a warrant on the individual. *Parliamentary Privilege in Canada*, 2nd ed., 337, 112n.

86. As reproduced in the Standing Committee on Agriculture and Agri-Food, Fourth Report (May 10, 2004), 2.

87. "Canadian Livestock and Beef Pricing in the Aftermath of the BSE Crisis," Report of the Standing Committee on Agriculture and Agri-Food, Fourth Report (April 2004), chairman's foreword, vii. (BSE stands for Bovine Spongiform Encephalopathy.) Note that the committee's work also prompted the Competition Bureau to get engaged on the matter, and it suggested to the auditor general that it review the Federal-Provincial BSE Recovery Program, a support program for the cattle and feedlot industry. Regarding the Competition Bureau, it conducted its own inquiry following a committee recommendation in April 2004; the bureau issued a statement that "We found no evidence of collusion or abuse of dominance by beef packers or grocers." Competition Bureau Canada, "Competition Bureau Concludes Examination into Canadian Cattle and Beef Pricing," press release (April 29, 2005).

88. All references in this section summarize content from the Third and Fourth Reports of the Standing Committee on Agriculture and Agri-Food to the House of Commons, May 4, 2004, and May 10, 2004, respectively.

89. See extracted quote from a letter, dated April 30, 2004, by Cargill to the clerk of the Standing Committee, in the Third Report of the Standing Committee on Agriculture and Agri-Food (May 4, 2004), 6.

90. *Companion to the Rules of the Senate of Canada: A Working Document* (prepared under the direction of the Standing Committee on Privileges, Standing Rules and Orders, 1994), preface, i.

91. In 1994, one deputy minister of justice could only question the effect, if any, of the charter on individual rights and the capacity of committees to undertake its powers against recalcitrant witnesses. George Thomson, Deputy Minister,

Department of Justice, Standing Joint Committee for the Scrutiny of Regulations (December 1, 1994), 10.

92. Maingot, *Parliamentary Privilege in Canada*, 2nd ed., 350. A recent case weighed in on the matter of privilege and the charter: see the Supreme Court of Canada in a May 20, 2005 decision. House of Commons v. Vaid, 2005, SCC 30, paragraph 30.

93. Privy Council Office, *Notes on the Responsibilities of Public Servants in Relation to Parliamentary Committees* (1990), 2-3. Says one authority: "Successive Governments have taken the view that officials giving evidence before select committees do so on behalf of their ministers and it is therefore customary for ministers to decide which officials should represent them for that purpose." May, *A Practical Treatise*, 629.

94. Department of Justice, *Appearances before Parliamentary Committees*, 20.

95. Maingot, *Parliamentary Privilege in Canada*, 2nd ed., 191.

96. Department of Justice, *Appearances before Parliamentary Committees*, 7. Public servants "have a general duty, as well as a specific legal responsibility, to hold in confidence the information that may come into their possession." Ibid., 20.

97. House of Commons, *Committees: A Practical Guide* (October 2004), 26. This document describes Crown privilege and ministerial responsibility as concepts that present "obstacles in the way of compelling a public servant to answer a question." Moreover, this document suggests that committees may excuse an official from answering a question, in addition to the above, "when the question is outside the public servant's area of responsibility or expertise; when the answer would involve a legal opinion; or when the answer could affect business transactions." Ibid., 25. See also the discussion on this matter in Marleau and Montpetit, *House of Commons Procedure and Practice*, 863-64.

98. Rob Walsh went on to say, "The committee's power to summon witnesses nonetheless applies, and the public servant might properly be found in contempt of the committee proceedings were he or she to simply not show up when summoned. Once before the committee, however, the public servant might be justified in declining to answer questions pertaining to internal government business without the authorization of the responsible minister.

99. Dunkley and Carson, *Parliamentary Committees*, 18.

100. Various government documents address the disclosure of information to committees: Canada, "Notices of Motion for the Production of Papers," in *Commons Debates* (March 15, 1973), app. B, 2288; Privy Council Office, *Notes on the Responsibilities of Public Servants in Relation to Parliamentary Committees* (December 1990); Department of Justice Canada, "Privileges and Parliamentary Committees," in *Memorandum from the Deputy Minister*, no. 168 (April 28, 1995); Department of Justice, *Appearances before Parliamentary Committees*, (January 16, 1996); Privy Council Office, *Guidance for Deputy Ministers* (July 20, 2003); and House of Commons, *Committees: A Practical Guide* (October 2004). The Access to Information Act (and the Privacy Act) are referred to from time to time. The Access to Information Act applies to departments that may have the

records in issue and seems to be used as a basis for determining what information can be made available to committees. See Special Senate Committee on the Pearson Airport Agreements, "The Power to Send for Persons, Papers, and Records: Theory, Practice and Problems," *Report of the Chairman and the Deputy Chairman* (1995), 3-4.

101. Canada, "Notices of Motion for the Production of Papers," in *Commons Debates* (March 15, 1973), app. B, 2288. In 1973, the government tabled general guidelines on what government papers or documents could be exempt from disclosure or production in the House of Commons. Although it has not been formally approved or adopted by the House, its 21 points are "soundly grounded on recognized parliamentary authorities" and "recognized practice." Ibid., 2262. For instance, determining what would be exempt from public production would be such items as "cabinet documents" and papers "received in confidence by the government from outside the government." Ibid., 2288. The guidelines continue to be used as a reference and are reproduced in Beauchesne, *Parliamentary Rules and Forms*, 129-30, and in a more recent Department of Justice memorandum (1996). Justice documents advise departmental lawyers on how to respond to committee questions, particularly on the matter of solicitor-client privilege. See Department of Justice, "Privileges and Parliamentary Committees," *Memorandum from the Deputy Minister*, no. 168 (April 28, 1995). This document identifies "reasons why disclosure of information would be problematic": (i) certain statutory provisions provide for the non-disclosure of information (e.g., the Access to Information Act); (ii) certain information covered by the Canada Evidence Act; (iii) the information outlined in "the 1973 exemption document" (noted above); (iv) information that would constitute providing legal advice to the committee, which the Department of Justice cannot do; and (v) information that is covered by solicitor-client privilege.

102. Privy Council Office, *Notes on the Responsibilities of Public Servants in Relation to Parliamentary Committees* (December 1990), 6.

103. Department of Justice Canada, "Privileges and Parliamentary Committees," in *Memorandum from the Deputy Minister*, no. 168 (April 28, 1995), 1.

104. Privy Council Office, *Notes on the Responsibility of Public Servants in Relation to Parliamentary Committees* (December 1990), www.pco-bcp.gc.ca.

105. In a discussion on legislation to provide public servants with whistle-blower protection (i.e., Bill C-11, an Act to Establish a Procedure for the Disclosure of Wrongdoings in the Public Sector, Including the Protection of Persons Who Disclose the Wrongdoings), it was noted that such public servants are already protected by parliamentary privilege; see the Standing Committee on Public Accounts, December 2, 2004, and the Standing Committee on Rules, Procedures and the Rights of Parliament, March 16, 2004.

106. Privy Council Office, *Notes on the Responsibility of Public Servants in Relation to Parliamentary Committees* (December 1990), www.pco-bcp.gc.ca.

107. Levy, "Summoning and Swearing of Witnesses," 6.

108. Dunkley and Carson, *Parliamentary Committees*, 17.

109. Maingot, *Parliamentary Privilege in Canada*, 2nd ed., 268.
110. Members have even formally lobbied ministers to co-operate with the requests of committees. Special Committee on Reform of the House of Commons, Report of the Special Committee on Reform of the House of Commons, Third Report (June 1985), 21, recommendation 4.11. Conversely, a chair—perhaps without cabinet aspirations—can take a bolder approach.

CHAPTER FOUR

Process and Opportunities

"Canadians may not know every rule. They may not know everything that this House of Commons does. They may not know everything about the committee structure... Many of us had to learn a lot of that after we were elected. I submit to this House that Canadians by and large know that their Parliament is a neutered and ineffective organization. It is incapable of operating properly under the present rules. That is why the issue of procedure is so important. It is one way of getting at the root cause and one way of making change."

– Mike Scott (R), House of Commons, April 21, 1998

While the parliamentary system can be criticized, Canadians should know that understanding the system presents opportunities to get heard and, perhaps, influence policy. It's more than digesting what's said on paper. It's what's done in practice that is essential.

POLITICAL SCIENCE FOR INSOMNIACS ... AND FOR YOU

"Dusting off old procedural books is usually of interest only to political science students wrestling with term papers, a wannabe Clerk or Speaker or perhaps an insomniac. But now (for the first time in ages) procedures and House Orders can make ideas and concepts leap from a simple theory to an actionable work-in-progress."

– Chuck Strahl (CPC), Deputy Speaker of the House of Commons,
Canadian Parliamentary Review, 2004[1]

Ultimately, decision making in Parliament is done on the basis of who carries the most votes.

> "It's a myth that the rules are fair… The rules are set up to guarantee that the minority will be heard but are weighted to allow the government to govern. That's the principle and that's the rub."
>
> — Camille Montpetit, Clerk Assistant to the House of Commons,
> February 12, 1996[2]

It also depends on how it's done. It can be participatory, conciliatory, or dictatorial, and a stew of all three. Each Parliament is unique. That's the challenge, and the opportunity.

> "A consultation in this type of Parliament is more of a consultation than it was before."
>
> — The Hon. Jean Lapierre, Minister of Transport,
> Standing Committee on Transport, November 4, 2004

Your task is to act on one question: how can the parliamentary situation work for me today?

This chapter highlights the key functions of parliamentary committees: considering bills, conducting inquiries, and reviewing departmental spending (see box ahead).[3]

SECTION ONE Committees and Legislation

THE LEGISLATIVE PROCESS: "SIX READINGS AND YOU'RE OUT"

> "I think the committee stage is absolutely important. It has a lot more impact than people assume."
>
> — Elizabeth Roscoe, Vice-President, Government Relations, Shaw
> Communications Inc., Interview, May 8, 1997

At first glance, the legislative process is fairly basic. Three readings, or stages, in the House, three in the Senate, then royal assent and a bill

INTERSECTING THE PROCESS

Standing committees intersect with the legislative process by:

- being asked essentially to draft a bill's principles, scope, and general provisions; this can be done either by a minister or by a private member;
- receiving a reference to review a bill prior to second reading;
- reviewing a bill following second reading, as is the usual course;
- and, in the case of Senate committees, reviewing the subject matter of a bill before it passes all stages in the House and prior to it receiving first reading in the Upper Chamber.

Committees can conduct reviews by:

- being ordered by the House to undertake a specific study;
- conducting a mandatory review of an act after a certain period of time;
- reviewing an existing act containing a "sunset" provision (or, essentially, an expiry date);
- monitoring the implementation of an act (after it receives royal assent);
- initiating studies within a committee's terms of reference or under any specific mandates (these can be very broad in scope);
- reviewing annual reports of government departments and agencies;
- examining departmental spending (estimates);
- considering a white or green (draft policy) paper that may form the basis of a future bill; and
- reviewing a bill's regulations.

becomes law. It's not quite so simple in practice. The discussion below reviews how committees fit into the legislative process and what this can mean for prospective witnesses.

A POLITICAL VIEW! 'Tis the Season

Keep watch on the legislative schedule. Committee work can be squeezed by scheduling bottlenecks (particularly just before Christmas or summer recess). End-of-session time pressures mean that bills may get priority; chairs may be urged to expedite the process; witness lists may be clipped to get closure on debate; clause-by-clause reviews can be fast-tracked and policy inquiries may be pushed to the back burner. The calendar becomes a critical constraint. All this can have an impact on your efforts. This explains why commentators often regard such periods as the "silly season."

A BILL'S FIRST STEPS

Before a bill receives first reading—the official start of the legislative process—much has already been done. The content of the bill will have long seized the attention of interest groups and bureaucrats especially. The draft bill may have lifted suggestions made in previous House or Senate committee reports. It could have been flagged in the speech from the Throne or in the budget.

In short, while first reading captures the subject matter in print, its tabling should never be "a surprise." All policy advisors would agree on one piece of advice: the earlier you bring your views to government the better, including before first reading (and well before committee stage!).

TIP To facilitate the passage of legislation, departmental officials prepare briefing books for committee members explaining the bill's intent and clauses. (The clerk ensures that members receive these prior to the committee's consideration of the bill.) This speaks to the importance of getting your concerns to the public servants as early as possible.

BILL DRAFTING PROCESS

In its most abbreviated form, the draft bill takes a number of steps before being tabled in the House, including the following.

- A department develops a policy proposal, known as a Memorandum to Cabinet (MC), and its minister takes this to a cabinet committee for consideration and approval. Then it is vetted by full cabinet. The matter may go back and forth if there is no agreement.
- If adopted, the bill is drafted by the legislation section of the Justice Department on the instruction of the sponsoring department, consistent with the MC. Privy Council Office lawyers will also be involved.
- Before the bill is tabled in the House, the bill is sent to the government House leader. The House leader (or his parliamentary secretary) reviews the bill's content in detail. Officials from the department will explain the intent and content of the bill. This is a last-chance *political sniff test* ensuring that the bill does not, for instance, contradict other legislative initiatives already under way.[4]
- The House leader decides when the bill should be tabled for first reading, which committee the bill will be referred to, and approximately when that committee would receive it.
- The House leader ensures that the "decks are clear" so that a committee has the time and the right mix of government members to properly consider the bill and turn it around within the allotted time frame.
- Also before a bill goes to the House, government caucus is briefed or informed on the intent of the bill.
- When the bill is introduced at first reading, the government must indicate which committee it will be referred to.
- Following the introduction of bills, departmental officials often offer technical briefings to all parties and to the media.[5]

All this reinforces the point that the bureaucracy, the minister, and his or her cabinet colleagues basically dictate the timing, parameters, and content of the legislative agenda. (In a minority government, accomplishing this is more challenging, although there is greater consultation involved with opposition parties.)

FIRST READING

First reading involves printing a bill and giving it an identifying number. There is no formal debate on the bill at this time.

Bills can be intentionally left at first reading for some time to allow for public reaction and to give committee members an opportunity to get briefed on their content.

Bills are usually introduced into the House for first reading, or the government can choose to do so in the Senate (to expedite the process). Elected members may not like having an unelected body get the first kick at the legislative can.[6]

 WHAT TO DO

- Parliamentary research staff will prepare *legislative summaries* of bills after they are introduced for first reading. The researchers, who staff parliamentary committees, may find your views helpful in identifying how a bill will potentially impact society or the marketplace.
- While the bill sits at first reading, key members must prepare themselves for second reading debate (when the substance of the bill is debated). In the lead up to second reading, key members should be advised about your concerns with the bill.

TIP Be wary of bureaucrats describing a bill as merely "technical" or "housekeeping" in nature. Such bills may be fast-tracked because they are positioned as non-controversial. Since when is somebody not somehow affected by anything government does?

DRAFTING A BILL IN COMMITTEE

Following Standing Order changes in 1994, sometimes committees become involved in actually drafting legislation. A minister can instruct a committee to essentially draft a bill, including its principles, scope, and clauses, and make recommendations to the House.[7]

THE PRIVATE MEMBERS' EFFECT

> "Opposition parties use such bills a lot now—it's a way to articulate policy. We now have an opposition private members' bill generation machine."
>
> — Derek Lee (L), Interview, May 10, 2005

A private member can prompt a committee to consider a bill drafted by that member (once the member succeeds in navigating through the rather tedious private members' business process).[8] But once achieved, it forces committees to deal with the private member's bill, or the matter is deemed to be reported to the House, effectively placing the burden on committee to squash the matter. Otherwise it is "endorsed." It should be added, however, that very few private members' bills actually make it through all the legislative hoops to become law.[9]

Either through the private member or committee drafting route, by accepting or concurring in the committee's suggestions for a bill (in the form of a report to the House), this becomes an order to introduce a bill. Without the usual second reading debate, the bill is adopted at second reading and goes directly to committee for consideration. It then proceeds on the usual legislative course.

REFERENCE TO COMMITTEE BEFORE SECOND READING

> "... under the new process of Parliament, this bill has been sent after first reading, so it gives greater latitude to MPs to make changes or improvements and revisions. Frankly, the process has been working rather well."
>
> — Paul Zed (L), Chair, Standing Committee on Procedure and
> House Affairs, October 31, 1996

House committees were given the authority in 1994 to review bills prior to second reading.[10] At this point, the principle of the bill has yet to be finalized. The committee can essentially rewrite the bill. However, under this approach, the House committee gets only one run at the bill. Clause-by-clause consideration occurs at this time as well, following witness testimonies. Second reading and report stage are combined, following the committee's review, and the bill proceeds directly to third reading.

"PRE-STUDIES"

> "Maybe we could consider doing a pre-study; and at the same time, the House of Commons Justice Committee will study the bill and hear the witnesses. Some of the witnesses appearing in the House could appear here before us the same day. I am sure it would require some logistics, but I think it would be a good opportunity to be exposed sooner rather than later to the different arguments involved in this case."
>
> – Senator Lise Bacon (L), Chair, Standing Senate Committee on
> Legal and Constitutional Affairs, February 2, 2005

Senate committees can conduct *pre-studies* of the subject matter of a bill prior to it passing all stages in the House and before first reading has occurred in the Senate.[11]

Containing both pros and cons, pre-studies might prevent members from committing to a position if the content of the bill evolves over the process, but pre-studies can offer members an earlier chance to shape content. For witnesses, the process can mean more trips to committee.

SECOND READING

After debate in the House, second reading locks in the government to the bill's principles. (Subsequent committee work on the bill is really left to discussing the details, not altering its principles.)

The sponsoring minister tables a motion to refer the bill to a standing, special, or legislative committee.[12] Only three types of amendments are possible at this stage. The bill's progress can be delayed by six months (the "six months' hoist"); there can be a "reasoned amendment" that indicates why the bill should not get second reading; and an amendment may suggest that the subject matter of the bill be referred to committee before second reading takes place.[13]

WHAT TO DO

Review the transcripts of second reading debate in the House. Members' speeches made at this time will be a useful reference to determine where political parties, and individual members, stand on the bill. This will be helpful in preparing for your committee appearance.

COMMITTEE HEARINGS & TESTIFYING

Preparing for your testimony and advice on appearing before a committee are fully discussed in Chapters Six and Seven.

"WORD FOR WORD ... CLAUSE BY CLAUSE"

> "There are new members at the table, and I don't mind having a reminder myself of what our responsibilities are when it comes to clause by clause."
>
> – Brent St. Denis (L), Chair, Standing Committee on Industry,
> Natural Resources, Science and Technology, February 2, 2005

After hearing from witnesses on a bill, clause-by-clause stage proceeds. This is a time of negotiation and decision for the committee.

Clause-by-clause stage is about approving, amending, or rejecting every word in a bill before reporting it back to the House. It can be a laborious process, or entire swaths of a bill can be concurred in and progress can be rapid. Quorum is required for this stage.

Incredibly, many interest groups may not pay enough attention to the opportunities presented at this time. Working informally through members, wins can be scored here or not as wording is added or discarded.

However, this stage can be well scripted. The chair knows which of the controversial clauses can or should be amended. The chair prefers opposition buy-in to the bill and should know in advance which major opposition amendments would be accepted.[14] Seasoned chairs will employ certain techniques to get bills through this stage, such as securing consensus on mundane clauses first but leaving the controversial provisions to the end.

> "I'm going to be blunt. I don't like beating around the bush. There has been discussion outside of this table about amendments. It's one of the reasons we've had the amendments circulated. Our time is valuable for all of us."
>
> — Ron MacDonald (L), Chair, Standing Committee
> on Fisheries and Oceans, December 5, 1995

The chair and parliamentary secretary do not want surprises. At the end of the day, the government (and the minister) must be assured that they can get their legislative agenda passed.

> "I find it deplorable that none of my amendments were passed here, but at least I can say so in the House, and I won't be embarrassed in any way."
>
> — Christian Gagnon (BQ), Standing Committee
> on Justice and Legal Affairs, December 4, 1996

This can be a time for partisanship. The government side may not want to be seen as giving opposition members the credit for suggesting useful amendments. It may pre-empt the opposition by tabling amendments before the opposition can get its say. Opposition members may filibuster, or slow down, the process by calling for a recorded vote on each provision. Or they may work together and embrace common amendments.

> "I recognize the position I'm in. I have to rely on the good graces of the government in order to get something passed. If that is the only way I can get the balance passed, I will."
>
> — Jim Gouk (R), Standing Committee on Transport,
> November 23, 1995

THE AMENDMENTS PROCESS AT CLAUSE-BY-CLAUSE STAGE

"If a bill is referred to committee after second reading, then amendments are admissable on its specific clauses providing the amendments don't go beyond the clauses' scope. If a bill is referred before second reading, the latitude to make amendments is far greater because you only have to stay within the long title of the bill. People just don't know when they should be speaking to one type of amendment or another."

– The Hon. Don Boudria (L), Chair, Standing Committee on
Procedure and House Affairs, Interview, September 9, 2005

Here is the process of amending a bill at clause-by-clause stage:
- In theory, amendments should be submitted to the clerk by members in advance of the committee meeting. This gives all members a chance to consider amendments. It also allows for translation and assurance that they are technically "in order."
- The clerk compiles these amendments in accordance to the number of a clause, line, and page number.
- In reality, because of last-minute deal making, amendments can often be tabled minutes before the committee sits. This means that they are unlikely to be translated (to the chagrin of some members).

TIP Watch for any discrepancies among amendments, in nuance or meaning between the French and English versions, particularly in key clauses of interest to you.

- Admissibility Rules: There are certain restrictions on the admissibility of amendments in committee,[15] e.g., they must not go beyond the scope of the bill. The committee cannot recommend changes in the provisions in the bill that undermine the very principles of the bill.[16] If relevant to the bill, however, it is possible that a committee can substitute every clause for a new one.[17] As well, amendments introducing a new expenditure or financial implications must involve a royal recommendation; only the government can do this;[18] an amendment creating or increasing a tax is inadmissible as the authority to tax requires a ways and means motion, and this is in the domain of the government. However, any amendment to reduce public spending or to reduce a tax is admissible. Amendments must also be "pertinent" to the subject matter of the bill in question. Clauses can't be deleted; the recourse here is to vote against the clause. With advice from the clerk, the chair determines the admissibility of amendments.[19]

- Once tabled, the chair will determine the process of reviewing and debating each amendment.[20]
- Departmental officials (from the lead department responsible for the bill) will sit at the table and assist the committee through this process. They will explain the intent of each clause if necessary.
- The member will read his amendment into the record and offer a brief explanation; after discussion, the amendment will be put to a vote.
- If it doesn't carry, the next amendment is considered.
- Finally, after all amendments and clauses are considered and voted on, the title of the bill and then the bill itself are voted on; once this has been done, the chair asks if the bill (amended or not) should be reported to the House.
- The bill is now ready for report stage.

The amendment-tabling process can be a tense time. Some committees will only allow amendments to be tabled 48 hours in advance—thus giving time for translation, legal consideration, and reflection by members. Still, provided there is consent from committee, amendments can be tabled at any time.

"When the department comes in with 20 amendments just 10 minutes before the meeting, there's nothing more frustrating. I'd like to ask you to tell us that you don't plan any amendments, and if you do, I'd like whatever we agree to here to be binding on both the government and the department side. It's too frustrating to get these 10

minutes before the meeting."
> – Raymond Bonin (L), Standing Committee on Transport,
> October 28, 2004

There is a prescribed method of tabling amendments (see shaded box above).

 WHAT TO DO

"Parliamentarians use their committee work in a political sense. They will work with groups to put forth amendments. The smart politician uses groups to build support for his or her cause."
> – The Hon. Audrey McLaughlin (NDP), former Leader,
> Interview, October 31, 1997

Interest groups (who are not officially part of the process) can still "participate" at clause-by-clause stage.

- Don't wait for the amendments to be tabled by members to suggest your ideas for changes or improvements to the bill (as the parliamentary secretary, the chair, and departmental officials will meet in advance to determine what changes can be made). Certain opposition members may also be part of these discussions.

- Members may be open to tabling an amendment on behalf of interest groups. After all, the member wants to be seen as participating constructively in the clause-by-clause process. This requires advance consultation and, above all, a working relationship with the member. Interest groups should also work with departmental officials in the same way.

- Keeping bureaucrats onside is wise. As one former MP put it, "Bureaucrats may feel that adopting substantive amendments acknowledges there are flaws in their drafting, and they will actually oppose changes to bills if it shows that they have missed something."

- Don't suggest amendments that argue against the very principles of the bill. Here, your work is to ensure that the devil is taken out of the details.

- There are times when amendments (or the bill) are so technical that members will turn to interest group representatives sitting in the audience to seek advice on wording revisions. It is wise to be in the committee room during this stage.
- Prior to the committee hearing, present your suggested amendment to a member in "near-perfect" legal drafting form. This could involve your own legal counsel's assistance. A technically correct amendment is harder to dismiss. This also makes it much easier for "allies" on the committee to table on your behalf.
- An amendment has a good chance of being supported by members around the table if:
- it is in the spirit of the government's intentions;
- it has been "vetted" by influential committee members or will be shepherded through the process by such members;
- it does not undermine the principle of the bill;
- it reflects witness testimony;
- it is properly translated;
- it is technically correct;
- it does not require a royal recommendation, noted earlier.
- A word of caution: this can be an unpredictable stage. As members wordsmith clauses to get consensus, they may not be fully aware of the implications of impulsive wording changes. Critical clauses, central to your group's interests, should be flagged to knowledgeable members in advance of the meeting. They might speak up on your behalf if a key clause is altered.

REPORT STAGE

"Tabling an amendment either in committee or at report stage in the House is an opportunity to make a point. By grandstanding, a member may want to become known for pushing a certain issue."

– Francis LeBlanc (L), former Committee Chair and Parliamentary
Secretary, Interview, November 13, 1997

A POLITICAL VIEW!

"Politics can take priority over procedure."

– Procedural officer, Interview, Spring 1998

Despite the rules and convention of approving amendments at clause-by-clause stage, the members can recommend any amendment they want, if the majority agrees. They have done so even contrary to the principle of the bill (which is a "no-no") in order to make a political statement, knowing full well that it will be turned over when the bill is reported back to the House. Attracting some notoriety may come at your expense (if the amendment takes aim at your issue)!

Following clause by clause, a committee reports the bill back to the House for "report stage," essentially a repetition of its consideration just done in committee. It's an opportunity for all the members of the House to have their say and table amendments and to consider those put forth by the committee, although the speaker will ensure that House time is not wasted with "excessive repetition," among other considerations.[21]

Despite all the committee's hard work on the bill, some or all of its amendments can be rejected at this point. The bill can even assume its original wording. Government amendments made at this stage in the House are first approved by a cabinet committee.

WHAT TO DO

- Report stage presents another legislative window. It's an opportunity to respond to the bill if problematic amendments were adopted in committee. (Senate consideration of the bill offers another chance—addressed further below.)
- Any committee amendment can be turfed out at report stage. So, your standing committee efforts should not be your last lobbying stop.

THIRD READING

Many observers believe that once a bill reaches third reading it has all but passed (although the same amendments that can take place at second reading can also be tabled here, such as the six months' hoist). A bill can be sent back to committee at this stage for further consideration.[22] Report stage and third reading can occur the same day by unanimous consent.[23] Once third reading is cleared, the bill is ready for the Senate.

THREE DOWN, THREE TO GO (SENATE PHASE)

Following from the House, Senate consideration of a bill also requires three stages. The Senate government leader hand-picks a sponsor (a senator) to shepherd the bill through the Senate process. Interested senators may also request being placed on the committee to receive a bill, although there will usually be a core group of committee members who will be present.

While a Senate committee is required by the Senate Rules to "report the bill,"[24] senators can filibuster, or delay, a bill somewhat. This can frustrate the government's legislative plans, particularly just before a recess when time lines are very tight. This is a handy way to wring some concessions out of the government.

IN AND OUT OF COMMITTEE

> "Here we are, having done second reading last night, we rushed the bill through the committee this morning. We are trying to help out the process. If the bill had reached us even a week earlier, we would not be in this position. It is not that the Senate has done anything by way of delaying the process."
>
> – Senator Donald Oliver (PC), Standing Senate Committee on
> Banking, Trade and Commerce, December 15, 1995

On most occasions Senate committees consider bills after they have gone through the House, although government bills can start in the Senate. By being second in line, the squeeze can be put on in a rush to complete a session's legislative agenda. Witnesses should know that the Senate phase can be accelerated. Still, amendments can be, and are, made at this stage.

"As I think you know, we had a sort of stare-down between officials in your department and this committee over the Bankruptcy Act. Ultimately, sense prevailed, and the department accepted a dozen amendments from this committee."

– Senator Michael Kirby (L), Chair, Standing Senate Committee on Banking, Trade and Commerce, March 26, 1998

Witnesses should also be aware that the Senate and its committees can be creative in addressing public policy issues, as elaborated below.

"... a [Senate] committee reports a bill with or without amendments and . . . the practice of attaching recommendations is more an exercise of poetic licence by committees than it is something provided for in the Rules of the Senate of Canada."

– Senator Noel Kinsella (PC), Standing Senate Committee on Legal and Constitutional Affairs, May 16, 1996

Instead of making amendments, Senate committees often make "recommendations" (or what is also known as "suggestions" or "observations") to flag their concerns when reporting the bill to the Senate chamber. While the government is not bound by these, senators like to remind the government that they will keep an eye on things.[25]

"My recommendation would be that the bill be reported without amendment... We may also wish to have included in this document the recommendation that we have the opportunity to do a watching brief on this bill. There is precedent for that, and I think we have good results in that precedent."

– Senator Jean Forest (L), Standing Senate Committee on Social Affairs, Science and Technology, April 24, 1997

Unlike in the House, there is no report stage in the Senate if the bill is reported from committee without amendments. If there are no amendments to a bill (at committee stage), then the committee's report is automatically deemed adopted before moving to third reading.

Another major difference between the House and Senate at this point: amendments suggested by Senate committees are not actually incorporated in the bill at hand until they are adopted by the Senate. Essentially, these are more like draft amendments awaiting approval, whereas in the House committee amendments are actually reprinted in the bill before going for report stage (although this may not occur if there have been very minor amendments).

THIRD READING AND BEYOND

> "Senate practice has been to allow a wide range of amendments at third reading. Unlike in the House of Commons, any clause may be reconsidered, and amendments defeated at committee stage may be moved again. The flexibility of third reading in the Senate gives senators, government departments, and others a final opportunity to fine-tune any piece of legislation. It's a safety valve to adjust the bill before it becomes law."
>
> – Heather Lank, Deputy Principal Clerk, Committees,
> Interview, June 17, 1998

Amendments can be made at third reading (which may deserve attention). However, Senate amendments must be considered and concurred in by the House and then returned to the Senate before royal assent can be received.[26]

Other than amending a bill, Senate committees have the option of holding a series of hearings after passage of a bill (assuming it has an order of reference to do so).

> "Hearings can be a useful tool to give the government a little poke. We want to let them know we are watching and that we want to know what progress has been made since we passed this bill… The principle of the Senate revisiting issues is useful to reinforce in the government's mind that, if they do not play ball with us, we can always come back to them."
>
> – Senator Colin Kenny (L), Standing Senate Committee on Energy,
> the Environment and Natural Resources, March 26, 1996

WHAT TO DO

- Similar to the House side, bring your ideas for amendments to senators as soon as possible.
- Consult in advance with the bill's sponsoring senator and, in particular, with the committee chair about your amendments.
- Persuading the Senate committee to issue a "recommendation" on a matter (if it won't agree to actually push for an amendment) puts your concern clearly on the record and may help position your issue for future consideration.
- Once the bill moves out of committee, continue to monitor the bill; it can still be changed.
- Keep the appropriate Senate committee informed about your issue even if a bill has passed and has become law of the land. The committee may be interested in reviewing the act down the road.
- For public servants, be advised that senators appreciate having the minister responsible for the bill in question appear before the committee (as opposed to the parliamentary secretary).

ROYAL ASSENT AND PROCLAMATION

When a bill passes all stages in both the House and the Senate, it receives royal assent.[27]

Having legislation come into force (or proclaimed) the day it receives royal assent means that there is little time to actually prepare for the new law's requirements. Proclamation, which is publicized in the *Canada Gazette*, Part III, can be held back so as to allow time to comply with the new law.

WHAT TO DO

- The sponsoring minister of the bill should be made aware of any implementation/compliance concerns created by the bill before it is proclaimed.
- See *Canada Gazette:* www.canadagazette.gc.ca.

PROROGATION/DISSOLUTION

Even when bills pass through most stages, they can still die on the Order Paper, when all business is quashed, whatever the stage, such as at prorogation, when the parliamentary session is terminated, or at dissolution, when an election is called.[28]

However, while prorogation would seem to nullify all work done to date, including committee work, the next session of the same Parliament can reinstate the bill back to the same point in the legislative process provided there is unanimous consent of all members.[29]

BYPASSING STANDING COMMITTEES

Standing committee consideration of a bill can be skipped altogether if there is unanimous consent in the House.[30]

Bypassing a standing committee means that the bill must be considered by the Committee of the Whole, whose membership includes all members of either chamber.

THE LAST STEP

A bill passes, but there may be work to do on its regulations.

REGULATIONS

"If we view the statute and the regulations as the human body, I would suggest, generally speaking—of course, not always—the statute would be the skeleton, and the regulations would be the flesh, the muscle, and the sinews."

– Tom Wappel (L), Subcommittee on Bill C-25, November 26, 1996

Rare is it that regulations are subject to the same committee scrutiny as a bill (as regulations are usually drawn up after the legislation passed). Regulations are critical.

> "Could you explain to this committee why, as a minister, you continue to institute regulations? You announce [regulations] or report them in the *Canada Gazette*, and we in the committee find out about it after the fact when it's too late for our input."
> – Val Meredith (R), Standing Committee on Citizenship and
> Immigration, March 18, 1997

Increasingly, regulations are getting the scrutiny they deserve, particularly on controversial bills if the meat of the issue is contained in regulation.[31]

Regulations take on increasing importance when governments introduce *framework legislation*. The bill's broad parameters are laid out in legislation with the "real substance of the law" found in regulations.[32]

House and Senate committees are usually limited in the time they can devote to the regulatory side. The volume of regulations would make it nearly impossible to review them all.

> "If you had to send every technical regulation to this committee to look at in a serious fashion, we'd never get a train across the country or a ship through the seaway... These regulations are changed on a regular basis, daily basis, on a monthly basis. That's the reason why they don't come to us."
> – Bob Nault (L), Standing Committee on Transport,
> November 22, 1995

Individual committees can look at a bill's regulations if they wish (particularly from a policy standpoint), although doing so significantly adds to the work burden. A separate committee, the Standing Joint Committee for the Scrutiny of Regulations, is charged with the responsibility of reviewing the technical applicability of regulations—discussed below.

There is a push toward greater transparency and accountability in regulation making. Departments are required to better inform parliamentarians and the public about their regulatory plans.[33] This, in theory, presents parliamentary committees with fuller opportunities to regularly review a department's overall regulatory initiatives. Moreover, the smart regulations initiative is trying to improve the regulatory environment. All this means that witnesses may have greater traction in getting their regulatory concerns heard at committee.[34]

"THE THIN GREY LINE"
The Standing Joint Committee for the Scrutiny of Regulations

"We need to take a regulation and strike it down if it cannot be corrected or is not corrected by the department, but we cannot use the review process as a lever to get into a policy or legislative discussion that is far better addressed by the people who are supposed to be doing that, which would be the House of Commons and the Senate."

— Sen. John Bryden (L), Joint Chairman, Standing Joint Committee
for the Scrutiny of Regulations, November 18, 2004

This is the last stop in the regulation-making process. The joint committee is authorized to receive all regulations for review. In fact, this is the only formal review point of regulations by Parliament. This committee's members usually cope with some 80 to 100 regulations at one sitting.[35]

The committee does not question the underlying policy. Its work is strictly defined—to the chagrin of some.

"I am holding here what, I believe, was submitted to every member in this committee meeting, that is, information on smart regulations, to improve the way Canada does business and to save our businessmen, our government, and our taxpayers money. If we have to burden them down with the status quo every time there is a regulation that comes here without question, then we will end up with a huge bureaucracy on every item that some bureaucrat or politician sitting in this place feels he wants to generate against someone else. For what? ... If we are not allowed to question the regulation that comes to bear on our community and the economy,

CASE STUDY: Busting Your Chops, Good.
Making an Illegal Regulation, Bad

In a nutshell, here is what the Scrutiny of Regulations Committee must zero in on:

"I only worry that we are busting the chops of some seed producer out there who wonders why he has to keep records for the government [i.e., for the Canadian Food Inspection Agency]."

— Rob Anders (CPC), Standing Joint Committee for the
Scrutiny of Regulations, November 4, 2004

"The answer to that is that, if it is considered a good idea that somebody should be busting someone's chops, it should be Parliament that gives the authority to do that rather than government taking it upon itself. That is the crux of the concern of the committee. If you want this kind of power, Parliament must give it to you expressly. Parliament has not done that yet. It is up to Parliament to decide whether it wants to give it to you. . . . The issue is not whether they should get the power; the issue is that now they have made an illegal regulation. That is the issue before this committee."

— Peter Bernhardt, Counsel to the Committee,
Standing Joint Committee for the Scrutiny of Regulations,
November 4, 2004

then we are all just rubber stamping it, and we may as well just go home. I might as well."

— Art Hanger (CPC), Standing Joint Committee for the
Scrutiny of Regulations, November 4, 2004

The committee does check whether regulations are supported by law, and it even has the power to disallow them.[36] This committee reviews regulations against a list of 13 "tests." Several of these are obvious, such as ensuring that the regulation complies with its enabling legislation or ensuring that there is no "defective" drafting. Others appear to be very broad and

potentially subject to varying interpretation, such as not having a regulation that "trespasses unduly on rights and liberties."[37]

A surprising 25% of regulations have been objected to by this committee, most on technical or translation problems. The balance may bump up
against the Charter of Rights or impose a change without the express
authority of Parliament.[38] This committee is not shy in criticizing departmental practices. It can press the department for an immediate amendment if necessary, it can advise the minister of a problem and request a
response, and it can draw attention to regulatory issues to the House.[39]

While the committee will usually recommend wording alternatives or
suggest that it be changed by the department, its "power of disallowance"
can actually lead to the rolling back of a regulation, if concurred in by the
House.[40] This substantial power has not been used frequently.[41] Still, the
work of this rather obscure committee has an important place in the legislative process.

> "[The regulations committee] represents the thin grey line between
> legal regulation and illegal interference with the lives of Canadians…
> Today, the regulations committee continues to find similar abuses in
> Canada's officialdom…"[42]
>
> – Andrew Duffy, *The Ottawa Citizen*, April 6, 1997

WHAT TO DO

- The Standing Joint Committee for the Scrutiny of Regulations
  rarely hears from outside witnesses. Nevertheless, the subject matter discussed here may be of significance to groups.
- Officials often consult with interest groups before the initial drafting of the regulation, which gives you a chance to provide input on
  its wording before it is adopted and well before it gets to the joint
  committee.[43]
- Before the bill receives royal assent, you should inquire with
  departmental officials as to when the regulations will be drawn up.
  Implementing regulations can be staggered according to priority.

- Witnesses should review the joint committee's terms of reference in order to determine if a regulation might infringe upon one of 13 tests that guide the committee's review of regulations. Committee members should be advised of your interpretation of how a regulation impacts your interests.
- The broader regulatory process is described in the Treasury Board of Canada Secretariat's website: http://www.tbs-sct.gc.ca.

SECTION TWO Committee Inquiries

"Public issues are like the food chain: they move along to the top. Committees often trigger the process."

– Gord McIntosh, Business and Finance Reporter, Canadian
Press, Interview, August 21, 1997

Apart from considering bills, another major function of standing committees is conducting inquiries.

TERMS OF REFERENCE

"As a committee member, in what would you like to see this committee get involved? It could be lobsters, shellfish, the east coast, or the west coast."

– Senator Gerald Comeau (PC), Chair, Standing Senate
Committee on Fisheries, March 26, 1996

Setting the terms of reference is one of the first important steps in a committee's investigation. The terms frame the discussion and set the parameters of the final report.

For House committees, the terms are either drawn up by the House, which instructs a committee to investigate a matter, or the committee will draft its own terms for a study it initiates (under authority of Standing Order 108(2)). Ministers can also suggest to the committee to study a matter.[44] Senate committees require a specific order of reference to conduct any study, although they may cast their net widely so they are not constrained by overly narrow terms of reference.

 WHAT TO DO

- While the terms are written behind closed doors without public consultation, committee members may be receptive to hearing the pros and cons of pursuing certain subjects as they formulate them.
- If possible, determine whether the committee's inquiry has been generally embraced by the responsible minister.

While ministers and their staff may be reluctant to talk about a committee's work, tacit or explicit interest may reveal how receptive the minister might be ultimately to the committee's report.

TIP Be aware of certain catch-all phrases inserted in the terms of reference, such as "to examine and report on related matters." This can substantially broaden the potential scope of the investigation.

THE INQUIRY

Responding to a committee's invitation to appear, preparing your submission, and testifying are discussed in subsequent chapters. The following sections highlight only the end product of the process: the committee's report.

THEIR REPORT OPTIONS

"The last committee adopted an idea that we would release a succession of reports having to do with various things and that they would be relatively small, not in their substance and not in their subject matter but not great, big, long, investigative reports, in order that they are more easily digestible and will have greater impact with respect to influencing public policy and government policy."

– Senator Tommy Banks (L), Chair, Standing Senate Committee on
Energy, the Environment and Natural Resources, October 7, 2004

There are three types of committee reports: *administrative,* reports on committee membership, expenses, requests, and budgetary approvals; *legislative,* reports on bills; and *substantive,* reports on special or major topics or issues.[45]

With respect to the latter category, committees are not obliged to issue reports after holding hearings or inquiries on a subject. When they do prepare reports, there are options.

They sometimes release *interim reports* (perhaps setting out key findings to date or posing new questions to help frame future discussion).

While infrequent, committees can also issue *supplementary reports* after a final report has been issued. A committee may table views on, say, a major development in the marketplace that prompts the need to revisit conclusions made in some earlier committee work.

Committees may, instead of writing a lengthy report, issue a *resolution* on a matter demanding immediate attention. This has rarely been done.[46]

Whatever the format, a unanimous report has greater sticking power.

"When a committee goes somewhere to study an issue, it does two things. It goes, it listens to the evidence, then it sits down in camera for however long it takes, and it listens to each and every member of Parliament—both those who were there and those who were not there—to canvass their opinions and, particularly in this committee, give those opinions to the researchers in an effort to draft what nine times out of ten on this committee is a unanimous report. That's what gives the credibility to this committee's reports—their unanimity. That's why we hope the department takes them seriously."

– Tom Wappel (L), Standing Committee on Fisheries and Oceans, December 9, 2004

REPORT WRITING

"There is always the danger that [in] the process of revision ... the committee will chip away, sentence by sentence, at the central ideas in the report... A word of caution: you may be less than thrilled with some revisions agreed to by the committee and tempted to

ignore or improve them on your own. You are strongly advised not
to do so."

— Advice for committee contract staff, in *So You're Going to Work
for a Committee? A Booklet for Contract Staff of the House of
Commons Standing Committees*, March 1989

Report writing is a political exercise. Drafting recommendations is the by-
product of dozens, perhaps hundreds, of hours of testimony. The report
and its recommendations get the attention, so members can jostle among
themselves to pitch their "pet" recommendations. They want them
inserted into the report.

Key conclusions or recommendations might be informally circulated to
ministers and departmental officials before being tabled. The chair may
want to ensure that the report's thrust is consistent with the minister's
views. The same can be done with caucus members before being publicly
released to ensure that party colleagues are onside (particularly on controversial matters).

"Always remember the recommendations. We are a committee of the
House of Commons, and we want to get our recommendations to
the House of Commons, for the whole Commons to consider, and
to the administration of this government."

— Joe Comuzzi (L), Chair, Standing Committee on Transport,
April 3, 2003

REPORT PRESENTING

"Mr. Chairman, perhaps you could ask our clerk what happens to the
reports that we issue, for our own information, even though we have
been here three years... Then we will know for the next time."

— Bernard Patry (L), Standing Committee on Aboriginal Affairs
and Northern Development, November 5, 1996

There are some procedural forks in the road here. Once adopted by the
committee, the report is usually presented in the chamber at a specific time
of the day. When the House is adjourned, a report can be tabled with the

clerk of the House (which requires approval from the full committee and an order from the House).

In the 38th Parliament, there are three ways to deal with a committee report. The committee can ask for a government's response under the so-called "120-day rule" (Standing Order 109)—this is dealt with further ahead. The chair can attempt to get unanimous consent of the House to concur in the report. Finally, any member of the House can seek concurrence in a report under a prescribed process to get the matter on the Order Paper, or the House's daily agenda; in doing so, this motion requires three hours of debate (Standing Order 66(2)).[47]

The latter course has become a stalling tool. Carving out a dedicated three hours of House time to one issue is always a challenge. By seeking concurrence in committee reports, this can end up delaying House business. As one committee official put it diplomatically: "It's more likely for the opposition to find favour in this practice." (Indeed, government members also used this tactic in the minority situation. But how things are done in a minority government might not be carried over in a majority government.)

A committee report can only be technically considered "final" when it is adopted, or concurred in, by the House—which then essentially becomes an order or resolution of the House.[48] While "concurrence" means that the House approves the report's recommendations, most committee reports are not concurred in or even debated.[49] However, concurrence does not oblige the government to act on the recommendations. (This explains why Standing Order 109 is so relevant; it is the means to get the government to at least respond to the report.)

While the finer procedural details of dealing with House business are outside the scope of this book, suffice it to say that witnesses should pay attention to what goes on here if the recommendations are important to you. Members should be informed of your concerns before the issue is raised in the House (although partisan politics can easily overshadow matters of public policy).

A committee report cannot actually direct government to introduce, or enact, legislation.[50] That being said, enterprising MPs have been known to base a private member's bill on an issue studied in committee. Indeed, reports are often legitimately exploited by many to support an interest.

"You have helped… We have used that report in fact by way of partial justification for our initiatives in attempting to convince the new government to give us a hand, an injection of capital, in order to address the most serious shortfalls within the fleet."

– Commissioner John Adams, Canadian Coast Guard (witness),
Standing Committee on Fisheries and Oceans, October 28, 2004

DISSENTING OPINIONS

"I very much appreciate the fact that the government did have the wisdom to look at the dissenting report of the Reform Party. I see that some of the recommendations were followed."

– Jim Hart (R), Standing Committee on National Defence and
Veterans Affairs, November 21, 1996

Commonly referred to as dissenting reports, dissenting opinions are frequent and are attached to the committee report. They reflect not only the partisan views of the opposition but evidence given by critical witnesses. Minority opinions must be included within the overall committee report and cannot be tabled separately in the House.

 WHAT TO DO

Determine if individual members, for their own partisan reasons, might table dissenting recommendations that support your position.

PRESS CONFERENCES AND PUBLICITY

"We had a press conference with hired public relations people, but no one came. It was a joke. There were a few little articles, three of which were negative."

– Senator David Angus (CPC), Standing Senate Committee on
Energy, the Environment and Natural Resources, December 2, 2004

Dealing with the media can just be frustrating. The point is, committees will hustle to generate news, and you have to be prepared.

> "… sending out a report to a library does not get you anything. You need to badger the *Vancouver Sun* … and you need to get on television there … and then work your way east to St. John's… If we do not do that, we may have wasted our time and effort."
>
> – Senator Colin Kenny (L), Standing Senate Committee on Energy,
> the Environment and Natural Resources, March 26, 1996

While many reports are tabled without fanfare, committees can hold press conferences to attract publicity (or, even, to initially launch their inquiries). Both government and opposition members could be included, unless dissenting members hold their own press conference. Press statements are usually drawn up by the chair and other lead members.

 WHAT TO DO

- Anticipate the committee's "headline." This will drive the media coverage.
- You may be able to tap into the committee's press conference by getting a live audio feed into the National Press Theatre. This can be televised (on CPAC or by other networks).
- On major issues, you may also consider holding your own press conference to reply to the report.

---

120 DAYS TO RESPOND

> "One of the problems you have with government is the fact that, despite all the good work committees do, and despite the soundness of the reports you give to government, nine times out of ten the darned things end up sitting on a shelf collecting dust, and nothing is ever done."
>
> – Dick Harris (R), Standing Committee on Fisheries and Oceans,
> October 7, 1997

A POLITICAL VIEW! Issue: Substance and Process

"Dear Mr. Prime Minister: … the amendments proposed by the Parliamentary committee will increase the bill's potential harm… Don't put B.C. businesses, workers and communities on the endangered species list."

– *The Ottawa Citizen*, March 12, 1997, C9

Sometimes groups express concerns not only with a report's substance (i.e., "what was said") but with the hearings process itself ("how the hearing was managed"). For example, in taking out this newspaper ad, a coalition of resource and community groups opposed to the Endangered Species Protection Act charged that the committee refused to travel to communities to get a sense of the bill's impact on local economies.

One thing committees can do is require the government to respond to its report within 120 days.[51] A response ensures that committee efforts are not totally ignored.

There are three types of government responses: it may make substantive responses to each recommendation; the government may instead make a policy announcement covering the same issue which could include tabling legislation on the subject or make a program announcement; or the government may make an interim response if the committee plans on making further recommendations in the near future. No matter the approach, a cabinet committee vets the response. Government responses can be pretty thin or substantive.[52]

When the House prorogues (when the parliamentary session ends), the government must still honour its obligation to respond to a committee's report within the 120-day period, although extensions are possible.[53] When Parliament dissolves (when an election is called), the government can avoid doing so. When the new Parliament begins, the reconstituted committee, if so motivated, can get the response it desires. It simply retables the report in the new Parliament and formally requests the minister to respond.

WHAT TO DO

- The appropriate minister may be asked about the report or the government's response in Question Period. The minister should be aware of your initial concerns as soon as the report is released. Opposition critics should be briefed as well.
- The 120-day response period allows the government to consult and consider its options, which include choosing the timing of its reply (does it want to get publicity for its reply or not?). Inform officials of your views.
- A government's response to a controversial report could attract the media. Your group may be called on for a press comment.

SENATE COMMITTEE REPORTS

Senate reports can only be tabled on the days that the Senate sits (i.e., Tuesday, Wednesday, and Thursday), although pre-approval can be sought for tabling when the chamber is not sitting.

The government has no obligation to respond to a committee report if it is "tabled" as it is considered for information purposes only. If a report is "presented," the Senate must debate the matter (and possibly for decision). Under a rule change in 2003 (Rule 131(2), (3)), the Senate can request a response—within 150 days—from the government on a committee report if that report has been "adopted" by the Senate. (This helps to ensure that the work of the committee is not totally lost in the ether.)

SECTION THREE The Estimates

> "My thinking is that, the more we discuss [the estimates], the more it becomes evident that the approach ... and the attitude of parliamentarians to the estimates is a major hurdle, and that part of what we would be trying to do ... is to give the estimates more relevance."
> – Marlene Catterall (L), Chair, Subcommittee on
> Business of Supply, December 14, 1995

"Estimates" are the spending plans for each government department and its agencies. About 5% of committee time is taken up by the estimates review process each year.[54] Still, the review process is frustrating.

Largely a spring event, departmental estimates (the "Main Estimates") are referred to their respective standing committees for review on or before the government's fiscal year-end (March 1) for report by the end of May, although the estimates review cycle can begin in the fall.[55] (Supplementary estimates may be prepared for additional funding needs and can be reviewed by the appropriate committees at other times of the year.)

This should be a significant opportunity for many. The minister, deputy minister, and other senior officials are captive, of the committee to discuss expenditure plans and priorities. Opposition parties have a golden opportunity to needle the government. Interest groups can get fresh insight into departmental activities.

> "There is no possible way for us to review such a sizable budget in just two hours."
>
> – Bernard Cleary (BQ), Standing Committee on Aboriginal Affairs and Northern Development, October 28, 2004

In practice, it is often a let down. Many agree that the review is not used to its potential.[56] The volume of material to consider is weighty. The time to sift through it is tight. The capacity to actually change departmental spending plans is, well, slim. Sometimes, members seem to be just going through the motions.

> "Most members of Parliament, and the average senator, vote on these estimates daily without even knowing what is in them, and sometimes I feel wrapped in shame that we are passing these billions of dollars and nobody knows. It bothers me deeply."
>
> – Senator Anne Cools (CPC), Standing Senate Committee on National Finance, November 17, 2004

It is understandable that members become frustrated. Committees cannot increase departmental spending. Committees can agree with, reduce, or defeat items, and suggested changes can be rolled back by the House once reported back to the chamber. Moreover, even if committees do not look at the estimates, they are "deemed to be reported" by the end of November.

To give members additional opportunities to comment on departmental spending (in theory), the Standing Orders were changed in the mid-1990s to allow members to make suggestions on a department's "future" expenditures. The change has resulted in departments issuing forward-looking "outlook documents."[57] As well, departments must table "frequently ignored" performance reports, among other documents, to improve public reporting and parliamentary scrutiny each fall.[58]

> "The simple truth that many find too shameful to admit is this:
> departments do not prepare performance reports that will embarrass
> their ministers and opposition MPs do not use departmental per-
> formance reports because they do not embarrass the ministers."
> – David Good, Professor, School of Public Administration,
> University of Victoria, *Canadian Parliamentary Review*, 2005[59]

The auditor general sees committees as an ally. Parliamentarians "close the accountability loop" when they delve into department and agency performance reports. The auditor general has been urging committees to do more and enhance their role in holding departments to account.[60]

Desiring greater input, MPs want the power to reallocate spending. This could be significant for public servants who would be appearing as witnesses in the future. As well, there has also been discussion about whether voting down a supply, or spending, matter in committee would be considered as a formal vote of confidence against the government itself—a serious issue, indeed.[61]

Unlike in the House, where each committee receives the estimates from its associated department, the Senate's National Finance Committee receives all departmental estimates.[62]

WHAT TO DO

"... last week, the CIDA minister advised this committee that Africa was the top priority of her department. When we checked her budget, we found that her department was spending more in Afghanistan than in any African country."

— Senator Percy Downe (L), Standing Senate Committee on Foreign Affairs, December 7, 2004

- Do you want to illuminate a particular issue, expose a problem with a government program, or publicize the benefits of another? Committee members may be amenable to posing questions on your behalf to ministers or officials appearing before the committee on such a program or initiative within the department.

PROCESS MEANS OPPORTUNITY

"I know some folks find this dry, but there are those of us who find this quite fascinating, the whole process of parliamentary procedure and how we go about the business."

— David Christopherson (NDP), Standing Committee on Public Accounts, December 14, 2004

Dry, yes. Important, absolutely.

As bills traverse the legislative process, as inquiries unfold, and as estimates are reviewed, there are many opportunities to engage the process. However, knowing how committees operate also depends on the personalities and motivations of the key players themselves, discussed next.

ENDNOTES

1. This member went on to write: "In the first weeks of Parliament, for example, the Health Committee unanimously passed a motion that said all victims of Hepatitis

C who contracted the disease through tainted blood should be compensated. That Report was brought to the House, where debate continued until the government used a procedural technique to squelch any decision or vote. Within hours, proposals to change (eliminate) the procedure were tabled in the Procedure and House Affairs Committee, and are likely unstoppable. Hundreds of millions of dollars may be at stake. Procedural issues finally matter!" Chuck Strahl, "Politics and Procedure in a Minority Government," *Canadian Parliamentary Review* 27, no. 4 (Winter 2004).

2. John Rainford, "Government to shift into legislative overdrive," *The Hill Times*, February 12, 1996, 7.

3. Standing committees also review Order-in-Council appointments discussed in Chapter Three (see "Reviewing Public Appointees").

4. The bill-drafting process can evolve; for instance, in June 1997, the Special Committee of Council (a cabinet committee) was assigned new responsibilities to oversee and manage the government's overall legislative agenda, objectives, and priorities, although the government House leader retained the day-to-day responsibility.

5. Privy Council Office, *Guidance for Deputy Ministers* (July 20, 2003), 11, www.pco-bcp.gc.ca.

6. Tim Naumetz, "Don't Introduce Bills in Senate, Reform Warns," *The Ottawa Citizen*, September 18, 1997, A3.

7. Standing Order 68(4).

8. See the Standing Orders' Chapter XI, Private Members' Business.

9. Once a committee is referred a private member's bill, Standing Order 97.1 requires a committee to consider the private member's bill within 60 days, and with an extension of an additional 30 days, otherwise it is deemed to be reported back to the House without amendment. There are other ways for members to bring attention to an issue, such as tabling a petition or question in the House; if that matter remains on the House Order Paper without a response after 45 days, then it is deemed to be referred to a standing committee and, once this referral is received by the committee, it is authorized to meet within five sitting days to consider the matter. Standing Orders 36(8)(b), 39(5)(b). One MP indicates that "… since the Liberals came to power in 1993, only 19 of 2000 bills introduced by backbench MPs were passed into law." Gurmant Grewal (CPC), http://www.gurmantgrewal.ca/house/bills.asp, accessed May 2005.

10. Standing Order 73(1). Reviewing a bill before second reading is sometimes referred to informally as "pre-study," although this description more appropriately describes a committee's consideration of a subject even before a bill is drafted and tabled for first reading—a practice undertaken in previous Parliaments. "Pre-study" more aptly describes a process undertaken in the Senate. See Robert Marleau and Camille Montpetit, eds., *House of Commons Procedure and Practice* (Montréal: Chenelière/McGraw-Hill, 2000), 632, 159n.

11. Senate Rule 74(1).

12. Standing Order 73(3).

13. House of Commons, Table Research Branch, *Précis of Procedure*, 5th ed. (1996), 57.

14. Discussion of parliamentary process here is described largely with a majority government situation in mind; in a minority, combinations of different parties can control the workings, and ouput, of committees which can alter the dynamic between committee members and chairs and therefore be less predictable.

15. A. Beauchesne, *Beauchesne's Parliamentary Rules and Forms*, 6th ed. (Toronto: Carswell Co. Ltd., 1989), 207, para. 698.

16. Ibid., 205, para. 689.

17. Ibid., 205, para. 689(2).

18. *Précis of Procedure*, 58.

19. The aforementioned rules are among the most common rules of admissibility, according to a summary of the amendment process. There are also other rules that dictate what is admissible, such as the "Parent Act rule," which refers to what amendments can occur for existing laws. Described in Parliament of Canada, Legislative Services, *Amending Bills at Committee and Report Stage in the House of Commons*, summary (October 2004), http://www.parl.gc.ca/information/about/process/house/Bills/AmendingBills-e.html.

20. For a fuller discussion on the prescribed process involved in dealing with amendments, see Marleau and Montpetit, *Procedure and Practice*, 651-58.

21. Beauchesne, *Parliamentary Rules and Forms*, 211, para. 713.

22. Ibid., 214, para. 737. Another source indicates that third reading is, indeed, a "decisive stage" and not "a mere formality." See Marleau and Montpetit, *Procedure and Practice*, 67.

23. Beauchesne, *Parliamentary Rules and Forms*, 214, para. 732.

24. Senate Rule 98.

25. Actually, a recommendation can become an order or decision of the Senate if the committee report is adopted by the Senate; therefore, procedural experts prefer to use the term "suggestion" or "observation." As for House committees, a bill is to be reported with or without amendments and cannot include recommendations. However, House committees can simply issue another report in order for it to make any further recommendations respecting that bill. See Marleau and Montpetit, *Procedure and Practice*, 659.

26. Should the House and the Senate not agree on the amendment, then, ultimately, a conference can be held to try to reconcile the situation. *Précis of Procedure*, 59-60. One procedural expert notes that the "ping-pong procedure" of going back and forth to try to secure an agreement on disputed amendments between the two chambers is the "most flawed error of the British North America Act as there is no deadlock-breaking mechanism between the two Houses."

27. Marleau and Montpetit, *Procedure and Practice*, 678. Interestingly, notes this source, the origins of royal assent reach back to the reign of Henry VI, starting in 1422. Ibid., 679.

28. *Prorogation:* The parliamentary session is terminated; bills die on the Order Paper, and committees cease all formal activities and, in fact, cease to exist; sittings of

Parliament are ended. (Note: Despite prorogation, some committees have been known to conduct "informal meetings" during this period.) *Dissolution of Parliament:* Calling of an election either by proclamation issued by the governor general or by the expiring of the Parliament's allowed term (five years). This is to be distinguished from adjourning and recessing. *Adjournment:* While in the same session, the House proceedings may be interrupted temporarily (e.g., Easter break) and resumed without upsetting the status of legislation before the House or the activities of committees, etc. *Recess:* The period of time between prorogation and its commencement in a new session.

29. Beauchesne, *Parliamentary Rules and Forms,* 66-57, para. 235(1).
30. In fact, in the Senate and unlike in the House, sending a bill to committee requires a separate motion at second reading; conceivably, without it, committee stage could be bypassed altogether.
31. One example of members wanting to see regulations on a controversial bill occurred during the heated debate on the tobacco bill in 1997; the government was able to keep caucus members onside by agreeing to committee review of its regulations. Mike Scandiffio and Terry McDonald, "Heard on the Hill: MPs call backbencher's amendment 'crucial,' " *The Hill Times,* March 24, 1997, 2.
32. *Report of the Special Committee on Reform of the House of Commons,* Third Report (June 1985), 35.
33. The Treasury Board of Canada Secretariat states, "Parliamentary Standing Committees will be able to review regulatory initiatives as they will be included in departments' and agencies' Plans and Priorities Reports, which are tabled in the Spring." See Treasury Board of Canada Secretariat, *Regulatory Process* (1998), website.
34. A 2005 report outlines broad steps to improve regulation making, such as using a "whole-of-government" approach which acknowledges that all government departments and agencies can play their part in reducing the unintended consequences of distinct and conflicting regulatory requirements. Parliamentary committees are not specifically flagged as playing a direct role in implementing these measures, however, in their normal review of departmental activities, legislation and regulations, committees (no doubt prompted by concerned witnesses) are likely to increasingly weave smart regulation thinking into their consideration of policy and programs. See Treasury Board of Canada Secretariat, *Smart Regulation: Report on Actions and Plans* (March 2005), www.regulation.gc.ca.
35. It is estimated that the government produces about 2,000 regulations per year (notes Derek Lee (L) on his member of Parliament website, January 12, 2005), which is an increase from about 1,200 regulations reviewed annually several years ago (noted Tom Wappel (L) before the Subcommittee on Bill C-25, November 19, 1996).
36. More specifically, the committee has the authority to initiate the revocation of a statutory instrument. See Standing Order 123(1), which says, "… the said Committee shall be empowered to make a report to the House containing only a resolution that all or any portion of a regulation that stands permanently referred

to the Committee be revoked." For a more thorough discussion on this matter, refer to Marleau and Montpetit, *Procedure and Practice*, 690-93.

37. The 13 tests or criteria to review regulations by the Standing Joint Committee for the Scrutiny of Regulations as approved by the Senate on November 27, 1986, and by the House of Commons on December 17, 1986: "Whether any regulation or other statutory instrument within its terms of reference, in the judgment of the committee: 1. is not authorized by the terms of the enabling legislation or has not complied with any condition set forth in the legislation; 2. is not in conformity with the Canadian Charter of Rights and Freedoms or the Canadian Bill of Rights; 3. purports to have retroactive effect without express authority having been provided for in the enabling legislation; 4. imposes a charge on the public revenues or requires payment to be made to the Crown or to any other authority, or prescribes the amount of any such charge or payment, without express authority having been provided for in the enabling legislation; 5. imposes a fine, imprisonment or other penalty without express authority having been provided for in the enabling legislation; 6. tends directly or indirectly to exclude the jurisdiction of the courts without express authority having been provided for in the enabling legislation; 7. has not complied with the Statutory Instruments Act with respect to transmission, registration or publication; 8. appears for any reason to infringe the rule of law; 9. trespasses unduly on rights and liberties; 10. makes the rights and liberties of the person unduly dependent on administrative discretion or is not consistent with the rules of natural justice; 11. makes some unusual or unexpected use of the powers conferred by the enabling legislation; 12. amounts to the exercise of a substantive legislative power properly the subject of direct parliamentary enactment; 13. is defective in its drafting or for any other reason requires elucidation as to its form or purport."

38. François-R. Bernier (general counsel to the Standing Joint Committee for the Scrutiny of Regulations), interview, July 8, 1997.

39. See Standing Joint Committee for the Scrutiny of Regulations, *Evidence* (May 6, 2004).

40. Marleau and Montpetit, *Procedure and Practice*, 693.

41. One MP has noted that "This Disallowance power has existed since 1986 and has been used eight times since then [i.e., to 2002]." (Derek Lee, MP, *Back Bench Exercises: Some Procedural Changes and Attitudes, to Strengthen Our House* (self-published, March 2002). In the late 1990s, one commentator noted that the use of the power of disallowance had been used only five times in the previous decade and mainly on Charter issues. François-R. Bernier (general counsel to the Standing Joint Committee for the Scrutiny of Regulations), interview, July 8, 1997. Note that, as of 2003, the power of disallowance applies to all regulations that are referred to the Scrutiny of Regulations Committee; however, both chambers must agree to a disallowance resolution for that resolution to be effective. See Statutory Instruments Act, section 19.1.

42. Andrew Duffy, "Amassing power one rule at a time," *The Ottawa Citizen*, April 6, 1997, A1-A2.

43. Watch for any changes in the regulation-making process. In the 35th Parliament, the government seriously contemplated giving departments the authority to exempt certain regulations from the regulatory notice and consultation process. This generated criticism and raised concerns about hindering the capacity of parliamentarians to adequately scrutinize regulations. Ibid.

44. Previously, before the mid-1980s, committees could only commence an inquiry if a minister had initiated the order of reference. Since then it has been argued that without such direct ministerial interference committee investigations and reports no longer always get the same attention as before. *Report of the Liaison Committee* (February 1997), as reported in Parliamentary Centre, *Occasional Papers on Parliamentary Government*, no. 4 (September 1997), 9.

45. See *Substantive Reports of Committees*, on the Library of Parliament website, http://www.parl.gc.ca. Committee reports can be drawn up when a committee completes consideration of a government or private member's bill and after its review of assigned estimates, Order-in-Council appointments, or any matter referred to the committee from the House of Commons. House of Commons, *Committees: A Practical Guide*, 7th ed. (October 2004), 33-34.

46. Greater use of issuing a *resolution* has been encouraged. See the *Report of the Liaison Committee*, February 1997, as reported in Parliamentary Centre, *Occasional Papers on Parliamentary Government*, no. 4 (September 1997), 13.

47. Standing Orders 66 and 109 are "provisional" until a certain period of time in the 39th Parliament; see Note to the Provisional Standing Orders, Standing Orders of the House of Commons, Consolidated Version as of June 30, 2005.

48. Beauchesne, *Parliamentary Rules and Forms*, 245; Marleau and Montpetit, *Procedure and Practice*, 886. Note also that, while a report may be seen as a "final" outcome of dealing with an issue, the committee can certainly revisit the issue, hold hearings again, or keep the matter front and centre in other ways. In this sense, the report in question may be a complete document, but the subject at hand may not be absolutely put to bed.

49. House of Commons, *Committees: A Practical Guide* (2004), 36.

50. Beauchesne, *Parliamentary Rules and Forms*, 241, para. 872(2).

51. Standing Order 109. See also Privy Council Office, *Guidelines for Preparing Government Responses to Parliamentary Committee Reports* (February 4, 2004), www. pco-bcp.gc.ca.

52. A familiar refrain is that members have been critical of the comprehensiveness of the government's reply. See Standing Committee on Procedure and House Affairs, *The Business of Supply: Completing the Circle of Control*, 64th Report (1997), 51-52. When responding, the government can just throw it back into parliamentarians' laps again; committees may recommend that the minister take action but the minister can, in turn, ask for committees to further engage Canadians. See, for example, the government response to the 12th report of the Standing Committee on Foreign Affairs and International Trade, *Reinvigorating Economic Relations between Canada and the Asia-Pacific* (April 2004).

53. Beauchesne, *Parliamentary Rules and Forms*, 243, para. 883.

54. The amount of time devoted toward estimates review varies year over year. The noted 5% figure is an average of the percentage of meetings from 1999-2000 to 2003-04 as reported in the *2003-04 Annual Report on Committees' Activities and Expenditures,* Five-Year Table of Committee Meetings by Type of Order of Reference 1999-2000 to 2003-04.

55. Standing Order 81(4); Standing Committee on Procedure and House Affairs, *The Business of Supply*, app. III, 95.

56. Standing Committee on Procedure and House Affairs, *The Business of Supply*, 24.

57. Standing Order 81(7) was adopted in 1994. One parliamentary report commented that it was too early to determine whether such changes will be fruitful. "Committee Effectiveness," *Occasional Papers on Parliamentary Government* (September 1997), 10.

58. "Improved Reporting to Parliament Project," Treasury Board of Canada Secretariat website, accessed July 28, 1998. The criticism was made by Leon Benoit, MP, quoted in Bill Curry, "Committee boss threatens to slash wasteful programs," *The Ottawa Citizen*, November 1, 2004, A5.

59. David Good, "Parliament and Public Money: Players and Police," *Canadian Parliamentary Review* 28, no. 1 (Spring 2005).

60. *Report of the Auditor General of Canada,* "Matters of Special Importance—2004," news release (2004), para. 22. The auditor general has suggested that committees develop guidance material for questioning senior public servants and ministers about their roles and responsibilities, departmental spending, and legislation. The auditor general has indicated that several documents have been prepared to explain accountability and responsibility: Guide for Ministers and Secretaries of State; Guidance for Deputy Ministers; the Management Accountability Framework; and the Values and Ethics Code for the Public Service. The auditor general commented on the lack of clarity of these documents. Ibid., paras 14, 15. "Closer scrutiny" of departmental documents by parliamentarians is regarded as a priority under democratic reform, as well. In short, improving the relevance of the entire process—the preparation, review, and reporting of the estimates and related documents—continues to be a work in progress.

61. Standing Committee on Procedure and House Affairs, *The Business of Supply*, 77.

62. The House Standing Committee on Government Operations and Estimates assumes an overall view and has "broad responsibilities relating to the supply process and financial reporting to Parliament by government organizations" (see this committee's mandate description on its webpage). Note that other Senate standing committees can consider departmental spending as well.

CHAPTER FIVE

The Committee Dynamic: The Key Players

"The contribution of the committee depends on the minister and its members, including the opposition. We had informal meetings in my office and formal meetings in committee. These resulted in good amendments, and there was no pride of authorship. We were all onside."

> – The Rt. Hon. John Turner (L), former Prime Minister,
> Interview, September 15, 1997

Committees have "personalities"—a cocktail of member personalities, interactions and political agendas. They can be congenial, well tuned, and clearly work as a team.

"Over time, it became part of the culture of the committee that because people involved in agriculture get up early in the morning to work the fields, et cetera, so too do members of the committee rise early in the morning for our meetings."

> – Senator Joyce Fairbairn (L), Chair, Standing Senate
> Committee on Agriculture and Forestry, October 7, 2004

Or committees can be unfocused, dysfunctional, and divisive with partisan fissures straining at every turn.

"With all due respect to our colleagues in the Transport Committee, often we don't agree with them, and in this case we vehemently disagree with them."

– Joe McGuire (L), Chair, Standing Committee on
Fisheries and Oceans, April 8, 1997

How the key players get along among themselves and with others affects the committee's capacity to get things done. Let's take a look at each player in turn.

THE CHAIR

"Committee effectiveness is determined by the chair. If they are nonpartisan, committees can be very effective. Otherwise, committees just become as partisan as the House."

– Jesse Flis (L), Interview, May 1, 1997

The chair is critical to a committee's success and reputation.

Basically, the chair's *job one* is to facilitate the party's legislative agenda.[1] But the chair is not always a pushover.

"I've had screaming matches with ministers on how we proceed with a bill."

– Chair (L), Standing Senate Committee, Interview, Spring 1997

Being a renegade can be career limiting.[2]

"If the committee chair continuously sticks his thumb in the eye of the minister, he will be removed as chair. After all, the government has to fulfil, its agenda. That being said, I always maintained an open dialogue with the Finance Committee chair, and this worked well."

– The Hon. Michael Wilson (PC), former Minister of Finance,
Interview, August 21, 1997

If the chair is prepared to attract some notoriety, he or she can undertake some controversial studies and chart a more independent course on non-legislative matters. Being obstructionist, however, does little to buy the political capital needed to advance committee ideas. A positive rapport between the chair and minister can be essential.

> "We're not a separate branch of government. It is probably smart for committees to get a sense of how their recommendations will be received by the minister. You can't operate in a total vacuum, or a committee risks being ignored."
>
> – Barry Campbell (L), Parliamentary Secretary to the Minister of Finance, Interview, May 23, 1997

The chair ensures that all runs smoothly, maintains order and decorum, and intervenes when necessary.[3]

> "... I don't want to interrupt you, but I guess I am going to have to. I question the relevance of this... I'm just trying to stay on topic."
>
> – Paul Zed (L), Chair, Standing Committee on Procedure and House Affairs, November 19, 1996

Chairs employ a string of techniques to manage committee business, including:

- levying a "time hammer" or "content hammer." They can dictate the time a witness has to make a case or set bounds to what can be discussed;
- organizing a "roundtable," which allows the committee to plough through a number of witnesses at one sitting;
- splitting the committee up to hold hearings in different parts of the country;
- inviting an association to appear rather than individual companies or groups;
- issuing a letter to the minister based on a handful of testimonies to profile an issue, instead of writing a full report;
- releasing an interim report to refocus the committee; and
- getting background or in-camera briefings from groups to help educate the committee on complex issues.

The chair has the scope to stickhandle the hearing process.

"The experience of this committee on policy issues has been that we like to have the minister appear after we have heard from witnesses, in which case we have more ammunition than if we have him appear at the beginning."

– Senator Michael Kirby (L), Chair, Standing Senate Committee
on Banking, Trade and Commerce, July 3, 1996

One of the most important powers of a chair is his or her capacity to "recognize" a fellow committee member, such as accepting a point of order or allowing a member to pose questions to witnesses.[4] The chair plays a central role in managing the summons process (outlined in Chapter Three). These powers combined with the capacity to lever his or her position (e.g., having the ear of the minister) give the chair a certain authority, indeed. A strong chair runs the show.

VICE-CHAIRS

"The fact that we [the BQ] are a vice-chair just gives us the right to ask the first question in the first 10 minutes. After that they [another party] are second."

– Pierre de Savoye (BQ), House of Commons,
March 4, 1996[5]

There are two vice-chairs on House committees; usually there is one government and one opposition member, the latter usually being, but not always, a member of the official opposition. It confers little formal power, although the opposition chair is part of the steering committee and may stand in for the chair in his absence. A vice-chair can head up a subcommittee.

Much depends on how the members use their position, combined with their knowledge of procedure, to influence the process. An astute vice-chair will negotiate concessions out of the chair. For instance, in return for not filibustering a bill, the vice-chair may seek assurances about having the committee study a certain matter. Committee members must become masters of political trade-offs.

Each Senate committee has one deputy chair.

MINISTERS

> "I always tried to play ball with the Finance Committee. I gave them as much information as possible. This didn't mean that the committee was in my pocket. But I knew that if they had all sides of an issue it would contribute to a better dialogue and usually support for my position."
>
> — The Hon. Michael Wilson (PC), former Minister
> of Finance, Interview, August 21, 1997

Ministers need the support of parliamentary committees. After all, their bills clear through committee before becoming law. A constructive relationship works for both the committee and the minister.

This relationship can also be a testy one.

> "I take very strong objection to this phenomenon of ministers taking for granted that they can run roughshod over everyone, give orders, take this person off committee, take that one off committee, and that they can just keep bills around there for one or two years and then suddenly, at the eleventh hour, invoke all the political reasons in the world why you would be a bad person to study this bill."
>
> — Senator Anne Cools (L), Standing Senate Committee on Social
> Affairs, Science and Technology, April 24, 1997

Ministers take a keen interest in who chairs certain committees. Years ago, a committee had to get ministerial approval to conduct an inquiry. Today, committees largely set their own agendas. So, who chairs and sits on committees is important. The minister's direct influence over the chair is based largely on moral suasion or through the parliamentary secretary.[6]

Ministers cajole, sweet-talk, and assuage committees into facilitating their agendas.

> "It's one thing for my colleagues and I to work together, but I think we should see some collaborative work on the part of committees like Natural Resources and Environment. Often they're seen as antagonis-

tic… Mr. Chair, I would ask you to have some joint sessions with them in order to share the views of the two groups…"

> – The Hon. Anne McLellan (L), Minister of Natural Resources,
> Standing Committee of Natural Resources, November 28, 1995

The rules actually allow ministers to sit as members, even chairs, of committees, although this is now rare.[7]

THE PARLIAMENTARY SECRETARY

"Mr. Chair, given the pool of ignorance of members around the table, I'm almost inclined to support the motion. However, we all know that this is just politics—nothing more, nothing less."

> – The Hon. John McKay (L), Parliamentary Secretary to the Minister of
> Finance, Standing Committee on Finance, February 9, 2005

The parliamentary secretary (PS) is the minister's permanent representative on the committee.[8] He looks out for protecting the government's political interests.

"As parliamentary secretary, I was a conduit. When the minister needed to know where the government might have it wrong, when the committee and its chair needed to know where the minister stood, what pressures he faced, I was the broker. It was a constructive approach."

> – Barry Campbell (L), Parliamentary Secretary to the Minister of
> Finance, Interview, May 23, 1997

Many see his or her presence as the long arm of the minister trying to direct what committees do (further demonstrating that committees really are not independent from the executive). When the PS speaks, the minister speaks—an oversimplification, but a common perception. (This being said, not all parliamentary secretaries are kept equally well informed by their respective ministers.)

"Normally, the committee should be independent from the minister. Parliamentary secretaries, even the most independently minded, are generally the extension of the minister."

> – Réal Ménard (BQ), Standing Committee on Citizenship and Immigration, October 21, 1997

The 2004 democratic reform initiative strengthened the role of the PS, who now sits in cabinet and has been given the nod to be even more active on policy matters.[9] These changes continue to feed the debate as to whether someone linked directly to the executive branch is good to have on a committee representing the legislative branch, MPs.

"As far as the PS role is concerned, the PS acts as a linkage between the committee, between membership, between members of Parliament and the minister. The role in this regard has been reinforced by the fact that he is sitting in cabinet, because the linkage is made even more official and more powerful now. I do not buy the argument according to which it's a weakening of the committees. I think it's a reinforcement of the message that the minister wants to be present in committee."

> – The Hon. Jacques Saada (L), Standing Committee on Procedure and House Affairs, February 19, 2004

The PS is charged with the responsibility of shepherding the minister's bill through committee stage. During clause-by-clause review, the PS sits as a witness (representing the minister) by fielding questions about the bill and discussing amendments. Parliamentary secretaries can also chair a committee, although not for a committee that relates to the portfolio of his or her position.[10]

MEMBERS OF PARLIAMENT

"Well, you have met a committee chairman and a group of committee members of Parliament that bloody well will ask questions ... and we won't let anybody dictate our jobs to us because we are here to represent the Canadian public."

> – Felix Holtmann (PC), Chair, Standing Committee on Consumer and Corporate Affairs and Government Operations, November 6, 1991

Members of Parliament (MPs) have several sight lines:

- "How am I perceived by my constituents?"
- "How do the media view me?"
- "How am I perceived by caucus colleagues, ministers, and the prime minister (or leader)?"
- "How do my actions affect my future political prospects?"

Serving the needs of their constituents is constant, and the riding is never far from an MP's mind.

> "Many of the members of Parliament from northern Ontario and Alberta sit on [the Natural Resources] Committee, with vested interests in mining, forestry, and oil. They will say they are representatives of their constituency... I don't see it as a conflict of interest..."
>
> – John Richardson (L), Joint Standing Committee on a
> Code of Conduct, December 4, 1995

Members face some daunting tasks. They are expected to evaluate complex issues, often at the last minute, and they jump from issue to issue throughout the year. They have House and caucus responsibilities, committees to sit on, and usually a handful of pet political projects to pursue. This requires talent, commitment, and energy.

The president of one national association sees the diversity of views found on parliamentary committees being their greatest strength: "MPs bring a mix of analytical and political senses to an issue."

OPPOSITION MPS

> "... I remember the estimates seemed to be more important to me when I was in opposition than they are now. At that time we approached the estimates with the idea of trying to dig further..."
>
> – Guy Arseneault (L), Subcommittee on Business of Supply,
> December 14, 1995

While the above discussion on MPs holds true for opposition members, too, the role of the opposition on committee can be a finicky one and deserves additional commentary.

A POLITICAL VIEW!

"For some MPs, their main priority is their constituents, and committee work is *a job they have to do*. Other MPs dive right into committee work. Different MPs devote varying degrees of attention to committees, and you have to know what category of MP you're dealing with."

– Francis LeBlanc (L), former Committee Chair and
Parliamentary Secretary, Interview, September 1, 1998

For witnesses, understanding how individual committee members approach their committee work can often explain why some members ask more focused questions than others or have a better grasp of the issues.

Members of Parliament (whether they are members of the committee or not) can employ a number of different techniques to influence House standing committees, including:

- acting as "inside lobbyists," to urge caucus colleagues to support a committee initiative;
- tabling a motion, or making a member's statement in the House, to flag an issue being considered in committee;
- writing an open letter to the chair (i.e., making it public) and asking that a committee investigate a matter;
- using a private member's bill to prompt committee (and House) consideration of a matter, as noted in the previous chapter;[11] and
- trying to get any four committee members to prompt the same committee's chair to convene a meeting to discuss an issue.[12]

Opposition MPs put tension on the system. They erect procedural roadblocks. They are compelled to oppose. The opposition may have long decided that they will table a dissenting opinion even before the witnesses show up! This is not surprising. After all, opposition parties must know their position on a bill for second reading debate. This underscores the point that interest groups should communicate with political parties well before committee stage.

Still, opposition members don't want to sink all bills. Legislation benefits their constituents, too. Opposition members can stand behind government members if they generally like the bill or agree with the study at hand.

Sometimes when pursuing inquiries, opposition and government members can jettison their partisan views. This can invigorate the committee.

"Committees give opposition members buy-in to an issue by giving them some responsibility for it as opposed to being totally partisan."
– Minister's assistant, Interview, March 5, 1997

 **WHAT TO DO**

- Supply information to opposition members as early as possible. They are often looking for an angle to expose or criticize the government position, on the substance of the policy and/or on the process in which it is considered (e.g., on choice of witnesses, scope of terms of reference, etc).
- When members coalesce around the same issue, opposition and government members can temporarily and seemingly "abandon" their party colours. Working with all parties is advisable.

CLERKS

Clerks are employees of the chamber and are assigned to committees. They wear the committee's procedural and administrative hats. They are essential to the day-to-day smooth functioning of committees. They organize the hearings, arrange the witness lists, and plan the logistics for most meetings, among other responsibilities.

Being information brokers, clerks disseminate briefs submitted to the committee. They ensure that all committee members are sent the right documents. (If you fail to get your submission to the clerk in time, members can blame the clerk for failing to do his or her duty!)

WHAT TO DO

- Respect the deadlines placed on you by committee clerks. They need time to circulate your brief to committee members (and translate the brief if required).
- Include the clerk on your circulation list. The clerk ensures that your submission is sent to all committee members.
- If a clerk rejects your application to appear, he or she is reflecting the wishes of the chair or committee to restrict the witness list. Don't take it out on the clerk.
- The clerk usually needs written confirmation of your intention to appear before a committee. (See Chapter Six on hearings preparation.)

THE LIBRARY OF PARLIAMENT (RESEARCH BRANCH)

"One of the major factors in the success and performance of a committee rests on the quality of the researchers or the research firm which has been hired."

— Senator Pierre DeBané (L), Standing Senate Committee on
Internal Economy, Budgets and Administration, August 6, 1996

"What's a librarian doing here commenting on tax policy?" No, standing committees are not staffed by a bunch of librarians, unlike what one accountant from a large national firm once thought.

Parliamentary researchers play an instrumental role in the life and work of committees. Researchers assist all members of the committee, irrespective of party, but they work through the chair.

The Parliamentary Research Branch sees itself this way:

"... [it] works exclusively for Parliament, conducting research and providing information for Committees and Members of the Senate and House of Commons. This service is extended without partisan bias in such forms as Reports, Background Papers and Issue Reviews. Research Officers in the Branch are also available for personal consultation in their respective fields of expertise."[13]

The researchers, and the committee clerks, are the foundation of professionalism for parliamentary committees. As politicians come and go, they are the committee's corporate memory.

Researchers prepare briefing materials for members, such as the document *Legislative Summary and Suggested Questions,* which contains background on a bill, commentary, and a list of questions that members could then use at the table.

> "We get very good research documentation now from our committee researchers but general questions. They have to be almost neutral-type questions rather than political questions, because they have to be careful as well."
>
> – Guy Arseneault (L), Subcommittee on Business of Supply,
> December 14, 1995

 A POLITICAL VIEW! Non-Partisans Catering to Partisans

Researchers usually draft the committee reports. However, as one researcher put it,: "The final report reflects political bargaining within the committee and may bear little resemblance to the first draft report."

Researchers are non-partisan; they are also pragmatic. They must be balanced in their approach but cognizant of who holds the majority on the committee, whether to government members in a majority government or to opposition members in a minority government. If the latter, then committee reports might have, say, a little more bite in the title (and content), thus reflecting the opposition's inclination of being harder hitting.

As committees evolve, so do their workloads. Feeding the information machine is incessant. Keeping in touch with those who support the committee is well advised.

"... the committees will be receiving bills earlier, parliamentary committees will be conducting specific studies, not unlike royal commissions and so forth, and there will be more consultation by electronic means. So there are two avenues for committees: the committees might hire more consultants or have the Library of Parliament play a greater role. . . . With the democratic reform, parliamentarians will be given specific responsibilities. They will tend to specialize in certain areas. In this new role, of course, they will require more information, which would be individualized, specialized, and continuous."

     – Senator Yves Morin (L), Joint Chair, Standing Joint Committee
     on Library of Parliament, March 24, 2004

WHAT TO DO

- It is good practice to send to these researchers copies of any relevant correspondence directed to committee members on the issue at hand.
- Researchers may appreciate receiving background briefings to help them to scope out the issues.

RESEARCH BUREAUS OF POLITICAL PARTIES

Not to be confused with the Parliamentary Research Branch, each political party has its own research bureau. They offer partisan advice to members. (They, too, should be briefed on your position.)

MPS' POLITICAL STAFF

"Lobbyists often think it is very important to talk to the minister. Frankly, it is more important to talk to the people who talk to the minister, such as the executive assistant or other staff."

> – Hon. Donald Johnston (L), former Minister of Justice and past President of the Liberal Party of Canada, Interview, August 24, 1998

Key staff are often information brokers between harried members (and ministers) and everybody else.

"Staffers" will look to you for information not only on how government policy affects your group (which they expect to hear) but on how you may bring solutions to their political problems (what they hope to hear).

"I used to rely on lobbyists for information as the bureaucrats don't have a monopoly of knowledge."

> – Ministerial assistant, Interview, February 1, 1997

To assist their boss, a member's staff may summarize issues such as culling through witness submissions and determining who is a supporter or opponent. Executive and legislative assistants will meet interest groups. These staff can dutifully transmit your concerns to the member or, if they are totally unimpressed, simply "file" your information in the office blue box after you go out the door, especially if you are totally self-serving.

✅ **TIP** Be careful in what you say. What is said to ministerial staff in private meetings can be passed on to departmental staff in their e-mail notes summarizing the contents of their meeting with you.

DEPARTMENTAL OFFICIALS

"When Paul Martin was the minister of finance, we went to him with some ideas. He was always open to new ideas at that time. However, it was the bureaucracy that was difficult to move. He once said to me that he could not start anything because the department had the engine of a lawn mower and the brakes of a Rolls-Royce."

— A witness, Standing Senate Committee on Energy, the
Environment and Natural Resources, December 2, 2004

A tension exists between public servants and politicians. Both see themselves as representatives of the public interest. The former see the public as *clients* (of government services), the latter as *constituents*.

Members become frustrated by officials for other reasons.

"My own experience is that there's a great range among senior officials from the department in terms of how forthcoming they are with the committee... On the other side of the question, I've sat in committees where I've seen committee members attack a senior official as if he or she were the minister. That's not right or fair either."

— Marlene Catterall (L), Chair, Subcommittee on
Business of Supply, December 10, 1996

Backbenchers want bureaucrats to be more accountable to parliamentary committees. Committee members also make the point that they do not want to feel manipulated by the civil service.

"I do not want to be giving the impression that the department is telling this committee what it should do; we should tell the department what it should do."

— Senator Lorne Bonnell (L), Chair, Standing Senate Committee
on Social Affairs, Science and Technology, November 21, 1995

It is a sweet-and-sour relationship. Officials take pride in having "their" bill become law. Going to a committee means suffering through the public's scrutiny and criticisms and member ideas to make improvements. The flip side is that officials look to the committee to air out tough political options or to facilitate a bill's passage. Says a former Finance Department employee,

"We almost ended up watching the committee ourselves like a lobbyist group. Departments become one of the interested parties during a committee inquiry, particularly if the chair is pushing the committee into new territory."

– Elizabeth Roscoe, Vice-President, Government Relations,
Shaw Communications Inc., Interview, May 8, 1997

Departmental officials interact with the committee in a number of ways: they brief members on upcoming bills; they can be placed on "loan" to committees on complex legislation; and they appear as witnesses on legislation, estimates, or during inquiries. Officials also include lawyers from the Department of Justice (and, as elsewhere, lawyers nuture fond reputations).

"Will you show this bill to Justice Canada now, after you talk to us? Because that's where the problem is. When you show it to Justice, they panic. They get paranoid. They're the ones who force the damn amendments."

– Raymond Bonin (L), Standing Committee on Transport,
October 28, 2004

Officials can wield considerable behind-the-scenes leverage (or can influence report writing) when committees consider amendments.

"I want to thank the officials, because you have been extremely flexible in not just saying no every time our witnesses come up and suggest an amendment to try to improve the legislation... I want to put on the record that I think that is exactly the type of approach that has to come from other departments as well... So I want to thank you for allowing us to have something other than a rubber-stamp role to play in the process."

– Ron MacDonald (L), Chair, Standing Committee
on Fisheries and Oceans, December 5, 1995

Sometimes referred to as *parliamentary relations officers*, certain departmental staff play a specific liaison role between the department, members of Parliament, its committees, and the minister's office. They brief their ministers, advise their departmental colleagues on how to appear before committees, and keep abreast of political and legislative developments affecting their department.

THE HOUSE LEADER

The House leader has many responsibilities. With respect to committees, and like a traffic cop, the House leader's office monitors committee workloads, assigns members to committees, and directs bills to the appropriate committee. The House leader will also act as a conduit between the minister, the Prime Minister's Office, and the committee chair.

THE WHIP

> "When the whip shows up in a committee, you know the fix is in. The whip is there to keep people in line... The whip is there to crack his whip."
>
> – Monte Solberg (R), House of Commons, March 4, 1996

Each party's whip acts as the central dispatch for his or her respective caucus members.

> "I apologize for having missed this morning's visit, but I was making a speech on the Quarantine Act, and my whip did not allow me to leave."
>
> – Réal Ménard (BQ), Standing Committee on Health,
> October 26, 2004

Responsible for day-to-day oversight of the committees, the whip deploys members to parliamentary committees and keeps attendance. (The government whip's reports help the PMO assess individual member performance, which is later used to consider backbencher promotions.) The government whip ensures—or should ensure—that votes in committees are not lost and that legislation is not derailed.

"But even though the Liberal whip's assistant has been hovering right outside the door with a cell phone to his ear—he is back there now—there's not a single Liberal here, so we don't have quorum to take these important votes."

— Pat Martin (NDP), Standing Committee on Government
Operations and Estimates, February 26, 2004

Knowing how members vote in committee can also signal potential problems when the bill gets back to the House. The whip's office also provides procedural advice to committee members.

"There is a political consideration which all parties have at heart. The whips have a lot to say with respect to who sits on what committee, who replaces who and when. Otherwise, the party system collapses. The whips are key to the proper functioning of committees under our partisan parliamentary system."

— Senator Eymard Corbin (L), Standing Senate Committee on
Internal Economy, Budgets and Administration, August 6, 1996

THE PRIME MINISTER'S OFFICE

"I know they have received marching orders from the PMO. I've seen them get their memos and whispers in their ears."

— Diane Ablonczy (CPC), Standing Committee on
Public Accounts, April 1, 2004

The Prime Minister's Office (PMO) is the government's nerve centre. It mulls over and implements political strategy and tactics, among a range of tasks. It monitors the goings-on of the entire government, including the overall functioning of standing committees (although the PMO would not ordinarily take a hands-on role in the operation of these committees). The PMO, in concert with the whip and House leader, manages the full range of House affairs and the government agenda.

THE PRIVY COUNCIL OFFICE

The Privy Council Office (PCO) acts as the cabinet secretariat and also gives strategic policy advice, among other responsibilities. The PCO supports the cabinet committee system (on which ministers sit), which, in turn, considers how to implement the legislative agenda and the government's priorities. Cabinet committee decisions ultimately affect the life and operation of parliamentary standing committees. Bills blessed by the cabinet eventually make their way to House or Senate committees for consideration. The PCO stickhandles the approval of government responses to committee reports, which must be approved by the appropriate cabinet committee.

THE TREASURY BOARD

"... we were very frank with the Treasury Board representatives. We told them that we were requesting funding because of the recommendation made by the committee."

— A witness, Standing Committee on Official Languages,
November 25, 2004

The Treasury Board is "the gatekeeper to the public purse," as one MP put it. Witnesses will not interact with Treasury Board officials at committee, but, like other central agencies (i.e., PMO, PCO, Finance), this department occupies an essential role—it funds government. Under democratic reform, the Treasury Board and committees have been tagged with the task to improve financial reporting to Parliament.[14]

THE AUDITOR GENERAL

"So I hope this is a wake-up call to you, to discuss this with your minister [of Indian Affairs]. You've heard the comments from all sides of this committee on the report by the auditor general. . . . If this committee passes a motion that you will be back here to present, we may set aside a whole afternoon, or maybe a whole day, for you to come and speak to us."

— John Williams (CPC), Chair, Standing Committee on
Public Accounts, January 31, 2005

Deserving special mention is the increasing role and profile of the auditor general. While not directly part of the day-to-day activities of committees, the auditor general's regular reports on departmental performance, spending, and programs feed members with juicy material to pursue in committee.[15]

CONSULTANTS

> "It's something that has been bugging me for a long time. That is, the role of consultants. Obviously, committees are their own masters. If a committee hires a consultant, you can pretty well determine what the report is going to say just by whom they hired."
>
> – Carolyn Bennett (L), Joint Chair, Standing Joint Committee
> on Library of Parliament, May 15, 2003

Contract staff are sometimes hired by the committee for a variety of reasons. They can be lawyers, university professors, public relations experts, or brought on to organize committee hearings, such as for a national tour (which requires plenty of logistical work). By playing a largely backroom role, consultants can influence the direction of the committee's inquiry, such as shaping the scope of the inquiry or suggesting certain witnesses to appear. At times, technical experts may even sit at the table and pose questions to witnesses. Or these experts will act as facilitators to guide discussion.

 **WHAT TO DO**

All "experts" have biases. They may have fairly fixed views. Your efforts to inform members might also include meeting with any relevant consultants.

THE MEDIA

"They have already called into question the good name of you, Mr. Chairman, and myself and the work of this committee, and I would find it appropriate along the way if this committee voiced its own concern about one-sided sloppy journalism."

– Garth Turner (PC), Standing Committee on Consumer and
Corporate Affairs, November 6, 1991

There is a long tradition of complaining about the media.[16]

"The [newspaper] story is full of lies."

– Yvon Godin (BQ), Subcommittee on Parliamentary Privilege of
the Standing Committee on Procedure and House Affairs,
November 16, 2004

Yet members thrive on media coverage and the visibility it gives them back home and on the Hill.

"Opening the window on what happens in committee opens up the democratic process … and ultimately allows parliamentarians more opportunity to show their constituents what they do in Ottawa."

– Gord McIntosh, Director, Parliamentary Press Gallery,
Subcommittee on Communications, June 2, 1995

With their deadlines, the media cannot afford to sit through hours of committee testimony to get the perfect 10-second clip. They don't show up at all or do so only for a slice of time. Their "coverage," then, is not usually complete. (See "The Media: Eyes and Ears," Chapter Seven.)

Yet, keeping an eye on hearings has its advantages. One national columnist sees committees as a "periscope into departments." When officials appear, it gives the media a chance to get access to a lot of people who may not ordinarily surface publicly.

The televised media face restrictions when covering committees, although the rules are changing. Television camera crews have been allowed to get only some initial shots of the committee in action or capture the entrance of a witness; after that, the TV crews have had to depart. However, the electronic media have been recently allowed to videotape any public committee meeting. Other media, such as print reporters, have been allowed to remain in the room during the entire meeting, and video feeds of committees are open to any member of the Parliamentary Press Gallery.[17]

CPAC

> "That [televised] coverage did an enormous service, not only to us, but to the issue and to the work of the witnesses. This committee is in the eye of a hurricane right now on a lot of issues... I will make every effort possible to have our proceedings televised..."
>
> – Senator Joyce Fairbairn (L), Chair, Standing Senate Committee on Agriculture and Forestry, October 7, 2004

Getting televised is a bonus for the committee; it provides a national pipeline to Canadians' homes. While much of the Canadian Public Affairs Channel (CPAC) coverage is of the House and Question Period, selected committee hearings, when televised, has prompted more favourable feedback from Canadians.[18] Committees jostle for CPAC coverage. Only about one in five House committees is televised on CPAC.[19] Televising House committee hearings is unpredictable, and many after-midnight broadcasts are not conducive to general viewing.

The Senate has been particularly astute in leveraging television. It actually lobbied the Canadian Radio-television and Telecommunications Commission (CRTC) to make it a condition of CPAC's licence to broadcast all taped Senate committee meetings.[20]

SENATORS

> "I have never understood why we call a member of the House of Commons a member of Parliament, because a senator is also a member of Parliament. However, there is no word for that."
>
> – Senator Gérald Beaudoin (PC), Standing Senate Committee on Legal and Constitutional Affairs, May 16, 1996

Few people realize that senators, too, are "members of Parliament." This masks a certain frustration: how to demonstrate relevance when some Canadians probably remember them better for playing kazoos (while filibustering the passage of the GST),[21] and others want to abolish the Senate outright.

Senators take pride in their contribution to policy making, but there is a hint of insecurity here. The Senate is often criticized for its very presence; if senators don't remind people of what they do, who will? They have been, and remain, determined to change the image.[22]

> "We are convinced an awful lot of good work is being done in committees, and it is being kept secret. We want to change that."
> — Senator Colin Kenny (L), Standing Senate Committee on
> Internal Economy, March 28, 1996

The Senate has embarked upon a campaign to better inform Canadians about what senators do, as demonstrated by their success in getting their committee hearings broadcast on CPAC. Senate committee budgets cannot even get passed now without including a communications plan.[23] One publicity-minded senator has even promoted the Senate's website and toll-free telephone number at the end of each day's televised hearing. Moreover, the Senate Committees Directorate has conducted surveys to probe service satisfaction among witnesses of directorate services—with an approval rating of over 95%![24]

Senate committees *are* different from House committees. For one, there is greater continuity on Senate committees.[25]

> "Senate committees are the heart of the Senate. With consistent membership, and with the time and resources to delve deeper into issues, they do top-notch work—work that can compare with that of U.S. congressional committees."
> — Gary O'Brien, Deputy Clerk and Principal Clerk,
> Senate of Canada, Interview, June 13, 2005

Questioning is often different.

> "Frankly, I have to say that I have found a greater opportunity in the Senate to ask questions in depth, to range further afield, and to have more latitude in my questioning than I ever did in the House of Commons."
>
> — Senator William Rompkey (L), Standing Senate Committee on
> Privileges, Standing Rules and Orders, October 3, 1996

Senators often compare themselves to their colleagues in the other chamber. As one Liberal senator said bluntly when referring to members of House committees, "I would not like to form a convoy with them and be required to move at the pace of their slowest ship." With greater subtlety, a Senate publication for witnesses reinforces the point: "Senators have always treated witnesses with a great deal of respect..."[26]

> "Senators are a diverse group of people who collectively have a great deal of knowledge and experience."
>
> — Senator Marie-P. Poulin (L), Standing Committee on Rules,
> Procedures and the Rights of Parliament, May 30, 2001

Seasoned witnesses appreciate the role of Senate committees and the commitment of many of their members. Ironically, the strength of Senate committees rests on what is commonly seen as most anachronistic about the Upper Chamber:

- without the need to get elected, senators check their partisanship at the committee door on most days;
- appointed senators have experience. From former premiers to business executives, senators bring depth to the issues;
- without the same constituency demands as MPs, senators can devote more attention to committee work. A senator's "constituency" is the province he or she represents;
- while House committee memberships are fairly fluid, Senate committee memberships change less frequently. Senate committee members retain an institutional memory of the issues;
- indeed, given that senators must work together over time, this promotes a more consensual approach to dealing with matters, such as running committees.

These attributes are often recognized as the ingredients for more thoughtful study and a finer calibre of questioning.

"In the Senate you've got extremely able and experienced people who are more interested in getting answers than in posturing."
— Dr. C.E.S. Franks, Professor of Political Studies, Queen's University, Interview, October 24, 1997

THE PLAYERS COUNT

"Minister, I think you know I am no flaming socialist."
— Senator Gerald Comeau (CPC), Standing Senate Committee on National Finance, December 8, 2004

The personality, philosophy, demeanour, and interactions of members and others shape the tone and style of committee proceedings. Committee hearings are, indeed, a sum of their parts.

The unique dynamic among the key players involved in parliamentary committees can work in your favour or not. Getting heard at committee involves knowing which players count.

ENDNOTES

1. Opposition members can occupy the chair's role for certain standing committees as a matter of course. This number has changed over time, although the Public Accounts Committee and the House chair for the Standing Joint Committee on Scrutiny of Regulations have long been occupied by members of the official opposition.
2. As noted in Chapter One, only recently have chairs been elected by secret ballot by the committee, thus insulating the committee somewhat from a certain amount of executive string-pulling.
3. *Fundamentals of Senate Committees* (October 2004), 5. See also Senate of Canada, Committees and Private Legislation Directorate, and Library of Parliament, Economics Research Division, *An Introduction to the Standing Senate Committee on Banking, Trade and Commerce* (January 1994), 10.
4. *House of Commons Debates* (September 20, 1995), 14650. Also Senate Rule 96(6) states, "A senator desiring to speak shall address the chair."
5. A reference to the 35th Parliament.
6. Before committee elections took place, and behind closed doors, as one former

MP put it, the minister could have attempted to veto the nomination of a committee chair by influencing the decision-making process within the PMO.

7. A. Beauschesne, *Beauchesne's Parliamentary Rules and Forms*, 6th ed. (Toronto: Carswell Company Ltd., 1989), 224, para. 770.

8. The parliamentary secretary is different from the "secretary of state"; the latter is a cabinet posting.

9. Office of the Prime Minister, *Democratic Reform* (December 22, 2003), http://www.pm.gc.ca. "In committees, they will support productive dialogue by sharing departmental information and acting as the Minister's representative to address political issues during departmental appearances." Parliamentary secretaries will be asked to play a more active role in policy development, will be given specific policy responsibilities by the prime minister, will be sworn in as privy councillors so they can be invited to cabinet and cabinet committee discussions as appropriate (and to support cabinet solidarity), and will be charged with a greater representative role between parliamentarians and their minister and within government generally. The two-year rotational duty for parliamentary secretaries will end so their work on policy and these relationships can be enhanced.

10. Beauchesne, *Parliamentary Rules and Forms*, 224, para. 769.

11. Standing Order 97(1).

12. Standing Order 106(4). Such requests can be publicized to further draw attention to the issue and the MPs' action. An example occurred when four opposition MPs attempted to get the House Justice Committee to consider reviewing the Airbus affair. Scott Feschuk, "MPs force mini-debate on Airbus," *The Globe and Mail*, November 20, 1997, A6.

13. Parliamentary Research Branch, *Current Issue Review* (1998).

14. See *Ethics, Responsibility, Accountability—An Action Plan for Democratic Reform* (February 4, 2004), 6.

15. The expectations of the auditor general as they relate to committees' roles can be found in the 2003 annual report and chapter two, "Accountability and Ethics in Government." See also the Auditor General of Canada before the Standing Committee on Public Accounts, February 12, 2004.

16. The Senate actually has a rule that allows a senator to bring an offending media report, such as a written article or newscast, to the floor of the Senate as a breach of privilege (Rule 45). This matter can be referred to a standing committee for consideration. This is a rare event, but it happens from time to time as reporters are threatened with summons to disclose their sources or threatened with contempt for the nature of their reporting.

17. In the early 1990s, the media were granted the privilege to record committee testimony for use on radio. In 1993, the Parliamentary Press Gallery, as well as Hill offices of members and some others, could get audio feeds of public committee meetings. Senate committees can be more flexible about allowing TV cameras to remain in the committee room during a testimony. In 2001, the electronic media were granted the ability to videotape any public committee meeting, with some restrictions, until the end of the first session of the 38th Parliament. See House of Commons, *Committees: A Practical Guide* (October 2004), 30.

18. Parliamentary Centre, "Televising Committees," *Occasional Papers on Parliamentary Government*, no. 6 (Ottawa, February 1998), 3-4.

19. About 18% of House of Commons committee meetings were televised in 2003-04. Committees Directorate, *Annual Report on Committees' Activities and Expenditures*, table on Activities by Committee. This is an increase over a previous period when fewer than 1 in 10 House of Commons committee meetings were televised in 1996-97. House of Commons, Committees and Legislative Services Directorate, *Activities and Expenditures, Annual Report 1996/97* (September 1997), 6. Getting more hearings televised seems to be an ongoing challenge. Members of Parliament have studied this issue. The Standing Committee on Procedure and House Affairs' Fifth Report (October 19, 2004) documents the desire for broadcasting committee hearings but also the frustration of not having the resultant increase in televised hearings.

20. Gary O'Brien, Deputy Clerk and Principal Clerk, Senate of Canada, interview, June 13, 2005.

21. Mark Kennedy, "Senate kazoo days over," *The Ottawa Citizen*, June 20, 1991.

22. Ann Sullivan, "Tory Senators say politics pressures Liberals to rejig committees," *The Hill Times*, October 28, 1996, 11.

23. Mike Scandiffio, "Sen. Kenny wants $4 million more for Upper Chamber," *The Hill Times*, April 15, 1996, 5.

24. *Fundamentals of Senate Committees* (October 2004), 9.

25. A remarkable example of this is to point to the length of one committee chairmanship: Senator Salter Haydon chaired the Standing Senate Committee on Banking, Trade and Commerce from 1951 to 1983, a 32-year run at heading up this committee. See An Introduction to the Standing Senate Committee on Banking, Trade and Commerce (January 1994), 27.

26. Fundamentals of Senate Committees (October 2004), 8.

CHAPTER SIX

"On Your Mark . . . "

"MPs uniquely stand between the Executive and the electorate, each representing the views of the other on a host of issues. MPs are fundamentally communicators, not decision makers. So, having a compelling story is preferable to compelling evidence. This should be the basis for your committee strategy."

— Peter Washburn, Vice-President,
Government Relations and International Trade,
Northern Telecom, Interview, July 17, 1997

There is a shopping list of decisions to make before actually sitting down at the committee table, such as deciding whether in fact to go, who will represent your group, the length of your brief, etc. The most important involves crafting your message. Is it compelling? If it lacks focus, if it does not resonate, then why are you going? This chapter is about getting prepared to appear.

SECTION ONE The Committee Gears Up

FINDING OUT WHAT COMMITTEES ARE UP TO

Sometimes just finding out what committees are up to can be a challenge. They rarely advertise in newspapers about upcoming hearings or studies. Individual members may even be in the dark about all the scheduling details until the last minute. Still, most committees have a general work plan for the session, including which bills are coming their way and how much time they will have for conducting other studies.

WHAT TO DO

- The clerk, researcher, and steering group members (primarily the chair and vice-chairs/deputy chair) should be the first points of contact to learn about committee plans.
- Check the committee's Internet site about upcoming meetings.

ORGANIZATIONAL MEETINGS

Before any witness appears, the committee has to get organized. If it is reviewing a bill, the committee may get some marching orders from the minister, such as the date to wrap up the hearings. If it is a general inquiry, the terms of reference must be decided upon. Other matters are hammered out, such as the meeting format (e.g., a roundtable or not), possible travel plans, report-writing deadlines, hiring consultants, etc. The choice of witnesses is also a key decision. These discussions are usually, but not always, done in camera.

GETTING ON THE WITNESS LIST

"I should tell you that I have been waiting to talk to you since 2001."
– A witness, Standing Senate Committee on Transport and
Communications, February 4, 2005

Your first act of lobbying a standing committee may be just getting on the witness list.

"If we decided to hear one group, you must hear all of them, and that will extend the hearings."
– Senator Allan MacEachen (L), Special Senate Committee on
Bill C-110, January 22, 1996

Time is limited. Committees must restrict the witness list. They may have heard already from "your type of organization." How many Boards of Trade can you hear from? Committees may also be wary of inviting a group if it only wants publicity. Committees want quality, not quantity.

> "Unfortunately, the minister, the chairman, and the parliamentary secretary have been unable to present us with witnesses who are able to present us with potential solutions to the problem."
> – Jim Abbott (R), Standing Committee on Canadian Heritage,
> December 12, 1995

The chair will closely manage the witness selection. The steering committee generally draws up the list of witnesses. Suggested names are provided by other members and research staff. To expedite a bill, committees may be pressured to restrict the witness list or to fast-track the bill.[1]

> "We were called in and told there would be no witnesses because, if we wanted the good stuff in the bill, we better not point out the bad things in the bill and make representations, which makes a mockery of the whole process."
> – Senator David Angus (PC), Standing Senate Committee on
> Banking, Trade and Commerce, April 24, 1997

A specific group may be asked to appear because it reinforces a particular point or view, or not.

> "It's no use listening just to witnesses who may be 100% favourable."
> – Sheila Finestone (L), Chair, Standing Committee on Human Rights
> and Status of Persons with Disabilities, November 26, 1996

While highly unusual, it is possible, with unanimous consent from the members, to appear before a committee in anonymity. The testimony of "a witness" before the Subcommittee on HIV/AIDS in November 1996 did just that.

The choice may not be yours. You may be summoned to the committee. (See Chapter Three, "Understanding the Authority 'to Send'".)

INFLUENCING THE AGENDA

"I don't know whether it is of concern to anyone else, but the textile and apparel industries are very worried about the abolition of quotas at the end of the year... My colleagues from areas where the industry is present have been asking me what the situation is. Perhaps it would be interesting for us to hear from officials at an ad hoc meeting dealing with this particular issue so we are better informed about what is being done at the present time."

– Pierre Paquette (BQ), Subcommittee on International Trade,
Trade Disputes and Investment of the Standing Committee on
Foreign Affairs and International Trade, November 16, 2004

At the end of the day, members are constituent champions. They may be willing to approach the committee on your behalf.

WHAT TO DO

- Contact the clerk about appearing; explain why you are a group that should be heard from on the matter. (The clerk will submit the list of interested groups to the committee.)
- Get a member to be your advocate. (Your issue might get better traction if it's couched in terms of a broader community, such as a whole industrial sector, rather than just about, say, one company.)

TIP Getting on the list requires salesmanship. Tell the committee how many people you employ in Canada or that your members represent x-number of Canadians.

ARE YOU AN "EXPERT" OR "JUST A PERSON"?

"There are witnesses we want to hear who are experts and can enlighten us on the way to understand the substance and the implications of the bill. There is, of course, another set of witnesses who are just people who want to be heard."

– Senator Serge Joyal (L), Standing Senate Committee on Legal and Constitutional Affairs, February 2, 2005

"Expert witnesses" often give members detailed insights.

THE ELUSIVE "ORDINARY CANADIAN"

"We must be careful to not let ourselves be influenced solely by very structured official lobby groups. They have their place, they are present and that is to be expected, but we must speak with ordinary Canadians…"

– Paul Crête (BQ), Standing Committee on Canadian Heritage, March 11, 1997

Members also like to reach for grass-roots input.

Committees can go the distance to be accessible. As part of a swing through the Atlantic provinces on the controversial Harmonized Sales Tax, for example, one Senate committee packed in full days of witnesses but reserved the last hour each day for people "off the street" to come in and comment on the tax.

WHAT TO DO

For associations, point out to members your group's links to constituencies, such as regional board members. ("Who represents you" is also important in this respect. This is discussed more fully below.)

AFFORDING TO GO

> "How is one to know if there is intervenor funding? We get called to
> appear with little notice. We shouldn't have to struggle to deal with fig-
> uring out how to afford to go in addition to writing our brief and get-
> ting prepared."
>
> – Ivan Hale, National Secretary, One Voice,
> The Canadian Seniors Network, Interview, July 8, 1997

Certain witnesses may be able to offset expenses when appearing before
committees. Discretion is left up to the committee.[2] For the not-for-profit
community especially, lack of funding can be a reason not to appear.

WHAT TO DO

Contact the clerk about the committee's policy on intervenor funding;
he or she will forward to you a Witness Expense Claim form for those
authorized to testify.

BEING REFUSED

> "On the final day ... the President of the [association] desperately
> pleaded to be called as a witness for a second time to speak against the
> Bill as amended. The committee denied him this right."
>
> – Roger Gallaway (L), *Notes for a News Conference on a Private Member's
> Motion*, September 4, 1996 (in speaking about a group's attempt to appear
> before the Standing Committee on Canadian Heritage)

As a major stakeholder, being publicly rejected can be a slap in the face,
although a refusal is not ordinarily a public affair. Many others are refused,
too, as witness lists are clipped to save time.

> "... if we're going to invite the group proposed by my honourable col-
> league, there may be several other groups who will then also want to
> have a hearing, and you begin to involve yourself in quite a commit-
> tee imbroglio."
>
> – Dan McTeague (L), Standing Committee on Citizenship and
> Immigration, March 11, 1997

WHAT TO DO

- If refused, see who else is appearing. The list may in fact be fairly representative. Committees want to be fair; they also must have closure in their consultations.
- Look for allies to carry your message. Form a coalition. (You may be offering the committee a "solution," especially if it faces a tight time line.)
- Suggest a roundtable format, which allows several groups to appear at once around the table.
- Do you have members of your group who live in the riding of one of the committee members? Your local MP might urge the chair that you are worth being heard.
- Submit a written brief in any case in order to get your views registered. A good brief may convince members that they should get your views on the record.
- Contact the committee researchers. They sift through all submissions. They may be interested in a fresh perspective on the situation.
- Ironically, being refused may force you to be more articulate. Have you clearly explained why your presence at the table has value?
- As a last resort, go to the media if you feel shut out, although "complaining" may get you nowhere. Yet media scrutiny might direct focus on the committee's handling of its hearings.

DECIDING NOT TO APPEAR

"For the record, I should probably say that representatives of the [association] were invited to appear as witnesses before this committee, and it was their choice to send a written submission but not appear in person."

– Senator Joan Fraser (L), Chair, Standing Senate Committee on
Transport and Communications, February 9, 2005

The decision not to appear is an option, particularly if the committee is not insistent that you appear. The committee may be simply offering you a time slot out of courtesy or because you have been previously active on the issue at hand. Your decision not to appear may be based on avoiding unwanted publicity. Or you may wish to save time and expense associated with appearing. However, saying "no" is tricky. If said too often, you may be turned down by the committee the next time you want to take your message to the Hill.

"ZERO" NOTICE

> "My hat is off to those people who were able to come on a day's notice. But really, Madam Chair, it is an affront to Parliament and to this committee to ask us to ram through like a sausage an important bill ..."
> – Chuck Strahl (R), Standing Committee on Justice and Human Rights, November 4, 1997

Frequently, witnesses are given very little time to prepare and appear. Legislation can move quickly through the House, sometimes to the chagrin of witnesses and members alike. You may have mere days to get ready or less. Some public sector witnesses have been called in the morning to appear in the afternoon! Committee members can seem unaware of the *panic* they create when they expect you to appear even with a week's notice. They are under the gun, too. You are being given the opportunity to voice your position.

COMMITTEE SET-UP

> "... I apologize for the size of this room. We will try to get a smaller room next time. This room looks like a battleship."
> – Senator Gerald Comeau (CPC), Chair, Standing Senate Committee on Fisheries and Oceans, November 4, 2004

There are various ways to hold a hearing. The format is important. It can influence your approach to the committee, such as deciding on the length of your opening remarks, how you field questions, etc.

Committees are usually set up in "horseshoe" fashion (see diagram).[3] The chair, researchers, and clerk will be directly opposite the witness table with members on each side. When facing the chair, government members sit on one side and opposition members on the other. (The members clos-

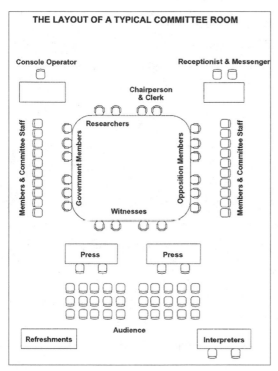

THE LAYOUT OF A TYPICAL COMMITTEE ROOM

est to the chair are generally the vice-chair and parliamentary secretary; the official opposition usually occupies the seats nearest the chair on the opposite side.)

"Roundtable" hearings allow several witnesses to be heard at once. Members can prod witnesses with opposing views to find a compromise. Some witnesses grab the opportunity to challenge other witnesses around the table—leading to confrontational exchanges.

"I have seen some committees very successfully operate roundtable discussion groups in which they have mixed people from the private sector with parliamentarians. Those roundtable discussions are quite different from the normal hearings where witnesses come and present a brief and are questioned. Instead, you see people from the private sector questioning parliamentarians and vice versa."

– Senator Colin Kenny (L), Chair, Standing Senate Committee on
Internal Economy, Budgets and Administration, August 6, 1996

Or a committee will have a "town hall" arrangement where a table of members faces an audience of witnesses and observers ("the public"). One town hall meeting, for instance, had witnesses break out into smaller discussion groups, each facilitated by committee members (which then "reported" back to the larger group at the end of the day).

"I think some of you coming to the microphones might have felt a little nervous. I promise you none of you were as nervous as we were. This was the first time that we have conducted a public meeting, and we did not know what to expect. I think the outcome is very positive."

> – Senator Colin Kenny (L), Chair, Standing Senate Committee on
> National Security and Defence, November 29, 2004 (the hearing
> took place in Kingston, Ontario, as part of a Canadian tour)

OUT-OF-TOWN HEARINGS

"Going out to various areas of Canada not only permits more witnesses to bring in more local flavour, it allows the general public to see us in action."

> – Guy Arseneault (L), Standing Committee on Canadian
> Heritage, March 11, 1997

When parliamentary committees take it to the road, this gives local representatives of your group a unique opportunity to voice their views. A "roadshow" may also attract local media that rarely get a chance to cover such events directly.

> **TIP** While a committee may use the end of the day to travel to the next city on their tour, you may offer to hold a plant tour, or hold a dinner event with committee members, if they remain in town.

APPEARING VIA VIDEO-TELECONFERENCE

Video-teleconferencing is used occasionally to hook in witnesses from afar.[4] It's cheaper than travelling. But it is less suitable for handling contentious issues.[5] Still, video-teleconferencing has its place.

WHAT TO DO

- Note that, when one witness speaks, the camera can pick up people immediately beside that person. Your yawn could be covered from coast to coast.
- Witnesses should make opening remarks especially short. Not being physically in the room makes it harder for members to focus on your soliloquy.
- Getting your submission and/or opening remarks to the committee in advance will facilitate members following along what you are saying.

E-CONSULTATION

"To tell you the truth, what the analysis has shown is that the experts' testimony is perhaps a little more sophisticated but not basically different from the recommendations Canadians were providing to us through the e-consultation. Instead of reaching the hundred-odd witnesses who might come before a committee on this study, we have managed to reach about two thousand people."

– Consultant, Library of Parliament, Standing Joint Committee
on the Library of Parliament, May 8, 2003

Committees are dabbling with web-based consultations. Some are intrigued by the possibilities.[6] Using technology to connect with "Canadians" is appealing for members, but its limited use suggests that the web's actual consultative value remains somewhat questionable. Nevertheless, more resources are being devoted to upgrade committee websites, provide on-line viewing of committee meetings, and enhance search features and content which supports the broader push to be, at least, more electronically accessible and useful.[7]

"I am sorry to come back to the question of modern technologies, but I do want to say that they sometimes do not work. I know, because I have attended meetings where the Human Resources Development Committee has tried to do interactive consultations. We will have to make sure that these technologies work."

– Diane St-Jacques (PC), Standing Committee on Procedure and
House Affairs, February 19, 2004

ACCESSING TESTIMONY

"Anybody dealing with legislation and wants to follow a bill through its stages, cover the speeches, and see the research can save a fantastic amount of time using LEGISInfo, which is part of the redesigned parliamentary website."

– Gary Levy, Editor, *Canadian Parliamentary Review*, Interview,
May 31, 2005

You can check out what a committee is doing this way:

1. Go in person (in-camera meetings excepted).
2. Read the testimony (the evidence) once posted on the committee webpage.
3. Access "LEGISinfo," a virtual parliamentary research assistant at your fingertips (www.parl.gc.ca/legisinfo); it is a quick way to access speeches, legislative summaries, and texts of bills at the various stages.
4. See it televised on CPAC.[8]
5. See it via the parliamentary committee's webcasting service (ParlVU), which provides live-stream video and audio of televised House committees and the audio of committees sitting in public.
6. Listen to certain hearings live via the web (Senate webcast).
7. Read it in sign language—a limited application. (A pilot program has provided two Senate committee reports in sign language with streamed Internet access (ASL and LSQ format); the Senate Committees Directorate is even prepared to loan DVD copies of these for those who don't have high-speed Internet access.)

SECTION TWO Your Appearance Checklist

Considering whether or not to appear should not be made lightly. Conduct the following top-line assessment of the committee's initiative. (This checklist assumes that the committee has contacted you to appear. Still, if you have initiated the contact, several of these sections should be relevant to getting prepared.)

STEP ONE: GET THE DETAILS

1. If the clerk has called you, what does it mean?

☐ Is it an actual invitation? Or is the clerk merely inquiring about your potential interest?

☐ You could get the same type of call from the chair's office. Is the chair insistent that you attend?

☐ Is it a summons? (If it is, see also Chapter Three).

2. What is the committee up to?[9]

☐ Is it a bill?

☐ Is it an inquiry on a subject?

☐ What type of committee is it: e.g., House, Senate, or joint committee?

(a) *If a bill:*

☐ At what stage is the bill? Is it being considered prior to second reading or after? (If the latter, then the principles of the bill have already been locked in).

☐ Has the bill originated in the House or Senate?

(b) *If an inquiry:*

☐ Are the terms of reference still under consideration, or are they final? (If they are still being drafted, should you suggest any issues to address?)

☐ Will it lead to a report being drafted (with recommendations), or is the committee just using the inquiry as a briefing to familiarize itself with a new issue?

☐ Is the inquiry designed to sound out ideas for future legislation?

☐ What has prompted the inquiry (e.g., a specific incident, constituent concerns, etc.)?

❏ Who has prompted the inquiry (e.g., committee members themselves a minister, etc.)?

(c) *Whether a bill or an inquiry:*

❏ In either case, are there particular issues that the committee wishes to hear about from you?

❏ Can a written invitation be sent to you (including any terms of reference)?

❏ Will there be a confirmation letter once you agree to appear (if you require one)?

❏ Is the committee travelling, or are these Ottawa-based hearings?

❏ Is the hearing televised?

❏ Is the hearing going to be undertaken in the traditional format (i.e., hearing from one group at a time), or is it a roundtable (i.e., hearing from several groups or witnesses at once)?

❏ Who sits on this committee? Who is the chair?

3. *What about timing?*

❏ Is there a choice of when to appear: various dates, times to appear?

❏ How much time will you have to testify in total, including time for questions?

❏ How much time will you have to make opening remarks?

❏ What is the time frame to wrap up all hearings?

4. *Will you have trouble actually getting there?*

❏ Is intervenor funding available?

❏ Can you testify via video-teleconference instead of making a trip to Ottawa?

5. *Who's appearing?*

❏ Is there a restriction on the number of presenters that can be at the table to represent your group? (The clerk may specify a limit, particularly if it is a roundtable meeting.)

❏ Does the committee prefer to hear from a certain representative (e.g., your president)?

❏ What other groups are appearing on the same day you may appear?

❑ Have witnesses already appeared on the matter?

❑ What witnesses are slated to follow you in the days ahead?

6. *What does the clerk want?*

❑ When can you accept the invitation? (The clerk wants your acceptance in principle, or your confirmation, as soon as possible.)

❑ Is it possible to submit your written submission in advance of the hearing? (This is optional.)

❑ When can you supply the names and titles of your group's presenters (and preferably in both official languages)?

❑ Do you have any audio-visual equipment needs (e.g., overhead projector)?

STEP TWO: ASSESSMENT AND DECISION

With a certain amount of background information at hand (Step One), your group now has tactical decisions to make (Step Two). Note that every committee visit requires a tailored response. These options, below, offer some preliminary prompts to assess what is needed to get prepared.

1. *What is your ultimate objective?*

(a) *Being idealistic, what do you want?*

❑ If a bill, do you seek passage of the bill with dozens of substantive amendments?

❑ Do you want the bill killed?

❑ If an inquiry, do you expect the committee to reflect all of your recommendations in its report?

❑ Do you seek to minimize any criticism of your group or to get a substantially positive profile?

(b) *Being realistic, what do you hope to get? Objectives vary.*

❑ Do you pursue only one or two key amendments in the bill?

❑ Are you seeking several technical (non-controversial) amendments?

❑ Do you suggest that a bill contain a *sunset provision* (so the bill can be reviewed after, say, three years) or suggest that it include a ministerial review instead (a less rigorous alternative)?

❏ Do you endorse a bill's principles yet reserve support until its regulations are available for scrutiny?

❏ Rather than adopting your legislative amendments, do you encourage government to adopt a regulatory change instead? (A regulation is more easily adaptable, whereas embodying a reference in legislation strengthens it.)

❏ Are you seeking to change the minds of members or just trying to heighten awareness of your ideas?

❏ Do you seek a favourable mention or recommendation in their report? (This could become a prospective lever and help make your point in future representations.)

2. What is the issue?

❏ What is *your* most essential issue to raise with members? (This must represent the backbone of your testimony. See Section Three, "Crafting Your Message," ahead.)

❏ What are two or three supporting points?

❏ How are committee members defining the issue?

❏ Whose definition of the problem prevails, theirs or yours?

❏ Do you have primarily a "technical" argument or a "populist" argument?

❏ By showing up to discuss your views, are you addressing the terms of reference (or the bill), or are you tabling extraneous issues?

> **TIP** The first witness frames the debate. The final witness gets the last word.

3. What is your group's reputation?

❏ Do committee members have a positive, negative, or unformulated view of you or your group?

❏ Do they have a positive, negative, or unformulated view of your issues? (You need to know how far up the learning curve you need to get members.)

❏ Is your organization held in high esteem by public opinion or not?

❏ Are the media sympathetic to your cause?

A POLITICAL VIEW!

"Take a longer-term perspective when appearing before a committee," advises one seasoned committee insider. "You are essentially building a relationship with members. Today's chair may be tomorrow's secretary of state."

Who really drives the committee's work: the chair or the parliamentary secretary? Is the chair close to a key minister or is he or she constantly offside? Understand who you are dealing with. Your testimony should be an "investment." Certain members could be streamed for cabinet or other positions. As well, you may need the committee on other issues in the pipeline. Taking a longer-term perspective is advisable.

4. What is your political assessment?

❏ Members must be given a reason to support your position. What "political cover" do you offer politicians? Why would they publicly endorse your view?

❏ Does appearing before the committee primarily serve the interests of the committee (i.e., does your appearance help it legitimize the consultative process)?

❏ Is the chair out to make a name for herself on this issue, or is there a less partisan issue to discuss?

❏ Is there a possible "hidden agenda"? (For example, a committee insists on having you appear in the morning. Why? Reporters are more likely to cover those hearings.)

❏ Do members gain by criticizing you?

❏ Are you in for a rough ride?

❏ Is your position generally consistent with the government's policy agenda? (Your point may be totally offside what the government is doing.)

❏ In presenting policy options, is the timing right? (Your solutions must be "doable" within the government's time frame.)

❑ What does the parliamentary calendar look like? (If your hearing date falls just before a recess, then the government may have little patience for any delay in the hearings or in any substantive amendments.)

5. Have you assessed the witness list?

❑ Who are your prospective "allies"/"opponents" among this list? Is the list stacked against you?

6. Are you available?

❑ Are you or your colleagues available to actually testify? Is your president on vacation?

7. Do you need more information?

❑ Can you get in and meet with the chair, parliamentary secretary or key members in advance of the hearing to talk about the committee's objectives and what the members want to hear from you? (See "Pre-Meetings," ahead.)

> **TIP** Unless the hearing schedule is locked in, it may be prudent to defer a decision to appear until a handful of hearings have taken place. This allows you to assess the tenor and substance of the committee hearing before committing.

8. So, do you go?

❑ Do you need to testify in person? Or is a written statement/submission sufficient?

❑ Does rejecting an invitation, or opportunity to go, mean that your issues will be decided in your absence?

❑ What do you achieve by going? What do you lose by not going?

❑ Based on the above, is it in your interest to give it a pass?

❑ Is it necessary to go just to defend your interests and get your views on the record?

❑ Do you have any option but to go? (You may be required to appear.)

❑ If you don't go, consider sending a letter to the committee, or just to its chair, outlining your position and explaining why not appearing is a valid course for your group.

❑ Ensure that you inform the clerk of your intentions.[10]

❑ As much as possible, choose the time that is best for you to appear.

STEP THREE: PREPARATIONS AND DETAILS

So, if you have determined that you are going (Step Two), now come the details (Step Three).

1. How important is your campaign (to achieve your objectives)?

❑ Going before a committee involves considerable work, or it can be a quick, in-and-out visit. How much time and resources can you devote to your effort?

2. Who represents you?

❑ What level of person should you bring (e.g., president, vice-president, etc.)?

❑ If you bring your most senior person, can he or she speak to technical matters that members may raise?

❑ By bringing your most senior person, could that only invite members to ask tougher questions on a broader array of issues (as opposed to a more technical expert who can only address specific areas)?

❑ What optics should be considered (male/female; French/English; regional representation vs. central Canada; etc.)?

❑ How many colleagues should be at the table?

❑ Will you show up with an "entourage"? (Striding into the room with several subordinates sends the signal that you need to orchestrate your visit with your public affairs gurus, lobbyists, lawyers, and media spinners.)

❑ If a committee is travelling across the country, could your group appear in more than one location?

❑ Does your visit to Ottawa involve lobbying? Determine the application of the Lobbyist Registration Act to your activities. (See "Regulating You," ahead.)

> ✓ **TIP** Select your spokesperson on the basis of his or her communications savvy, not title. But seniority is important, too. Is your top person media-trained?

3. How do you support your testimony?

❏ Do you prepare formal opening remarks or refer to bullet points? (See "Opening Remarks and Your Submission," ahead.)

❏ Do you prepare a lengthier written submission?

❏ Develop a Power Point presentation? Distribute handouts? (Note: You may have to bring the necessary equipment to make "high tech" presentations. Check with the clerk.)

❏ Are these materials translated?

❏ Do you conduct new research, commission a fresh public opinion survey, or get a legal opinion to table at the committee?

❏ Do you conduct focus groups to test your key messages?

❏ Do you hire expert outside advice (e.g., a public affairs or media relations specialist)?

❏ Does your industry association appear or its individual members? (See "Internal Politics," ahead, for advice in managing your organization's own members and preparing them for the upcoming hearing.)

❏ Do you create a coalition with another group?

4. What are your broader efforts?

❏ Are there other witnesses to suggest to the clerk or committee chair? ("Third parties" can reinforce your position.)

❏ What should you be doing to assist coalition members, or sympathetic "third party" groups, who may be appearing as well?

❏ Do you meet other interest groups who may also be appearing?

❏ Do you brief ministerial staff, or ministers, about your issues to be tabled at committee?

❏ Do you meet beforehand with the public servants who manage the issue?

❏ Do you conduct caucus briefings for the political parties?

WHAT'S YOUR HEADLINE?

"Ministry accused of hiding key data."

— *The Globe and Mail,* May 26, 1998, A7

Environment Canada was tarred with this headline after its appearance. What could be yours?

☐ Is another standing committee interested in the same issue? Should its key members be briefed as well?

☐ Is it necessary to brief members of the relevant Senate committee? (Or, if a Senate initiative, brief House committee members?)

5. Do you know the committee's members?

☐ Is there a core group of members who attend most meetings?

☐ Is the committee working in a collegial manner, or is it highly partisan?

☐ Do you expect any non-committee members (with a special interest in the subject) to show up?

☐ Are committee members likely to raise any constituent concerns?

☐ Do you have biographies of members? What are their likely dispositions on the issue at hand?

☐ Do you have the transcript of what members have said at second reading debate (if a bill)?

6. How will you manage your committee relations?

☐ Do you set up a "quick response team"? (By monitoring the hearings, a dedicated staff person or group can address erroneous information being tabled by other witnesses, respond to member comments and identify emerging issues.)

☐ Do your pre-meetings with committee members flag any adjustments that should be made to your key messages (or opening remarks)?

☐ Do you have any information on your group's activities in member constituencies (e.g., number of employees working in member ridings)? (This can be sewn into your opening remarks.)

❏ Can you get a sympathetic committee member to pose a "prepared" question at the table?

❏ Be aware of the committee's future business. A member could ask for your opinion about some upcoming committee initiative.

7. How will you manage the media?

❏ What's the "media spin" of your position?

❏ Who is your media spokesperson?

❏ Should you brief certain key media about your position prior to the hearing?

❏ Do you entice interest by publicly releasing a survey result or legal opinion the day before your committee appearance?

❏ Do you issue a press release the day you appear?

❏ Do you hold a press conference following the hearing?

❏ Do you require a media monitoring company to assess media coverage during the full hearing period? (See "The Media: Eyes and Ears," ahead.)

8. What's your image?

❏ Conduct a simulation of appearing before a committee, including the reading of your opening remarks, and hold a mock question and answer session. (Record your remarks on your video camera and play it back. Are you slouching? Reading too quickly?)

❏ This role-playing can be conducted by a professional. Better to blunder in private than on the record…

❏ Will members face a wall of blue? Red ties, white shirts, and blue suits may be too heavy on the Bay Street look. Is your group too colour-co-ordinated?

❏ If the hearing is being televised by CPAC, holding up your papers to read may not come across well on camera.[11]

TIP Committee proceedings may be televised and replayed on the parliamentary television channel (CPAC). Watching any committee in action can be a useful training tool, such as observing how other witnesses handle questions.

Of all the preparations and decisions to make, getting your message right is the most important.

SECTION THREE Crafting Your Message

> "Committees look at big issues. Often witnesses think they have to come and address the big picture when they know nothing about it. We want to hear what people know, their experiences. This is what is interesting. Knowing their individual experiences helps us understand the big picture."
>
> — Francis LeBlanc (L), former Committee Chair and
> Parliamentary Secretary, Interview, November 13, 1997

Use facts and anecdotes to help members understand your slice of the bigger problem. Doing so requires defining the issue. This is the linchpin for success.

D-E-F-I-N-E THE ISSUE

> "It seems to me that back in 9/11 it was not 9/11 itself that troubled Canadians but 9/12, when the border clanked shut and our economy seemed destined to go down the tubes."
>
> — A witness, Standing Senate Committee on National Security
> and Defence, November 15, 2004

On the Hill, key words can make a big difference.

- Are Canada-U.S. border issues primarily about ensuring *access* or *security*?
- Is health policy about *curing* sickness or *preventing* it?[12]
- Is science policy about *pure research* or *product commercialization*?
- Is climate change about *energy efficiency* or *environmental protection*?

Of course, it can be about all of these matters. The point is, which issue predominates?

> "I know that the senator across from me is my good friend. He will dis-
> agree with me on this, but we like to use the sponsorship 'issue' as
> opposed to sponsorship 'scandal.' I am making a little joke here."
>
> — Senator Jim Munson (L), Standing Senate Committee on
> Transport and Communications, February 4, 2005

The advantage goes to the group that defines the issue.

If members share your view of the problem, then they will be open to your solutions. If your opponents frame the issue, your position could get sandbagged.

You really have only two options.

Option A: If the issue is defined against your interest, then you must change the way it is perceived.

> "I've seen some businessmen say it's in the national interest to pay less
> taxes or change some tariff. Nothing could make less sense than that.
> The average politician wants to know how this change will help his
> riding or the economy and not just help make the businessman more
> money."
>
> — The Hon. Doug Peters (L), former Secretary of State,
> International Financial Institutions, Interview, June 9, 1997

Option B: If the issue is defined correctly, then you must reinforce it.

> "… would it be fair to say that you have come back here tonight to
> sound a little warning to us: *Hey, senators, before you start recom-*
> *mending big changes in the tax breaks, take note of these things?*"
>
> — Senator David Angus (CPC), Deputy Chair, Standing Senate
> Committee on Banking, Trade and Commerce, December 8, 2004

Every issue can be viewed through this prism.

> "NHL's bid for aid gets cold shoulder: Public subsidies won't sell, MPs
> say."
>
> — *The Globe and Mail,* April 29, 1998, A1

Representatives of the National Hockey League just couldn't score when they appeared before a Commons subcommittee in the spring of 1998. They tried to impress upon members the apparent tax burden and business disadvantages facing Canadian hockey clubs versus their American counterparts. MPs (and the media) inevitably focused on the political unpopularity of granting tax concessions to clubs that pay players "runaway" salaries.

In the end, your message must be politically saleable.[13]

 WHAT TO DO

- Reinforce your key messages throughout your presentation (in your opening statement, your written submission, your answers to member questions, and your media interviews).
- Back up your key messages with research, a public opinion survey, anecdotes, etc.
- When contemplating your key message, consider how it will be received. This may help you to adjust your messaging.

HOW WILL YOUR MESSAGE BE RECEIVED?

"Witnesses tend to talk about what they want to talk about."

– Barry Campbell (L), Standing Committee on Finance,
March 11, 1996

Witnesses can say what they want. But that is not the point. You are there to be listened to, not heard.

Do your opening remarks have substance?

"When committees call witnesses—at least this is my impression—we want witnesses to give us the answers; we don't want to listen to 20 minutes of rhetoric from them on their opening statements."

– Darrel Stinson (R), Standing Committee on Natural Resources
and Government Operations, October 9, 1997

What is your bottom line? (Politicians certainly don't mince words.)

> "Mr. Chairman, I will tell you, the people in this committee, the government, and any government members who are listening that I feel strongly about this. If this change takes place … the second largest employer of people in the area, in the district in which I live, will go under."
>
> – Harry Verran (L), Standing Committee on Public Accounts,
> November 29, 1995

✓ **TIP** Boil down your issue to one word. Was it "salaries" or "taxes" that defined the issue in the public's mind in the NHL case (mentioned above)?

Do you overstate your case?

> "I am least impressed with witnesses when they play the unity card. It isn't helpful for a witness to say that if we don't agree with his position we're against Quebec. Then I roll my eyes. We're sensitive to the issue, but not when it is inappropriately thrown on the table."
>
> – Senator Wilfred Moore (L), Interview, September 22, 1997

✓ **TIP** Avoid making grandiose statements. "If we only do 'x,' Canada would be a great country." Nothing is quite so simple when governing a country.

Are you only being critical?

> "I get the feeling … that often *les hauts fonctionnaires* come here almost on the defensive. In your case … it was exceptional that you gave suggestions and recommendations. We appreciate that."
>
> – Eugène Bellemare (L), Vice-Chairman, Standing Committee
> on Government Operations, December 7, 1995

Are your solutions practical?

> "You are suggesting something called an impartial public inquiry. We politicians are familiar with impartial public inquiries, and Rip Van Winkle will wake up, and it still will not have been reported."
>
> – John Rodriguez (NDP), Standing Committee on Finance,
> December 4, 1990

> **TIP** Avoid elevating a concern to a parliamentary committee prematurely. You may be asked if you have approached the department first about the problem at hand.

Do you have a true grasp of the issues and of what others have said?

> "With the greatest respect, I have difficulty understanding how you can support a bill until you know what the overall ramifications are going to be… Certainly the testimony of the witnesses who appeared on Bill C-68 is there for all to see."
>
> – Jack Ramsay (R), Subcommittee on the Draft Regulations on
> Firearms, February 4, 1997

Can you back up what you want?

> "Are you alleging that this is happening, or do you have proof that it's happening? You're asking legislators to pass a law, and we don't even know how much money you're saying is involved here."
>
> – Jim Silya (R), Standing Committee on Finance, September 24, 1996

Are you asking for preferential treatment? (This is an enduring source of frustration for members.)

> "OK, well I just found it somewhat ironic that you are just like everybody else. Coming up here rhetorically suits you to tell us that we need more competition, we need benefits for the consumers, and then you

turn around and say except for some things I really believe in that's where the government must prohibit competition. Strange."

– Herb Grubel (R), Standing Committee on Finance, September 24, 1996

> **✓ TIP** Avoid the habit of feeling obliged to comment on every clause of a bill, unless of direct concern to your group.

Are you standing alone on the issue, or are others reinforcing the message?

"What strikes fear in us is having wave after wave of witnesses saying the same thing."

– MP (L), Interview, June 11, 1998

Are you launching a campaign at the wrong time? Parliamentarians might not be ready to embrace new ideas late in the parliamentary timetable.

"… we're going into year four of the [35th] Parliament, and people are not going to want to launch into major initiatives as much as in years one, two, and three. It's a political reality."

– John Duncan (R), Standing Committee on Aboriginal Affairs and Northern Development, December 3, 1996

Give members a handy means to pursue an issue. A key statistic can capture the scope of an issue and force discussion.

"I met with the Ontario Chamber of Commerce just about two weeks ago. They indicated that border delays are costing the Canadian and U.S. economies about $13.6 billion annually. I'm just wondering what the priorities are. What are your priorities? How are you going to continue to reduce these border delays?"

– Belinda Stronach (CPC), Subcommittee on International Trade, Trade Disputes and Investment of the Standing Committee on Foreign Affairs and International Trade, November 16, 2004

SECTION FOUR Opening Remarks and Your Submission

"We need a short, punchy presentation. Tell us something new, something neat or important. Otherwise we drift off into La-La Land."
– Jennifer Fry, Parliamentary Reporter, CBC Radio, "The House,"
Interview, November 10, 1997

With your messages in hand, you need to craft your opening remarks and, perhaps, a longer written submission. Make them worth reading (and listening to).

Your options: you are not required to write any remarks or a submission. Sometimes witnesses go in and speak from the heart. Many read a brief statement. Polished witnesses can speak to three or four essential points and then table a supporting written submission.

BREVITY COUNTS...

"Thank you, senators, I appreciate the invitation. I did not time these remarks, but I will do my best to stick to around 10 minutes."

– A witness

[. . . over 3,600 spoken words later . . . !]

"I neglected to mention that [the witness] is an award-winning writer, and you can see why."
– Senator Joan Fraser (L), Chair, Standing Senate Committee on
Transport and Communications, February 4, 2005

AN EFFECTIVE DELIVERY

"Unfortunately, you used up all 40 minutes of the time allocated. There will not be time for questions."
– Raymond Bonin (L), Chair, Standing Committee on Aboriginal
Affairs and Northern Development, March 18, 1997

It is fatal to go before a committee and just read a lengthy submission. You will lose your audience. It eats up time for questions.

> "… Twenty minutes seems like a long time. Your attention starts to wander after 20 minutes."
>
> – Daniel Turp (BQ), Standing Committee on National Defence and Veterans Affairs, October 9, 1997

There is an inverse relationship between the length of time it takes to read your remarks and the capacity of anyone to identify your key messages.

> "Persuade them why they should read your submission, don't read your submission."
>
> – Jayson Myers, Chief Economist, Alliance of Canadian Manufacturers and Exporters, Interview, May 8, 1997

One lobbyist was congratulated for having only a two-page opening statement. "It was amazing how many members congratulated us for our short remarks."

✅ **TIP** Be sensitive to the committee's situation. If you are the last witness to appear after a long day, do you really think that members will be attentive to listening to your lengthy set of remarks?

 **WHAT TO DO**

- Confirm with the clerk how much time there is available to make opening remarks (e.g., 10 minutes). It can vary.
- Your opening remarks should highlight your key messages. Why are you appearing?
- Consult the committee's terms of reference. They may pose questions or themes to be addressed.

- Use a larger font type and double- or triple-space sentences to make your remarks easier to read.
- Or use bullet points and key phrases. If you know your material, you can speak more freely to the committee by only referring to your notes, not reading them word for word.

TIP This isn't a comedy hour, but revealing your personality helps to avoid being stiff, monotone, and dull.

WHO ARE YOU?

"… I think for many members of the committee perhaps some of the statistics you have quoted in your brief … come as a bit of a revelation in terms of the size and importance of your association."

– Senator Michael Meighen (PC), Standing Senate Committee
on Banking, Trade and Commerce, April 4, 1996

When writing your opening remarks, inform people who you are and whom you represent.

Establish a constituency connection with the committee members, if possible.

Your position may have greater credibility if members understand the process in which you developed your position. Did your board of directors endorse your position? Is it based on a survey of your membership? (Or is this merely a personal view?)

TIP Go easy on the use of acronyms or avoid them altogether. Your group's jargon is not readily known to outsiders. Spell out acronyms in your written brief and identify them fully the first time you use or say them.

BEST AND WORST PRACTICES[14]

In the opinion of parliamentary research officers (those who must read all submisions)…

Well-written submissions are:

1. brief and to the point;
2. simple to understand;
3. logically presented;
4. specific in their recommendations (not vague complaints);
5. well laid-out (e.g., includes table of contents, executive summary, endnotes, subheadings, etc.).

Poorly written submissions are:

1. unfocused: do not address issue at hand;
2. too long;
3. wishy-washy in their positions;
4. rambling;
5. lacking solutions.

STYLE AND FORMAT

"First may I congratulate [the association] on something. The format in which you do your briefs is the best of anyone around by a long shot. I am emphasizing format as opposed to content. The marginal notes are helpful."

– Senator Michael Kirby (L), Chair, Standing Senate Committee
on Banking, Trade and Commerce, October 2, 1996

Write for quality, not quantity. Your material should be succinct and inviting. Does your brief really have to be more than 10 pages long?

When using slides or overhead presentations, it seems that the information is often too detailed or cluttered to read. (Imagine the effect when the lights are dimmed during a late-afternoon session!) Visual presentations should be punchy.

With respect to a supporting written submission, members often do not have the time to read all briefs submitted to the committee. An executive summary is essential. Highlight your key points.

When drafting the committee's report, parliamentary research staff will cull through hearing transcripts (and submissions) to find "quotable quotes"—representative statements that sum up a group's position. They also look for key statistics, such as the cost of any proposal. These should leap out from your pages.

> **TIP** Politics is a verbal business. As one MP put it, "Talking to people is their personal market research." Your written submission should be a supporting document for your oral testimony.

Good presentation helps readers grasp your key points. Imagine reading dozens of lengthy briefs and trying to determine what each group stands for on multiple issues. To assist them, sometimes committee researchers will boil down all these views in a matrix format (i.e., the pros and cons). Using unequivocal language helps members and committee researchers to understand and summarize your positions.

WHAT TO DO

- Pages and pages of endless paragraphs in a submission are brutal to read. The layout should be inviting. Include a succinct executive summary and use bullet points. Perhaps highlight key messages in the margins. Use charts. Use bold type for headings. (Don't use too many font types.) Be creative.
- When commenting on a bill, identify the specific clause that you are addressing. Otherwise it can be a guessing game to link your concern to the actual provision.

- The Committees Directorate suggests that briefs longer than 10 pages "must" include a one-page summary; that endnotes are preferable to footnotes; and that recommendations should be summarized at the end, although many groups do so at the beginning of their submissions.[15]
- Use appendices to elaborate upon detailed issues or provide supporting documentation. Keep the body of your submission uncluttered.

> ✔ **TIP** When writing your submission, think of crafting "sound bites on paper."

TONE

"If we were here to engage in rhetoric, the tone of our presentation would be considerably different from what it has been."

– The Hon. Eric Cline (NDP), Minister of Health for
Saskatchewan, Standing Committee on Industry, April 17, 1997

How you express yourself should be a conscious decision. One company's government relations officer warns not to try to show members how smart you are. Arrogance does little to bend a sympathetic ear.

LANGUAGE

"First, I would like to thank [the witness] for sending us his brief in both official languages. I would have liked the other witnesses to do the same… I will nevertheless try to make do as best I can with the interpretation…"

– Gilbert Fillion (BQ), Standing Committee on Public Accounts,
November 29, 1995

Canada has two official languages. You could be bluntly reminded of this. Respecting the language needs of members comes down to common courtesy. Usually the criticism is directed at lack of translated written materials, but bureaucrats have been criticized for speaking only in English.

"... the Official Languages Act clearly states that citizens may deal with the Government of Canada, which would include this committee, in the language of their choice [French or English]."

– Lee Morrison (L), Standing Committee on Transport, October 7, 1997[16]

Despite the act, members may try to prevent committee staff from circulating an untranslated brief. Much depends on the preferences of each committee. Your opening remarks are not obliged to be handed out. If you do and they are only in one official language, you could be criticized for not having them translated. As one committee official put it: "Move heaven and Earth to have at least a one-page summary translated!" Good advice.

For a large technical document, members may accept the fact that translation may be unnecessary given the cost. A synopsis in both official languages may be sufficient. The clerk can offer advice on what would be appropriate. For some, there is the expectation that all documents are to be translated all the time.

"... the committee has always accepted submissions in either official language, but often national associations and groups provide their documents and submissions in writing in both official languages."

– Derek Lee (L), Standing Committee on Justice
and Human Rights, November 4, 1997

WHAT TO DO

- It is a courtesy, especially for large organizations and for public servants, to have portions of your opening remarks in both official languages.
- For written submissions, public servants must submit their briefs in both official languages.[17] National organizations or associations are expected to do so as well.
- Sending material to the committee well in advance of the hearing may give the committee time to translate your documents for you (e.g., two weeks ahead). Consult the clerk on whether this course can be pursued, if, of course, you can actually have your submission ready so far ahead of your appearance.

INTERNAL POLITICS

"A lot of associations have an internal consensus. A lot freak out if they have to go further."

— David Walker (L), former Chair, Standing Committee on
Industry, Interview, June 25, 1997

Ironically, preparing for a parliamentary committee may involve "lobbying" your own organization or your board of directors. For associations, the fastest way to undermine a committee performance is for its own members to publicly contradict the main message delivered that day. Internal solidarity is fundamental to effectively delivering the message to government.

COALITIONS

"I've seen coalitions go to committee that aren't coalitions at all. They don't mesh. There has to be a particular purpose in mind. There's got to be a dynamic."

— Lynn Toupin, Executive Director, The National Anti-Poverty
Organization, Interview, June 4, 1997

Managing coalitions is especially challenging. Groups must embrace a common objective, share information, and be prepared to compromise. Representatives have to get positions endorsed from their respective organizations. All this takes time. Credible coalitions cannot be thrown together overnight.

For both associations and coalitions, any dissention among the members on the message may allow your critics to "divide and conquer."

> ✓ **TIP** Show your group what you are doing in Ottawa. With the clerk's permission, have your photographer take some pictures of your group at the outset of the committee appearance for use in your newsletter or annual report. Note: Pictures are not allowed to be taken during the actual proceedings.

WHAT TO DO

Internal Consensus

- Associations need room to manoeuvre without getting each word approved. There are various ways to maintain solidarity among association members, or to minimize the fissures, including getting association members to develop consensus on principles of the position and keeping groups or companies well informed about your preparations, the hearings process and its follow-up.

- Asking the committee clerk for a *letter of invitation* to testify may be useful. Showing it to your group may help to spur preoccupied or reluctant colleagues to focus on the task at hand.

The Briefing Binder: A Checklist

Include the following basic elements in a briefing binder for yourself and your team (for "night-before" reading and for use at the hearing)

❑ Table of contents to facilitate use while at the hearing

❑ Logistics: location and time of meeting

❑ Clerk's name and office telephone number

❑ One page highlighting your three to four key messages and supplementary points (this can be used for media interviews following the hearing, too)

❑ Copy of your opening remarks

❑ Copy of any slides or handouts

❑ Summary of key statistics you will use at committee

❑ Q&As: key questions you can anticipate being raised and their answers (Use highly visible headings and bullet-point answers—not sentences!—for quick reference. No answer should really have more than three bullet points.)

❑ Supporting documentation/briefing notes on main issues

❑ Committee's terms of reference

❑ Overview of the committee hearings to date, or a summary of the second reading debate, etc., which identifies the context of the key or controversial issues already discussed (or expected to be raised)

❑ List of committee members that includes some background on each member (where they are from; relevant biographical information, i.e., what they did prior to entering politics; and an indication as to their support for your issues, etc.).

> **TIP** Each section should be well marked (use tabs) and be in binder format for easy access at the hearing table.
> But go easy on constantly flipping through the binder. It can be a distraction. It might signal your lack of preparation if you rely on this crutch too often. Also, a super-thick binder itself might create some fascination and be seen as the source of all answers.

"I know that your aides have binders filled with information about Africa. I wonder if, before February, they could provide our staff with information that could be circulated to members of the committee."

> – Senator Peter Stollery (L), Chair, Standing Senate Committee
> on Foreign Affairs, December 7, 2004

Public Servants and Estimates Preparation

"On estimates, they can ask you about anything under the sun. Members don't just stick to the numbers but anything under your department's purview. This is why it's one of the harder briefings to do."

> – Debbie Kilmartin, Co-ordinator, Parliamentary Relations,
> Finance Canada, Interview, July 9, 1998

- For public servants, appearing before a committee on the department's estimates can involve considerable preparation and internal co-ordination within the department. Good thing, as members can take aim at any departmental initiative, policy, or program. Prepare a good briefing binder where key points can be easily retrieved for reference at the committee table.

SECTION FIVE Know the Committee

THEIR INFORMATION NEEDS

> "I wonder how this committee can properly evaluate the work of the [Law Commission of Canada] if we don't have the powers to do anything but ask questions at a setting like this within a limited period of time… I guess the right way of putting it is how can we ask questions about things we may not know anything about, but which the commission has been involved in?"
>
> – Jack Ramsay (R), Standing Committee on Justice
> and Legal Affairs, December 13, 1995

This revealing quote points to two significant "truths." First, the essence of committee work pivots on the quality of the questioning. Second, to launch probing questions, members require a certain knowledge of the subject.

Members need information. Offering to do a background briefing may help.

> "Perhaps we could renew our profile in the energy sector. I do not know that there are specific issues out there, but it seems they want to tell us about what is going on. It seems appropriate, if this committee is of that mind, to organize a trip out west to meet officials in the oil and gas sector to see what they are facing and what their prognosis is for the future."
>
> – Senator Ron Ghitter (PC), Chair, Standing Senate Committee on
> Energy, the Environment and Natural Resources, March 26, 1996

PRE-MEETINGS

> "We sit down and identify what we need to communicate. We pull out a list of committee members and look at their background. We consciously set out to know how to position ourselves. All this is done so we can educate MPs and help them to do their jobs."
>
> – Michael McCabe, President and CEO, Canadian Association of
> Broadcasters, Interview, May 27, 1997

A POLITICAL VIEW!

"I may want an issue on the record so that I have the option of addressing it in my final report."

— Committee chair (L), Interview, Spring 1997

There is often a symbiotic relationship between witness and politician. Both may need each other to advance an issue. By consulting beforehand with sympathetic members, witnesses may even be encouraged to flag certain issues at the hearing. Getting on the record gives members the option to use the reference later on.

Don't assume that committee members will read your written submission. They may only scan its summary (and sometimes only minutes before you appear or as you speak!). Pre-meetings allow for a verbal briefing. Members might flag controversial issues. (Better to hear it privately first than on the record.) Pre-meetings help to build a mutual understanding on issues and may make the actual hearing a more productive exchange.

Some members may refuse your invitation. Are you lobbying or offering a background briefing?

"I'm uneasy about pre-meetings. I feel, almost irrationally, that the water is being prepared for the baby."

— Senator (L), Interview, August 1997

 WHAT TO DO

Pre-Meetings with Committee Members

- Many groups operate in a non-partisan way and meet members of all parties. Even your critics need some understanding of your position. And vice versa.
- In pre-meetings, the message should not be delivered only by the

paid lobbyist who recites the pre-packaged policy lines.

- Avoid going over your full presentation in a pre-meeting. The member will hear it anyway. Highlight your key points and talk about your solutions.
- A member's expression of support for your position in private may not translate into any vocal support in public. Then again, a sympathetic member might agree to lob an easy question at you during the hearing to help you get a point on the record. (Note: Individual members could be pulled from the committee by the whip at any time to sit at another committee meeting.)
- Keep a "scorecard" on where individual MPs stand on the issues. This helps to identify critical, moderate, and supportive members.
- Feedback from these pre-meetings could lead you to adjust your opening remarks.
- You might have representatives meet with the member in his or her riding office. This helps to localize the issue and the contact.
- Above all, remember that members have very little free time after committee, House, and constituency responsibilities. A pre-meeting takes up valuable "free" time. Make it worthwhile.

Pre-Meetings with Others

"Know your enemies, if you can. Meet them. For consumer groups, you need to gather information from all sides. Cultivate these relationships. Get intelligence from them."

– Ivan Hale, National Secretary, One Voice, The Canadian
Seniors Network, Interview, July 8, 1997

- Meeting with committee researchers prior to the hearing can also be a good idea as they prepare issue summaries for members. Conducting presentations to caucus committees may also be useful.
- Cast your net wider. Pre-meetings could include allies and critics. You need to know what other groups will say at committee. Such exchanges might even elevate the quality of the debate.

> ✔ **TIP** Keep your webpage up to date. "The first thing I do with a witness is to go to their website," notes a parliamentary researcher.

SUBMITTING THE SUBMISSION

> "If you could encourage people to give us those written submissions as soon as possible, that will help every one of us, and similarly if you ask those people who are coming in with information to try to give us a synopsis rather than read any document to us. We can probably read faster ourselves than it can be read to us."
>
> – Jerry Pickard (L), Standing Committee on Natural Resources
> and Government Operations, October 9, 1997

Getting your submission to the clerk as early as possible is preferable (i.e., two weeks ahead of time is suggested). As noted earlier, this could allow the brief to be translated, if appropriate. It also enables researchers time to summarize it. Even getting your brief to the clerk two to three days ahead of the hearing allows time for photocopying and circulating to committee members.

Most witnesses would struggle with these deadlines. Many table their submission as they sit down to testify. Getting your brief in earlier may improve your chances of securing a place on the witness list (but not always).

> "Obviously those who have already sent briefs will be privileged as witnesses because they have taken the trouble to send briefs on their own. We can take it for granted that we will be inviting them in the first place."
>
> – Clifford Lincoln (L), Chair, Standing Committee on Canadian
> Heritage, April 8, 1997

WHAT TO DO

- Give full details on who is submitting the brief (name, title, address, telephone number, and organization name). It is suggested that the author or head of the organization sign the submission (a covering letter would do).
- Electronically submit your brief. "E-mail simplifies everything," urges one clerk.
- Logos, graphs, tables, diagrams, and photographs should be in black and white (as briefs are photocopied).[18]
- When supplying video, a written script must be included.

TIP The cost of producing a brief in both official languages can be prohibitive for smaller and not-for-profit groups. The next best thing? Use excerpts of the verbatim transcript from your appearance, which is translated, to circulate later to parliamentarians.

DISTRIBUTING YOUR MATERIAL

"The committee was considering the bill on the financing of political parties, and a representative of a major accounting firm ... arrived to testify and asked the clerk to distribute his document. The clerk realized that the document was unilingual English and informed the witness that he could not distribute it because it was in English only. The witness then proceeded to place copies of his paper on the table, and members helped themselves."

– Michel Guimond (BQ), Standing Committee on Procedure
and House Affairs, October 21, 2004

The clerk is responsible for distributing documents to members. Not you.

The clerk may need 25 copies of your presentation in English and 10 copies in French (these figures will change depending on the committee; others suggest it is 20 and 20, respectively, or more). This is to distribute

enough copies to all the members of the committee, researchers, transla-
tors, etc. Additional copies should be brought along, too, for media and
observers.

The clerk is not allowed to release your brief beyond the committee
until the date of the hearing.[19]

Sometimes groups themselves selectively pre-release their submissions
beyond the committee (or have a copy sent by courier the moment they sit
down to testify) as a way to nurture a rapport with others.

> "Committee appearances were a useful way to build a relationship with
> officials. For example, in one case, we sent them our submission in
> advance of the hearing to give them a heads up on what we were going
> to say. Over time, they started contacting us in advance with informa-
> tion on issues they knew we were interested in. For an organization
> with limited resources, this was a real bonus."
>
> – Marnie McCall, former Executive Director, The Consumers
> Association of Canada, Interview, August 15, 1998

 WHAT TO DO

- Consult the clerk about the committee's policy about circulating
  submissions to members.
- You can ask that the brief not be publicly distributed and be classi-
  fied as "confidential"; this is at the discretion of the committee.[20]
- Members are constantly migrating from office to chamber to committee room. If your brief was circulated to members in advance of
  the hearing, they may not carry the day's submissions around with
  them. So be prepared to have enough copies available at the committee for members and others.

WHAT'S TABLED IS PUBLIC

"Before we conclude, the committee has decided that we're going to seize this map here… It's a marvellous map, and we'll return it in about a week."

– George Baker (L), Chair, Standing Committee on Fisheries and Oceans, February 12, 1998

Whatever documentation is tabled in committee or sent to the clerk should be considered as public information. Committees can append copies of your correspondence, complete with your group or association's letterhead, right in the *Proceedings of the Committee* or in its final report. The "test": make sure that what you send to the committee is what you would feel comfortable with on the front page of a newspaper.

> **TIP** Be careful of what you bring to the committee table. "If you refer to a document with sensitive information in it, you may be asked to table it," advises a parliamentary relations officer in one large department. "We ask any departmental witness: *What are you bringing to the committee?*"

SECTION SIX Regulating You

In conducting your parliamentary committee activity, be aware of some of the rules that could guide your activities.

THE LOBBYIST REGISTRATION ACT

"Lobbying is a legitimate part of our democratic system. People, organizations and businesses have the right to communicate, to decision makers, information and views on issues that are important to them. However, it is important that this happen in a transparent manner— that Canadians have the opportunity to know who is lobbying public office-holders and in which context."

– Michael Nelson, Registrar, *Message from the Registrar of Lobbyists*, LRA Website, June 21, 2005

The broad pursuit of transparency in government is reflected in an updated Lobbyist Registration Act. Anyone communicating with government should be aware of (and compliant with) its requirements.[21]

Communication with parliamentary committees is one of the handful of "exclusions" from needing to register.[22] Yet many witnesses regularly interact with government at multiple levels and would be required to register other communications and activities—doing so is a fact of lobbying life. While the actual committee event does not require registration, pre-meetings with members, dealings with departments, and other types of related activity might well fall within the registration requirements.

Lobbyists are also required to abide by the *Lobbyists' Code of Conduct*. The code includes a number of rules, including the use of "accurate information." As well, lobbyists "should not knowingly mislead anyone and shall use proper care to avoid doing so inadvertently."[23] To say the least, this code should guide your behaviour at all times.

The act's disclosure requirements mean that far more information is, or should be, available on lobbyists who appear before committees as witnesses. As one official advised, "Ensure your declarations are in good order before you appear at committee." One can expect that committee members can more fully peek into the backgrounds of those who testify before them. Expect committee members to ask you whether you are registered under the act; if you are a paid lobbyist you may be asked about the nature of your client list. Members simply like to know with whom they are dealing.

THE INCOME TAX ACT AND REGISTERED CHARITIES

How charities communicate with government is subject to certain requirements set down by Canada Customs and Revenue Agency (through the Income Tax Act). It distinguishes between charitable and political activities relating to the nature of communication that charities can have in advancing an issue. A detailed policy statement outlining these requirements is available on its website.[24]

COMPETITION ACT

"It might be an offence under the Competition Act for me to reveal what our pricing strategy is going to be with respect to this issue or any other … I really can't comment on whether there will be a price increase in the near future to reflect this."

> – A witness, Standing Committee on Health, December 14, 2004

What you say may invite scrutiny of another sort—from officials with the Competition Bureau. Moreover, forming coalitions (to promote public policy changes) could also catch the eye of this government marketplace watchdog. "Most strategic alliances do not raise issues under the Act," notes the bureau.[25] Its litmus test is whether any behaviour intends to diminish competition. Committee proceedings can provide the bureau with a view of the marketplace players. They may monitor certain hearings. Are you suggesting regulatory changes that would unduly restrict competition?

REGULATING THEM: ETHICS GUIDELINES

"Ethics is busting out all over."

> – Dr. Bernard Shapiro, The Ethics Commissioner for the House
> of Commons, Remarks to The Ottawa Evening 2005, co-hosted
> by Friends of the Canadian Institute of Health Research and
> Partners in Research, May 11, 2005

The pursuit of transparency and accountability is seizing Ottawa's (and the public's) attention. It's certainly shaping parliamentary activity: a new Standing Committee on Access to Information, Privacy, and Ethics has been set up; MPs, senators, and public office holders must comply with separate conflicts of interest codes, and there are new and separate ethics officers for the House of Commons and the Senate. The push for greater transparency of member financial interests is focusing members on the practical application of the requirements and the expectations. This suggests that members may be even more particular about their receiving—or being perceived to receive—any inappropriate benefit from anybody on anything.[26]

"Mad cow disease has proved to be a major headache for farmers. The House of Commons is set to pass legislation to award each farmer $100,000. An MP who also happens to be a farmer will receive $100,000 if the bill is adopted. Must that MP abstain from voting?"

– Yvon Godin (NDP), Standing Committee on Procedure and House Affairs, October 14, 2004

For witnesses, the desire to avoid a conflict might explain why a member excuses himself from the table or abstains from voting on a matter. Indeed, the ethics commissioner pays attention to changing committee memberships as shifting responsibilities may create real or potential conflicts of interest for members as they move to their new committee.

A final point here: ethical behaviour applies to everyone. The expectation crosses all institutions in our society these days. Members will expect witnesses who come before them to exhibit the highest ethical standards, whether it is what is said at committee or in how witnesses conduct themselves in business, in organizations, or in society at large.

"Canadians want the truth, the whole truth, and nothing but the truth, and an unwillingness or inability to conduct themselves in an acceptable, ethical manner will incur the wrath of voters and shareholders down the road."

– Chuck Strahl (CPC), Deputy Speaker of the House of Commons, *Canadian Parliamentary Review*, 2004[27]

ACCESS TO INFORMATION AND PRIVACY

"… material which cannot be provided under the Access to Information Act or the Privacy Act cannot be divulged."

– Privy Council Office, 2003[28]

Public servants must tread carefully in what they can or can't say (keeping in mind the principle of *ministerial responsibility*, as addressed in Chapter Three) given the existence of the Access to Information and Privacy Acts. Public servants must adhere to the requirement that "… the provision of information to committees beyond that normally accessible to the public must be a matter of ministerial decision and must be consistent with statutory obligations."[29]

Parliamentarians' currency is the exchange of information—they desire more of it and don't want to restrict it. Public servants are holders of information—they use it to implement programs (or policy) and don't necessarily relish sharing it. Inevitable conflicts ensue.

Officials are given some rather blunt internal advice to parry parliamentarians' information pursuit: "… parliamentarians cannot be required to keep information private, and accordingly parliamentarians should only be provided with information that can be made public."[30]

SECTION SEVEN Last-Minute Checklist

HOLDING A FINAL STRATEGY MEETING

"I think it would be wise for us to advise these national groups that we expect them to address the regional concerns as well as the national ones."

– Guy Arseneault (L), Standing Committee on Canadian Heritage,
April 8, 1997

Just prior to your appearance, you should review your approach. Are you truly ready to go?

WHAT TO DO
Ready? Set? Go to Your Pre-Hearing Checklist!

While there are many factors to consider before deciding to appear and preparing (noted earlier), the day or morning before you appear, conduct this last-minute checklist.

Hearing Logistics

❏ Telephone the clerk (the day before) to confirm the meeting details (i.e., location, time).

❏ Confirm the time available to read your opening remarks and the length of the question-answer session to follow.

❏ Are there any member substitutions on the committee?

❏ Are there any last-minute new witnesses slotted to appear before or after you?

❏ Is the hearing going to be televised (on CPAC)?

❏ Review the committee room layout and seating arrangements of members for colleagues who have not previously testified.

❏ Plan to leave for the hearing early enough to clear security, find the room, and get settled.

Your Key Messages

❏ What are your objectives in appearing before the committee?

❏ Review your key messages that support these objectives.

❏ For public servants, this must be done by *explaining* the government's policy decisions, not *defending* them (as ministers are responsible for policy decisions).

Opening Remarks

❏ Do your opening remarks capture your key messages?

❏ Do the remarks clearly identify who you are and what you are responsible for?

❏ Read aloud your remarks to colleagues. How long does it take to read? Is your voice monotone? Do you look up? Do you show conviction?

❏ If you go over your allotted time and are cut off, how would you conclude? (Your ending should include your essential message.)

❏ Delivering these remarks with sections of French and English makes a positive impression.

❏ Before saying a word at the committee table, pause, take a breath, relax, and then begin.

Political Context
- ❏ Will committee members be generally receptive or critical of your position or recommendations?
- ❏ Is the government generally supportive of the committee's inquiry (if it is not a bill)?
- ❏ What are the prevailing political priorities of the government? Do any of your messages mesh with these?

Identify the Minefields
- ❏ Anticipate the two or three areas of discussion that could present the most difficulty for you. Script those answers now.
- ❏ Do members of your own association or group (or for the public service, other government departments) disagree with any major issue being presented by you that day?
- ❏ What are other key witnesses likely to say, or have said, at committee that could potentially undermine your position?
- ❏ Do you have the authority to commit your group (i.e., if a member asks you to conduct further research or to appear again before the committee)?
- ❏ For public servants, could you be criticized for inadequately briefing members prior to the bill in question coming to committee or for rushing its consideration at committee stage?
- ❏ Also for public servants, what you say at committee could, for partisan reasons, be raised by a member in Question Period. Advise the minister's office of any relevant exchanges with members. (Private-sector groups in the political spotlight may also consider giving the minister a "heads up.")

Questions and Answers
- ❏ Estimate the number of questions you could get within the time allotted to you.
- ❏ Consider the main concerns of each committee member.
- ❏ What is likely to be the lead question from the official opposition? They ask the first question.

❑ What issues have come up in previous testimony that could also be raised with you?

❑ Has an issue come up in Question Period, or in House debates, that will prompt questions?

❑ Have the national media recently reported on a news story that could generate any critical questions? Check the day's newspapers.

❑ Have any local stories in member ridings come up recently that could be raised at the table?

❑ If you appear with colleagues, agree beforehand which type of questions will be handled among your team.

❑ Be prepared for the chair to cut off your long-winded answers.

❑ Conduct a simulation. Get a colleague to ask tough questions. Even a 20-minute Q&A session will help to polish your answers. Suggest more appropriate responses. (The next chapter addresses the handling of an array of question scenarios.)

Bailouts

❑ Handling particularly aggressive questioning requires a measured response. Speak directly to the chair. The chair is responsible for maintaining decorum in committee. (The next chapter reviews this in more detail.)

❑ Use the tag-team approach. A colleague at the table could offer a supplementary point if your response does not hit the mark.

❑ Expect members to pose any question they like. Politely defer to the chair to determine the relevance of questions which stray consistently well beyond the inquiry's terms of reference or bill at hand.

❑ Offer to get back to the committee in writing on a question that requires a more thoughtful response.

❑ Suggest talking to a member "off-line" following the meeting to address a specific constituent complaint, although the member may prefer to address the principle of the matter at the table.

❑ For public servants, there may be issues best left to the department's deputy minister to handle and should not be addressed by more junior officials appearing before committee.

Attitude

❏ Are you prepared to step into the committee room with a positive, constructive attitude? Help members understand your position; don't confront them with it. A conscious decision here will affect your tone and manner in committee.

Media

❏ Who will conduct media interviews if you are scrummed before or following your testimony?

❏ One off-the-cuff or negative statement made during your testimony could become the headline. Assume the media are monitoring your testimony.

❏ What you say to the media should parallel what you say before the committee.

❏ If the hearing is televised on CPAC, be aware that your message is being carried nationally.

Handouts

❏ Are your slides, charts, etc., in order? Are they easy to read?

❏ Do you have enough copies of your materials, in English and French, for all members, the media, and others sitting in the room?

❏ Referring to internal documents in your testimony may prompt members to request that you table them for the record. Are you sure that what you take to the table is what you want on the public record?

❏ For public servants (and national groups), do not table any document, such as your opening remarks, unless it is translated.

WATCH YOUR FLANK

"Before giving [the witness] the floor, I would like to draw your attention to a poll published in the local newspaper yesterday."

– The Hon. Charles Caccia (L), Chair, Standing Committee on Environment and Sustainable Development, March 6, 1997

Your submission is polished. You are ready to testify. Surprises happen. An unexpected poll (perhaps commissioned by an opposing group) hits the headlines prior to your appearance. Your key point is undermined. An opponent plays up public misconceptions about your group. He could even feed members with questionable, perhaps erroneous, information.

All witnesses compete for the ears of committee members. Some will stop at nothing to beat you.

You may have even lost before saying your first word at the committee table.

ENDNOTES

---

1. Sometimes committees will not hear from any witnesses other than ministers and their respective officials, such as on a bill. See Robert Marleau and Camille Montpetit, eds., *House of Commons Procedure and Practice* (Montréal: Chenelière/ McGraw-Hill, 2000), 648, 283n.
2. Senate Rule 102 specifically allows for reimbursement.
3. The committee room diagram is reproduced from the Committees Directorate, *A Guide for Witnesses Appearing before Committees of the House of Commons*, House of Commons Committee Website (appendix), www.parl.gc.ca
4. Video-teleconferencing occupied less than 1% of committee time on the House side. House of Commons, Committees Directorate, *2003-04 Annual Report on Committees Activities and Expenditures*, 5. The number has been higher; in use since 1994, video-teleconferencing consumed less than 4% of total meeting hours in the mid-1990s. House of Commons, Committees and Legislative Services Directorate, *Activities and Expenditures, Annual Report 1996-97* (September 1997), 6.
5. *Report of the Liaison Committee* (February 1997), 14.
6. The Sub-Committee on the Status of Persons with Disabilities launched its own dedicated four-month web consultation on the Canada Pension Plan disability program in December 2002. It was a parallel initiative to the "usual process" (a roundtable consultation) undertaken in Ottawa. In testimony describing the process, it was noted that some 15,000 Canadians participated, and feedback was received from over 1,400 people through its polling tool through a dedicated web address, www.parl.gc.ca/disability; the committee apparently had a feedback target of 200 people. Some 135 personal stories were posted, and the target was 40; the committee wanted 10 solutions to be tabled and received 28; however, the committee did not hear fully from one target audience: doctors. While this glimpse into web consultations is provided, it is beyond the scope of this book to evaluate

e-consultation. There are pros and cons. How can the integrity of the information on-line be assured to be genuine? Is one group co-ordinating the dumping of feedback into the process? Can the committee be assured it is getting a representative sampling of feedback? Still, this mechanism seems to have an appeal in allowing "real" Canadians to share their "heart-touching" experiences, such as those experienced with the Canada Pension Plan disability program. See Standing Joint Committee on the Library of Parliament, *Evidence* (May 8, 2003).

7. Under the democratic reform initiative, it has been suggested that new e-consultation mechanisms be considered, including "greater use of modern technology by Committees for citizen engagement, greater use of webcasting and videoconferencing, and electronic filing of motions and questions." Privy Council Office, *Ethics, Responsibility, Accountability An Action Plan for Democratic Reform* (February 4, 2004). Note also resources being devoted to upgrading House of Commons e-capabilities in House of Commons Administration, *Reports on Plans and Priorities 2004-05* (Spring 2004).

8. Fewer than one in five House committee hearings is televised. House of Commons, Committees Directorate, *2003-04 Annual Report on Committees Activities and Expenditures*, 1.

9. Committees also review departmental estimates and Order-in-Council appointments. While these are not specifically considered in this checklist, key questions/points flagged here could assist a witness in preparing to appear for such hearings.

10. In addition to confirming your appearance, the clerk needs your name and title for a number of reasons: to have security passes ready; to publicize the witness list; to enable CPAC, if a televised proceeding, to flash your name on the screen; to ensure that a translation of your title and company name is available for the record; and, possibly, to have nameplates printed for the committee table.

11. The following publication offers tips on dealing with televising a committee testimony and proceeding. Parliamentary Centre, "Televising Committees," *Occasional Papers on Parliamentary Government*, no. 6 (February 1998), 7-8.

12. A shift in public policy focus can have a profound impact; e.g., taking an interest in disease prevention in turn leads policy makers to consider the causes of illness, such as obesity, smoking, pollutants, and workplace stress. See Don Lenihan and Graham Fox, "Governing from the centre: What's the alternative?," *The Hill Times*, January 31-February 6, 2005, 14.

13. Another example of effective messaging in campaigns: Defining your issue may involve massaging your opponent's key point. Take the debate between the multinational pharmaceutical industry and the generic drug manufacturers in the patent drug review in 1997. This issue pivoted on the doubly important priorities of funding long-term drug R&D and getting short-term lower-cost drugs. The Pharmaceutical Manufacturers Association of Canada (PMAC) wanted to maintain adequate patent protection, and drug profitability, so long-term R&D could take place in Canada. It also had to take on the drug cost issue being advanced by the opposing generic drug lobby. PMAC had a means to do so. Since drug misuse

was costing Canada's health care system billions of dollars annually, it had created a national program to promote public education about appropriate and responsible use of medication. (The program: "Knowledge Is the *Best* Medicine," 1994.) Wise use of medications contributes to lowering health costs. To PMAC, the issue was not only "cost containment" but proper "drug utilization." By pushing its main message (patent protection), PMAC had also addressed its opponent's key issue (drug costs). In another case, there always seems to be an alternative view of the same issue. Banning tobacco advertising in 1998 may have been an obvious health issue, but it also became a burning issue because of the ban's perceived impact on sponsorships of sporting and arts events. The government had to reconcile both concerns. Another example of politically positioning messaging: one Liberal MP introduced a private member's bill that would have banned negative-option billing by cable companies in 1996. He positioned it as a consumer-friendly bill. However, others wanted it viewed differently. Opponents profiled it as a cultural issue. It was seen as infringing upon the capacity to deliver new speciality French-language channels in Quebec. It was defeated.

14. The features of good and bad submissions received from witnesses are ranked in order (from the author's survey of parliamentary research officers, May 1996).

15. Committees and Legislative Services, *Preparing a Submission to a House of Commons Committee* (March 1998), website.

16. See Treasury Board of Canada Secretariat, *Official Languages Act*, Section 4(1), Annotated Version (1989).

17. Senate of Canada, Committees and Private Legislation, *A Guide for Witnesses Appearing before Senate Committees* (January 1994), 4.

18. Ibid., 5.

19. Ibid., 6.

20. Committees and Legislative Services, *Preparing a Submission to a House of Commons Committee* (March 1998), website.

21. The act now states that lobbying will consist of "any oral or written communication made to a pulic office holder." Industry Canada, Lobbyist Registration Branch website, *Important Notice to all Users of the Registration System*, June 9, 2005. The act came into force on June 20, 2005.

22. It is noted that "Preparation and presentation of briefings to parliamentary committees" is an example of communication that would not normally require registration. See Industry Canada, Lobbyist Registration Branch website, *Interpretation Bulletin—Communicating with Federal Public Office Holders*, June 20, 2005.

23. Industry Canada, Lobbyist Registration Branch, *Lobbyists' Code of Conduct*, Rule 2, "Accurate Information."

24. Revenue Canada, *Political Activities*, policy statement, reference number CPS-0222, September 2, 2003. Charities should review the current guidelines around what is deemed to be a "political activity"; for instance, "a charity must not single out the voting pattern on an issue of any one elected representative or political party." Ibid., section 6.1.

25. Director of Investigation and Research, Minister of Supply and Services Canada,

Strategic Alliances under the Competition Act (Information Bulletin 1995), iv.

26. Says one parliamentary observer: "Many senators historically, and still at present, have had distinguished careers in business and the professions, and retain business and professional activities after becoming senators. The Senate has accepted the potential conflicts of interest inherent in having senators who retain strong connections with business and other groups not only participate in proceedings but also hold positions of responsibility and influence such as chair of the Senate Banking and Finance Committee. It is not yet clear how the Senate will resolve these potential conflicts of interest. As of January 2005 the Ethics Officer for the Senate had not been appointed, nor had a code of ethics been promulgated for the Senate." C.E.S. Franks (Professor Emeritus at Queen's University in Kingston), "Parliamentarians and the New Code of Ethics," *Canadian Parliamentary Review* 28, no. 1 (Spring 2005). Note that Senate rules specify that senators cannot sit on a committee examining an issue where they have a pecuniary interest; other Senate rules apply as well (Rule 94(1), (3), and (10)).

27. Chuck Strahl, "Politics and Procedure in a Minority Government," *Canadian Parliamentary Review* 27, no. 4 (Winter 2004).

28. Privy Council Office, Guidance for Deputy Ministers (July 20, 2003), 11, reproduced on www.pco-bcp.gc.ca.

29. Ibid., 10.

30. Ibid., 11.

CHAPTER SEVEN

The Hearing

It is a sobering thought that the overall quality of written submissions delivered to parliamentary committees rates about a C+.[1]

Some do a superb job. For others, members grit their teeth and politely bear it. Going before a committee is not an "appearance." It is a "performance." You should aim for nothing less than an A+.

SECTION ONE Before You Start

GETTING THERE

> "I apologize for being five minutes late. I might say to you, as chair of the Transport Committee, that, if the elevator transportation in this building were a little quicker, I might be here slightly earlier."
>
> – The Hon. Paul Martin (L), Minister of Finance, Standing
> Committee on Transport, December 4, 1996

Go to the committee room with time to spare (e.g., 60 minutes beforehand). On busy days it may take 30 minutes just to clear security and get to the hearing room. Many witnesses go much earlier. They want to get the flavour of the debate and check the mood of the members.

In the winter, if you have an early morning hearing, it may be wise to get to Ottawa the night before. Being snowed out and stalled on the Pearson Airport tarmac is not enjoyable.

> ✓ **TIP** Novice witnesses can familiarize themselves with a committee room and minimize anxiety. Check with the clerk about visiting the committee room in advance, such as the day before. It takes the mystery out of the layout and where you are going.

YOUR INTRODUCTION

Introduce yourself to the clerk. He or she needs to ensure that you have shown up! The clerk can tell you what members are present, introduce you to the chair, and outline any last-minute details on the hearing schedule and format.

Inform the clerk beforehand if you have a plane to catch. However, avoid booking flights too close to your appearance as there is always the possibility of a delay.

WHAT TO DO

- Upon your arrival at the committee room, give the clerk copies of your opening remarks/submission (to be distributed to members, researchers, interpreters, etc).
- Distributing copies of your remarks can prompt members to follow along; it can also result in members having to flip through them as you read, which can be distracting.
- Wait for the hearing to begin before making your submission available to those in the audience.

> ✓ **TIP** If time and the occasion permit, you should personally introduce yourself to all members of the committee. Shaking hands with members is a small courtesy.

WHO'S IN THE AUDIENCE?

"You will be interested to note that a number of [the finance minister's] representatives are present here in this room this morning. I urge you to take the opportunity to find out whether, indeed, there is some milk of human kindness in these individuals."

— Senator David Angus (PC), Standing Senate Committee on
Banking, Trade and Commerce, March 3, 1997

Committee hearings can be popular spots for a whole raft of people: competing interest groups, departmental officials, media, etc. Between witness testimonies, there may be some networking opportunities to pursue with these folks.

TIP "I always try to go and see the minister when he and his staff appear on a bill. It's an opportunity to say a few words to the minister."
— Elizabeth May, Executive Director, Sierra Club, Interview, June 13, 1997

SIMULTANEOUS INTERPRETATION SERVICE

"First, to save money on the length of the wire for the earphones just about took my ear off. Perhaps that could be brought to someone's attention and something done about it."

— Senator Consiglio Di Nino (CPC), Standing Committee on
Rules, Procedures and the Rights of Parliament, February 4, 2004

The real jeopardy is missing the translation. French and English simultaneous interpretation is available at the committee table (and for those in the audience). Ensure you get the earpiece ready before you commence.

WHAT TO DO

- Set up your earpiece as soon as you sit at the table so you can be ready to receive the French/English translation or the "floor" discussion—the latter may be helpful just to hear certain members.

- As Interpretation Services points out, "You can help ensure the clear communication of your message" by providing interpreters with a copy of your opening remarks before you begin to speak, or in advance of your testimony. This way, they can faithfully communicate your message in the other official language and accurately use technical terms, acronyms, etc.

CELL PHONES: OFF

"I'll start with a friendly reminder to members of Parliament, staff, our leaders from the military, anybody and everybody here. Please do us all the courtesy of disarming your cell phones…"

– Pat O'Brien (L), Chair, Standing Committee on National
Defence and Veterans Affairs, October 20, 2004

Say no more.

SECTION TWO What to Expect

"We sat here, and we watched the disrespect of Bloc members as they walked out of this meeting; we sat here, and we listened as the Bloc members badgered witnesses."

– Randy White (R), Standing Committee on Procedure and
House Affairs, April 21, 1998

What happens in parliamentary committees can be unpredictable. Following are some things to expect.

MEMBERS GONE MISSING

"Given that there were no opposition members here to ask questions, I've played rather fast and loose with the time. That was a good 27-minute round, but don't tell them."

– Paddy Torsney (L), Vice-Chair, Standing Committee on Justice
and Legal Affairs, April 17, 1997

Presuming that it is not boycotting you, an opposition party may not be present for any number of reasons. There may simply be fewer members of some opposition parties to attend all hearings. As well, opposition members sometimes storm out of a hearing because of a procedural dispute with the chair. Don't let these partisan games rattle you. The hearing will usually proceed in any case.

Members see hundreds of witnesses. Missing your testimony may be nothing more than "just not being available that day." On the rarest of occasions, no one shows up!

> "Because of the members of Parliament not being here, the witness is denied testimony. Then they have to go back to wherever they came from. That has happened at least three or four times in the last three or four years. It's an embarrassment."
>
> – John Richardson (L), Standing Committee on National
> Defence and Veterans Affairs, October 9, 1997

WHAT TO DO

Personally follow up with absent committee members and ensure that they have received your brief.

QUORUM

> "If someone were testifying at a meeting and because of a snowstorm only a couple of members showed up, you could still hear the evidence. However, you could not take a vote."
>
> – Senator Mabel DeWare (L), Senate Subcommittee on
> Post-Secondary Education, August 6, 1996

You're there, but few MPs or senators are. Quorum or not, the chair may ask that you proceed with your testimony. Each committee has its own policy about accepting testimony.

LIGHTS, BELLS, AND DELAYS

"… let me apologize one more time for the fact that we were not able to complete our hearings last Thursday. Unfortunately, as committees, we are creatures of the House. It's a shame when people come from a distance and those disturbances happen."

– Reg Alcock (L), Chair, Standing Committee on Transport,
December 2, 1996

You have spent considerable time and effort getting ready. You may have flown in from across the country to testify. Expect interruptions or delays.

"I first want to extend my apologies to the committee members and witnesses who did make it on time. The prime minister was speaking in the House on perhaps one of the most important issues of our time, so we were delayed."

– Wayne Easter (L), Subcommittee on Grain Transportation,
November 29, 1995

You can expect lights to flash and bells to ring. This signals a vote in the House or a quorum call. The hearing may be put on hold if members must leave to vote—possibly delaying the hearing by at least half an hour (or postponing it).[2]

"I'd like to just interject briefly, and then we'll have some more questions. We do have quorum now, and there is something we need to do on almost an emergency basis. We need to approve the budget for the study of Bill C-9."

– Werner Schmidt (CPC), Vice-Chair, Standing Committee on Industry,
Natural Resources, Science and Technology, February 7, 2005

If additional members arrive and quorum can be secured, then the chair may preempt, even interrupt, your opening statement to conduct committee business. Or the committee can opt to discuss any matter within its purview regardless of what is scheduled at that meeting.[3] Be patient.

HEADLINE HUNTERS

"The lack of anything successful to do in the Commons or Committee (an average MP's likelihood of influencing a bill cobbled together by Cabinet and the Public Service is about as certain as Sir John A. Macdonald sweeping into power . . .) has made getting on T.V. the only diversion."

– *Frank's Millennial Guide to Ottawa*, 1995, by Geoff Heinricks, 17

This satirical view of committee work aside, there is an underlying truth to the matter.

Members can grandstand for the press. They may also spare little effort to get attention. From a Liberal member leaping over committee chairs during a hearing to block the exit of a former Conservative cabinet minister[4] to day-to-day partisan antics among members, some crave media coverage no matter what people may think.

"We had our chairman come from Vancouver and he saw all the partisan nonsense. This doesn't instill a lot of respect for the system. MPs should be more cognizant of this."

– Michael Makin, President, Canadian Printing Industries
Association, Interview, July 3, 1997

 WHAT TO DO: PARTISAN SHOTS

"Without getting into a political fight, I would still like to reply to the comments made by my Conservative colleague, since he did bring up a past incident."

– Odina Desrochers (BQ), Standing Committee on Official
Languages, November 25, 2004

Calmly wait out partisan banter and stay out of the crossfire.

SECTION THREE You're On

> "I remember the farmers. They spoke from the heart. But those professional lobbyists, all they did was hand out volumes of paper. It all comes down to how an issue affects people, the family; after all, this is what counts."
>
> – Jesse Flis (L), Interview, May 1, 1997

FIRST WORDS

> "I don't want to cut you off, but perhaps just slow down. Our translators are having difficulty keeping up to you."
>
> – John Maloney (L), Chair, Subcommittee on Solicitation Laws
> of the Standing Committee on Justice, Human Rights, Public
> Safety and Emergency Preparedness, February 9, 2005

After inviting you to sit at the table, the chair may leave it up to you to introduce yourself, or he may do so. As well, even before you say a word, the chair may make an introductory statement, perhaps summarizing the point of the inquiry.

 **WHAT TO DO**

- When introducing yourself and your group, include names and titles and note the geographic location of the organization, if appropriate. This sets an immediate context for the members opposite.
- And don't talk too fast. The interpreters are very good at keeping up with the discussion, but they will interrupt you if they cannot translate an excessively rapid delivery. You're there to communicate. Don't put your mouth into overdrive.

GETTING ON THE RECORD

"We can always put in a motion that their written record be included in the record of the committee."

– Mac Harb (L), Standing Committee on Public Accounts,
October 8, 1997

Members want to get to questions. But you want your opening remarks to be formally registered or tabled. One technique accommodating both is to have your opening statement, summary, or list of recommendations "considered read into the record." The committee must pass a motion to print your text in the committee transcript or proceedings (as if you had actually read them). Or it could be appended to the proceedings.[5]

ETIQUETTE

It is parliamentary etiquette to address members through the chair. This has several purposes. It reinforces the chair's authority. It maintains formality. It also helps you keep your cool when faced with aggressive questioning.

WHEN HONOURABLE MEMBERS ARE NOT "HONOURABLE"

Properly addressing members can sometimes be a challenge.

- The chair: "Mr. Chairman" or "Madam Chair" (*"Madam Chair, thank you for allowing us to appear"*).
- All other committee members: "Member" or "Senator" (*"Could the Member [Senator] please repeat that question?"*).
- A member can be addressed as "Mr." or "Ms.," although it is less parliamentary.
- Using "Honourable" is acceptable. (*"I'd like to point out to the Honourable Member [or Senator]..."*).
- However, in correspondence, only ministers, former ministers, privy councillors, and senators have titles including the word "Honourable."

YOUR BEHAVIOUR

"Every damned time we have a serious issue to discuss in this country we're under time frames. We're a little tired of it."
— Wilfred Harder, Chairman, Advisory Committee to the
Canadian Wheat Board, Subcommittee on Grain Transportation,
December 6, 1995

You are there to help members understand your position, yet your behaviour can make indelible (and possibly negative) impressions.

WHAT TO DO

"If this is the Standing Committee on Finance, something that's very important to the federal government, why have there been no more than five MPs here?"
— Narman Hassam, Vice-President, Internal, University of Alberta
Students' Union, Standing Committee on Finance,
November 30, 1995

- Don't complain. It can be very disappointing, but whining about their low attendance gets you nowhere; criticizing members for their lack of attentiveness is a cheap shot. Members have many duties to perform other than sitting in committee.
- Members must also endure hundreds of hours of testimony, and momentary distractions are inevitable. They suffer from the occasional diversions (whether it's reading the newspaper, signing correspondence, or heckling each other). Take the hint: maybe you are rambling. Get focused. Offer snappier replies to members' questions.

"I ask that you make your presentation to the committee, and your judgement of my attention span will have to be put aside. I can hear what you are saying."
— Raymond Bonin (L), Chair, Standing Committee on
Aboriginal Affairs and Northern Development, March 18, 1997

- Be respectful. Members will respect you if you treat the committee professionally and if you can diplomatically parry rudeness or tough questioning by one of their colleagues. Members have been known to slam books on the table and shout to make a point. It may be a ploy. They may want to get you flustered, shake your confidence, and get you to say things that you will later regret.
- Hearings have been known to be disrupted by boisterous protestors.[6] Of course, misbehaving is unacceptable. Disrupting a committee proceeding is actually contemptible, such as shouting and even waving placards.[7]
- Be responsive. At times, your testimony may require a little *mea culpa* if members feel that the actions of your group have not been doing enough for consumers or constituents.
- Don't be arrogant. You're "the expert" but avoid hitting MPs over the head with that fact. You are there to help them understand the issues, not reveal their ignorance.
- Be interesting and capture members' attention. Inject a little humour into your testimony.

"As a nurse, I wondered if I needed to bring a bit of stimulant to get you people ready for this presentation, but there's some passion at this end of the table, so I don't think you'll need medication."

– Kathleen Connors, Chairperson, Canadian Health Coalition,
Standing Committee on Industry, March 4, 1997

QUESTIONING FORMAT
(OR, *Stuffing in as Many Questions as You Can*)

"If it's agreeable, in the near future I'll introduce a motion to change the speaking rotation from what it is now … In the spirit of co-operation in the Christmas festive season, maybe you can reflect upon it as you're opening up your gifts and stuffing your gullets with turkey. Maybe you can help out the good old NDP down here at the end."

– Peter Stoffer (NDP), Standing Committee on Fisheries and
Oceans, December 9, 2004

Members are very particular about carving out time to ask their questions.

Done in "rounds," questioning will be led by the official opposition, who will get 5 to 10 minutes. Depending on the committee, each party represented around the table gets an equal amount of time. In subsequent rounds, members will have less time to pose their questions. Time permitting, members may even get a third go at you. Everybody wants a turn.

> "In the last Parliament we gave the first question to the official opposition, as a rule, religiously respected. Then we went to the government. Then we went to another opposition party. In this case, with a new Parliament we will alternate between opposition and government, zig-zagging, like a nice slalom."
> – The Hon. Charles Caccia (L), Chair, Standing Committee on Environment and Sustainable Development, October 7, 1997

Some chairs allow for a looser approach. When pursuing an interesting line of questioning, members will sometimes just jump in and follow up on each other's questions. The Q&A format depends entirely on the committee chair.

In a roundtable format, several groups or witnesses appear at once and must share the floor with the others. Answering is more of a free-for-all. It can pit witnesses against each other and stir up debate (which is why members like this approach).

WHAT TO DO

Check with the clerk before the hearing about how the Q&A format will be conducted.

QUESTIONING IN HOUSE VS. SENATE COMMITTEES

> "You have to be really nimble to get your point across, especially at a House committee. Before you know it, one member's line of question-

ing ends and another's begins. You must get your point across each time; otherwise you can lose your opportunity."

– Dr. C.E.S. Franks, Professor of Political Studies, Queen's
University, Interview, October 24, 1997

With several parties around the table, each with a prescribed amount of time to pose questions, House committees often lack cohesiveness during questioning. A line of questioning can suddenly be cut short as the floor is passed from one party to another.

Senate committees are less stringent about setting time limits for questions. Being less partisan, senators will often play off each other's questions and probe much deeper on issues.

Both styles can be a challenge. A generalization, but expect more partisan shots in House committees and more detailed questioning in Senate committees.

QUESTIONING STYLE

"If you asked 295 parliamentarians where they want to go, you would get 295 answers."

– John Williams (R), Subcommittee on Grain Transportation,
November 29, 1995

Questions from members can be largely anticipated or totally unpredictable. Questioning can be personal, abusive, erratic, incomprehensible, and seemingly totally irrelevant.[8] Questioning can also be thoughtful, well researched, laser-focused, and effective in rooting out the essential issue. Your challenge is to deal with each style as best as you can (even if your replies get a cool reception).

"I have no further use of the witness. I know how biased they are."

– Ghislain Lebel (BQ), Subcommittee on Bill C-25,
November 26, 1996

Members will ask witnesses whatever they want. But, if a bill, expect the obvious: how will the proposed legislation really affect you?

"I'm not an international lawyer; I'm a housewife from Mississauga. When I'm lectured at I just glaze over and stop listening."
— Carolyn Parrish (L), Standing Committee on Industry,
March 4, 1997

BEST AND WORST PRACTICES[9]

Good answers are a combination of *what you say* and *how you say it*. To answer questions *effectively*, be:
1. clear, short, and to the point;
2. in command of issues and facts;
3. honest;
4. relaxed;
5. confident.

But *poorly delivered* answers are:
1. unfocused;
2. defensive;
3. insincere;
4. ideological;
5. taken personally.

"I'd like to know from you, without divulging what your revenues are, but just ballparking, what the legislation as it stands represents in terms of additional costs. Just guestimate what the … percentage of revenue might be."
— Mauril Bélanger (L), Standing Committee on Canadian Heritage,
October 8, 1996

Members may preface their questions with rambling monologues and finish with a series of quick-snappers. Members might draw upon their personal experience and constituent anecdotes to frame their questions. Or members may rely on the list of prepared questions drawn up by researchers—a *Coles Notes* approach.

Like a student before an exam, anticipating the questions is critical. The oral testimony is more important than the written brief itself. It is the tone and substance of what you say, not the written submission, that sticks in the minds of committee members. Also, what you say gets quoted in the newspaper.

GOOD ANSWER

"Answering tough questions can depend on personalities. Those witnesses trying to evade a question get members in a snarl."

– Senator Finlay MacDonald (PC), Interview, May 21, 1997

Answering questions at committee requires skill. The situation requires tact, indeed, when you must respond to a committee's call for "persons, papers, and records." (See "Understanding the Authority 'to Send,'" Chapter Four.) The section below offers some guidance in answering questions and delivering your testimony.

WHAT TO DO

Responding to Members' Questions

- Witnesses must answer all questions posed to them.[10] Answers are not always black or white.
- Being familiar with the committee's Orders of Reference should give you the context in which to respond.
- Members can sense weakness in a witness's faltering presentation. As generalists, members are frequently deferential to the expertise of witnesses. However, if the witness contradicts himself, or is unclear, or the statistics are suspect, then members can be relentless in exposing you. The witness may quickly lose credibility. This is why it is imperative to (i) understand where members' potential concerns may lie; (ii) stick to your "key messages"; and (iii) ensure that any use of statistics is accurate or that your story is plausible.

Brevity

"I remind all questioners to make their questions brief and the minister to make his answers brief."

> – Lyle Vanclief (L), Chair, Standing Committee on Agriculture
> and Agri-Food, December 12, 1996

- When answering, be brief.

Working It Out

- When you are facing tough questioning in a highly charged atmosphere, your capacity to explain and be reasonable will be your life jacket. Sometimes this may involve working with members to pinpoint exactly the issue of concern.

"You have to go to individual committee members and ask them what they really want to know. What's behind their interest? You want to point out the implications of where they may be headed. You will want to point out alternative ways of how they can get there."

> – The Hon. Doug Peters (L), former Secretary of State,
> International Financial Institutions, Interview, June 9, 1997

Get Back in Writing

- If you get a question that takes you off guard, or if you do not have a position/opinion on the matter at hand, take the question "under advisement." Pledging to get back to the committee in writing enables you to offer a more thoughtful answer.

"I'm happy and anxious to answer all these questions, but I'm just looking at my watch. I could provide them in writing. I would rather talk with you about them, but the time is almost up."

> – The Hon. Art Eggleton (L), Minister for International Trade,
> Standing Committee on Foreign Affairs and International Trade,
> April 10, 1997

- In offering to get back to the committee, you do not want to be perceived as avoiding the matter. Use this approach judiciously.

  "… I look forward to your written response, but I think you're ducking the question…"
  – John Solomon (NDP), Standing Committee on Industry,
  February 11, 1997

Work as a Team
- Use the "tag team" approach. If there are two or three of you representing your organization, one of you can offer a general reply. This gives your colleague time to think of a supplementary comment.

> **TIP** When consulting your colleagues at the table, remember that the microphones may be turned on (usually the red light signals a live mike). Whispers can be picked up if there is a lull in the conversation and the mike is on.

- They ask about apples, you talk about oranges. This is not to suggest you dismiss the question; rather, you want to get your key messages across.

Appeal to the Chair
- Members can call into question your personal integrity or the credibility of your organization and may level totally unfounded allegations against you. Do not rise to the bait. Reply to the member only through the chair. The chair is responsible for keeping order and decorum during the proceedings. In fact, the Standing Orders require the chair to "maintain order."[11] You can appeal to the chair for fairness and for keeping it relevant.

  "I always advise my members that if some question is too personal then appeal to the chair about its relevance."
  – Association President, Interview, July 9, 1997

- If ever a member declares that you are in "breach of privilege" because of something you have done or not done, it appears that the most immediate course of action would be to appeal to the chair for thoughtful consideration of the situation.

> "The good judgement of the Chairman is one of the most important protections enjoyed either by witnesses or by third parties whom witnesses mention."
>
> – Katharine Dunkley and Bruce Carson, Library of Parliament Research Branch, 1986[12]

Appeal to the Committee, Too
- Should a member pose a question that is clearly difficult for you, you can get out of the tentacles of a persistent member by throwing yourself to the will of the majority. The prospect of this working may very well depend on whether members feel that the witness has treated the committee with respect.

> "The witnesses from the SIRC [Security Intelligence Review Committee] literally don't give a hoot about the members of Parliament elected by the people of Canada… I think [they] really should review the fundamentals of the parliamentary system and learn to show respect."
>
> – François Langlois (BQ), Subcommittee on National Security, June 20, 1995

Explain and Be Respectful
- Witnesses can make a solid case for not answering a question. (The right tone helps, too.) Says one parliamentary authority, "A witness who is unwilling to answer a question, after stating the reason for desiring to be excused from answering, may appeal to the Chair whether in the circumstances, for the reason stated, an answer should be given."[13] Arrogant behaviour on the part of the witness would surely isolate him or her from moderate committee members who may even be willing to temper a colleague's insistence for inappropriate information.

Correct the Record
- Nasty words or misrepresentations can sometimes be thrown around the table. If necessary, you can send a letter to the committee to correct the record afterwards. Still, what is said in committee (by members or witnesses) is protected by privilege: meaning you cannot sue for defamation.

> "On occasion, unfounded or unfair allegations may be made and widely publicized or damaging information may be exposed, with no recourse available to those whose reputations suffer."
> – Katharine Dunkley and Bruce Carson, Library of Parliament Research Branch, February 1986[14]

Strike from the Record
- If a statement is highly inflammatory and personal, you might ask that it be stricken from the record. However, this is rarely done, and a witness should think very hard before asking that anything be stricken.

Restrict the Use or Dissemination of Information
- If highly sensitive information is to be tabled, the witness can ask the chair that such evidence not be published.[15] A witness could suggest revealing sensitive information to the chair only.[16]

Go In Camera
> "… I'd like to remind my friend that it's not for the protection of the committee … that we go into in-camera meetings. It's for the protection of witnesses who may wish to appear before us and provide information that they don't necessarily want to …"
> – Mike Scott (R), Standing Committee on Aboriginal Affairs and Northern Development, October 2, 1997

- If the committee agrees, going in camera allows information to be delivered to the committee protected from the public's view. This can be an option more suitable for answering incriminating or highly confidential information or if the subject matter involves a pending or ongoing criminal trial.[17] Asking to go in camera without real cause may be treated as suspect by committee members.

- When meeting in camera, witnesses should ask the chair in advance whether the evidence/testimony of such a meeting will be eventually circulated.

Choose Your Words Wisely

"I cannot guarantee you that the information you put on the record will not be used [by the public]. I don't have the power to do that."

– Raymond Bonin (L), Chair, Standing Committee on
Aboriginal Affairs and Northern Development, March 18, 1997

- Answering questions is on the public record. Carefully choose your words.

Special Considerations for Public Servants: Matters of Policy

"With the greatest respect … I don't think it's appropriate at this point for me or my colleagues to enter into a debate about that policy. We are here to assist, if we can, with these regulations."

– Richard Mosley, Assistant Deputy Minister, Department of
Justice, Subcommittee on Draft Regulations on Firearms,
February 6, 1997

- In addition to keeping the above points in mind, public servants must always walk a fine line. They can explain policy decisions but not interpret them or debate them. These should be left to the minister.[18]

- Internal advice to staff appearing before committees:
  1. give straight answers;
  2. respect the committee;
  3. avoid controversy and partisanship;
  4. Avoid the "divergent views" question (never support an alternative policy position on which the department has yet to decide).[19]

Accountability
- Deputy ministers are advised that they should acknowledge an error before committee, and how it was fixed, if a matter falls under their responsibility.[20]

Keep "QP" in Mind

"You're exposed. You make a gaffe, and you have to prepare a QP card for the minister the next day."

— Departmental official, Interview, November 28, 1996

- What is said by a public servant in committee could rebound. An exchange here could prompt an opposition member to raise an issue in Question Period. (A "QP card" refers to a briefing note prepared for a minister to handle a question during Question Period.)
- Officials should inform the department's parliamentary relations officer (or the minister's office) about upcoming appearances.[21] They should receive a copy of your opening statement.[22]

Respect Official Languages

"People who hold important positions in the Public Service must be bilingual or at least make an effort along this line. Personally, when I am in English Canada, I always or nearly always speak in English, although I am not an anglophone."

— Osvaldo Nunez (BQ), Standing Committee on Citizenship and Immigration, March 11, 1997

- Members will expect public servants to address the committee in both official languages, or at least make the effort.

SECTION FOUR Questioning Scenarios

Here is a sampling of questions that could be launched at you.

SITUATION ONE: THE POLITICAL LOB

"There are concerns … that you have fairly strong Liberal connections—contributions perhaps, party membership, I'm not sure—that you are a confidante and friend of the minister."

— Elwin Hermanson (R), Standing Committee on Agriculture and Agri-Food, December 21, 1995

✅ **TIP** Be ready for the political lob. The member may be looking to shake your confidence, establish a potential conflict of interest, or undermine your credibility.

Your personal political involvement or affiliation should be irrelevant. Our political system depends on participation in the political process. You can acknowledge your political affiliation or not, but you should politely remind the committee that the real issue is to discuss the topic of the hearing.

SITUATION TWO: THE CONSTITUENT ANECDOTE

"I just want to put something on the record that might assist you in understanding members of Parliament, where they are coming from and our constituency... This letter came to me just recently, I think for the sake of confidentiality I won't release who it is, but it's typical of the kind of things that come to us. This lady says..."

– Felix Holtmann (PC), Chair, Standing Committee on
Consumer and Corporate Affairs, November 6, 1991

✅ **TIP** An anecdote lends credibility to the member's point. You can't be expected to know the specifics. Speak to the principal issue underlying the grievance. Deal with personal anecdotes "off-line" and offer to look into it following the hearing.

SITUATION THREE: STATISTICS

"Am I missing something on this context, or are we going on a wing and a prayer here on these numbers? Do you have backup that can be substantiated to support all the numbers you have brought forward?"

– Senator Ronald Ghitter (PC), The Special Senate Committee
on the Cape Breton Development Corporation, May 27, 1996

✅ **TIP** If you use statistics at committee, be prepared to substantiate them. Pledge to get back to the committee with the appropriate source if it isn't readily at hand.

SITUATION FOUR: TABLING SURVEYS

"I just want to point out to the witness that, if you're going to introduce a public opinion survey, either you introduce it or you don't. You don't introduce it and say it's proprietary."

– David Walker (L), Chair, Standing Committee on Industry,

February 11, 1997

> ✅ **TIP** Be prepared to make a survey available to the committee, if you refer to one.

SITUATION FIVE: BUREAUCRATIC COMPLAINING

"You made some mysterious allusion to great confrontations within the federal bureaucracy. We'd like to have some of the dirt on that one… If there's something we can do to address it, we will."

– Roger Simmons (L), Chair, Standing Committee on Health,

December 12, 1995

> ✅ **TIP** Exercise caution in complaining publicly about the bureaucracy; you may need it in the future. On the other hand, if the officials are "blocking" your efforts to move forward on a file, the committee should know if a matter is being stalled and may be encouraged to assist you.

SITUATION SIX: FOLLOW-UP REQUESTS

"I have some other questions here. I do not want to mention that on television. I will give you some information personally. Most of it concerns DFO and how they are treating some of the people and the fishermen, especially the Natives. Perhaps I can give you that later, and you can answer it by letter."

– Senator Willie Adams (L), Standing Senate Committee on

Fisheries and Oceans, December 7, 2004

> ✅ **TIP** When asked to supply further information, there is really only one answer: "Yes, we would be pleased to."

SITUATION SEVEN: GOVERNMENT FUNDING AND YOUR CREDIBILITY

"I want to ask what has changed for you since 1986. Is it the $2 million bail-out you got from the department...?"

– Don Boudria (L), Standing Committee on Consumer and Corporate Affairs and Government Operations, June 27, 1989

> **TIP** Directed at a consumer group, the suggestion that government funding had compromised its position on a variety of public policy issues was rejected by the group's representative. If you have received government funding or a grant, being transparent is important. Be prepared to establish your credibility by demonstrating what positions your group has taken.

SITUATION EIGHT: BEING CUT OFF

"... I appreciate that you came all the way from Richmond [BC], but you've had a 20 minute presentation so far... Unfortunately, there are time constraints and the members do have other committees or responsibilities they have to get to."

– Eleni Bakopanos (L), Chair, Standing Committee on Citizenship and Immigration, November 30, 1995

> **TIP** No matter how far you have travelled, time constraints affect everyone. Apologize for taking up so much time. Ask for one minute more to conclude. Cease reading your text and quickly summarize your key message(s).

SITUATION NINE: POLITICAL BIAS

"I want to know what your political or philosophic bent is. Are you one of these raving socialists like we have over here, or do you lean more towards the capitalist...?"

– Leon Benoit (R), Standing Committee on Finance,

May 16, 1996

> **TIP** When faced with a question as to his political leanings, this university professor replied appropriately that his academic publications are open to scrutiny. He then moved on to talk about the issue at hand. Stay focused so you can address your key messages, whatever the question.

SITUATION TEN: GIVE THEM RECOMMENDATIONS

"What is the one thing, if all else failed, that you think we could include in our first report or be the subject of our first report, which would have the greatest effect?"

> – Senator Tommy Banks (L), Chair, Standing Senate Committee
> on Energy, the Environment and Natural Resources,
> December 9, 2004

> **TIP** Don't blow an opportunity to table some useful ideas.

SITUATION ELEVEN: FROM THEORY TO PRACTICE

"… I've seen people who have developed things in theory. They look like a million bucks, but in practice they aren't worth 50¢."

> – Bernie Collins (L), Standing Committee on Citizenship and
> Immigration, November 28, 1995

> **TIP** Grand ideas look good on paper. Members want a practical assessment. Be ready to spell out how your idea will truly work (whom it will affect and what it will cost).

SITUATION TWELVE: ARE YOU WELL BRIEFED?

"The clearer your answer to this question, the better friends we will be. You know that I tabled a bill concerning humanitarian access to drugs… Would you be willing to commit [the association] to supporting that bill...? Some members of your association are extremely open and generous, while others have reacted very negatively."

– Réal Ménard (BQ), Standing Committee on Industry,

March 6, 1997

TIP You should be aware of any other parliamentary activity being driven by individual members on the committee, such as a relevant private member's bill. Still, if asked, you can "take it under consideration." The member will expect you to submit your position when it becomes available.

SITUATION THIRTEEN: THE OPTICS OF GENDER

"[Sir], something bothers me. I am terribly sorry to interrupt you so early in the thing [opening remarks], but all I see is an array of men here."

– Chuck Cook (PC), Chair, Standing Committee on Privileges

and Elections, November 29, 1990

TIP There were four men sitting at the table representing the Canadian Broadcasting Corporation. Its president actually pointed to a female colleague sitting in the audience to demonstrate supposedly that the CBC entourage was not all-male. This witness also went on the offensive and pointed out the ratio of men to women on the standing committee itself. Whether you perceive a double standard or not, you are the witness, and taking a shot at the committee will not endear you to the committee members. Be aware of how you are perceived by members.

SITUATION FOURTEEN: KNOW WHAT WAS TABLED IN THE PROCESS

"I appreciate the opportunity to answer the questions that might come forward ... Some of these questions have been raised by at least one party in the House of Commons and, of course, the debates that occurred at second reading, at report stage, and at third reading."

– The Hon. Joseph Volpe (L), Minister of Human Resources and

Skills Development, Standing Senate Committee on Banking,

Trade and Commerce, December 8, 2004

> 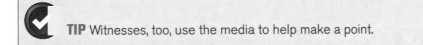 **TIP** Know what's been said at other stages of the bill—it will help you to be better prepared.

SITUATION FIFTEEN: WHAT'S IN THE NEWS? (PART ONE)

"I was just reading in the *Chronicle-Herald* about a situation where the debit cards that customers use to pay for whatever goods or services often show the entire number of the card on the receipt. In your opinion, is this a breach of the act, to allow that information to be exposed openly on a receipt?"

> – Art Hanger (CPC), Standing Committee on Access to
> Information, Privacy and Ethics, December 1, 2004

> **TIP** Members read the same papers you do; what's in the news could be the subject of a question to you.

SITUATION SIXTEEN: WHAT'S IN THE NEWS? (PART TWO)

"… I took a clipping out of *The Vancouver Sun* last week. It talks about discrimination and harassment in the Department of Fisheries and Oceans. I brought that along only to make the point that…"

> – A witness, Standing Senate Committee on Fisheries and Oceans,
> December 7, 2004

> **TIP** Witnesses, too, use the media to help make a point.

SITUATION SEVENTEEN: YOUR PRIORITIES

"I know the Coast Guard is responsible for a tremendous number of activities, but if as the head of the Coast Guard now you were asked to pick the three issues that you feel most important for the Coast

Guard to address, to be responsible for in this country, what would they be?"

> – Loyola Hearn (CPC), Standing Committee on Fisheries and
> Oceans, October 28, 2004

TIP Members want to know your priorities. Be ready to deliver for them.

SITUATION EIGHTEEN: PREDICTABLE QUESTIONS

"I will end on one question at which my colleagues will groan because I ask it everywhere."

> – Senator Michael Meighen (CPC), Standing Senate Committee
> on National Security and Defence, December 2, 2004

TIP Members often have pet questions. If you have monitored the hearings, you should have no excuse but to be ready for it (but don't roll your eyes when you hear it).

SITUATION NINETEEN: "WHAT IFS"

"I have a hypothetical question for you. Given the scope of the corruption associated with the Sponsorship Program, if you had the authority at this time to lay criminal charges, would you be able to do so, in light of the facts you have uncovered?"

> – Benoît Sauvageau (BQ), Standing Committee on Public Accounts,
> February 12, 2004

TIP Parry what-if questions. As the witness, the auditor general replied to this one that she doesn't like to answer hypothetical questions. She also noted that responsibility rests with the RCMP and the courts to pursue such a course.

SITUATION TWENTY: KNOW WHOM YOU ARE UP AGAINST

"I had the honour of being the minister of fisheries ... Can you be candid with us?"

> – Senator Pierre De Bané (L), Standing Senate Committee on
> Fisheries and Oceans, November 4, 2004

> ✓ **TIP** Getting a sense of the members' backgrounds is a good idea. Otherwise, you might get caught replying to an answer that could invite a highly informed retort.

SITUATION TWENTY-ONE: THE LAST WITNESS TO TESTIFY

"There's a lot of pressure on you—I want you to know that—because this is the very last day we will be hearing witnesses. So it's all up to you. This is your chance to make a big impression on this committee."

> – Jim Hart (R), Standing Committee on National Defence and
> Veterans Affairs, December 7, 1995

> ✓ **TIP** Being the last witness presents you with an opportunity to offer a rebuttal to a previous witness's testimony, and it enables you to offer concluding commentary before the committee turns to writing its report.

Particularly for Public Servants:
SITUATION TWENTY-TWO: IMPLEMENTING THE GOVERNMENT'S AGENDA

"A couple of you are ADMs [assistant deputy ministers]. I'm told that ADMs make the government move forward at a practical level. I want to ask you the question whether the department has developed specific action plans ... that are being developed to put into reality what was put forward in the throne speech?"

> – Andy Mitchell (L), Chair, Standing Committee on Natural
> Resources, May 9, 1996

> ✅ **TIP** Members are curious about what the public service is doing to implement the government's agenda. An informative answer should not let members down.

SITUATION TWENTY-THREE: THE CONSULTATIVE PROCESS

"I know you think I am being difficult, but I am trying to be practical here… It does not make much sense for us to have a consultation on that subject without knowing what the process is… The political implications and the public policy implications and the business implications rest in the details, not in the objectives."

– Senator Michael Kirby (L), Chair, Standing Senate Committee
on Banking, Trade and Commerce, July 3, 1996

> ✅ **TIP** Announcing a consultation process may lead members to question officials about what preliminary work has been done to understand the impact of policy changes on the marketplace. In this case, the officials pledged to supply further information to the committee after consultations with industry groups.

SITUATION TWENTY-FOUR: WHO'S IN FAVOUR? WHO'S AGAINST?

"When a bill is introduced, I always pay a lot of attention to the opposition that is voiced to the bill. When there is no opposition, which is the case here, there is a risk that it can get passed very quickly. The people who should have opposed it then start turning up when the work is over, and that is when the problems begin… Do you know if anyone is against it?"

– Raymond Bonin (L), Standing Committee on Transport,
October 28, 2004

> ✅ **TIP** Officials should reassure members that due process was taken to prepare a bill.

SITUATION TWENTY-FIVE: DEALING WITH THE SENATE

"That is not acceptable. You people are paid very handsome salaries not to make those kinds of junior-civil-servant mistakes which exclude certain members of Parliament from a list… I hope you are not trying to shield the minister who may have given a direct order to deliberately exclude senators. I want to know."

– Senator Gerald Comeau (PC), Standing Senate Committee on
Social Affairs, Science and Technology, October 24, 1996

TIP Senators don't like to be left out. Have they been treated by the department in the same way as members of the House?

SITUATION TWENTY-SIX: TATTLING

"In ten seconds, tell me, which is the worst department?"

– Jim Silye (R), Standing Committee on Procedure and House Affairs,
December 5, 1996

TIP This was posed to a senior public servant who respectfully replied that parliamentary scrutiny should be focused on the business plan of the department and not on such subjective measures. Avoid making judgemental comments.

SITUATION TWENTY-SEVEN: BEING RESPONSIVE

"I have a concern … that, when officials come before the committee, they often say they don't have the information we need. Then we ask them to undertake to provide it to us, but that kind of never happens."

– Diane Ablonczy (CPC), Standing Committee on Citizenship
and Immigration, October 20, 2004

TIP This member suggested that the clerk keep track of such information requests. So should you.

Before going to committee, it is prudent to ensure that there are no outstanding requests from members.

SITUATION TWENTY-EIGHT: *Mea culpa*

"… I'm just letting you know that we were most disturbed to find that the presentation offered by the Department of Fisheries and Oceans in Vancouver was in one official language only, in this case English…"

– Tom Wappel (L), Chair, Standing Committee on Fisheries and Oceans, December 14, 2004

> ✓ **TIP** The witness, a deputy minister, had only one response: "On behalf of the department, I apologize. You certainly can be assured I will do my utmost to ensure it doesn't happen again."

SITUATION TWENTY-NINE: THE BOOK OF RIGHT AND WRONG

"In your mind, is the rule book clear for public servants as to what's right and what's wrong when you're working for the Government of Canada?"

– Brian Fitzpatrick (CPC), Standing Committee on Public Accounts, December 2, 2004

> ✓ **TIP** Asked during an inquiry into the Sponsorship Program, this public servant noted that she adhered to the ethics policy. In this era of increased scrutiny, knowing the policies—even if you always adhered to them in practice and in spirit—is just a good idea.

SITUATION THIRTY: CONGRATULATIONS ON YOUR APPOINTMENT

"You understand that qualified cronies are still simply going to be perceived as cronies."

– Joe Preston (CPC), Standing Committee on Government Operations and Estimates, December 2, 2004

> ✓ **TIP** By being selected as the head of a Crown agency or board, some members might start from the premise that your appointment stemmed from a personal or professional connection to a minister. Presumably your qualifications should stand on their own, and be prepared to demonstrate how.

SITUATION THIRTY-ONE: WHAT HAVE YOU DONE WITH THE $?

"You seem to be in the hot seat this evening. I am not clear on what percentage of funds you have disbursed from what you have received from
the government to date."

– Senator Percy Downe (L), Standing Senate Committee on
National Finance, February 2, 2005

> **TIP** Federally funded agencies and foundations can expect very
> specific questions about their budgets. Know your numbers.

NO QUESTIONS

"When there are no questions, it's because we know everything or we
don't know very much and don't want to be embarrassed."

– Raymond Bonin (L), Chairman, Standing Committee on Aboriginal
Affairs and Northern Development, October 31, 1996

You might get few, if any, questions. Members may simply be exhausted if
they have been sitting for hours. They may also have a string of other witnesses to hear and just don't have time to engage you. Or, if you are a
highly controversial witness, members may feel uncomfortable giving you
any more of a platform.

SECTION FIVE The Media: Eyes and Ears

"Don't be McKenna'd"

– Laura Peck, Vice-President, Barry McLoughlin Associates Inc.,
Interview, June 1, 2005

Despite 90 minutes of committee deliberations, media coverage can focus
exclusively on what's said just outside the committee doors.

"PM to say 'no' to missile shield—McKenna's musings that we'd already
joined U.S. defense program force Martin's hand."

– Front page headline, *The Ottawa Citizen*, February 23, 2005[23]

If media are present, always assume you are being taped, even though a formal interview may not have started. The same holds true after the interview ends. A stupid, off-the-cuff comment can become the news story.

> "'An imbecile, an idiot, a perfect idiot [that's what Indian Affairs Minister Ron] Irwin is,' Mr. Bouchard said ... before yesterday's cabinet meeting, apparently unaware that microphones on television cameras were picking up his comments."
>
> – "Bouchard says Irwin 'An Idiot,'" by Rhéal Séguin,
> *The Globe and Mail,* February 15, 1996, A1

Reporters can remain in the room during the proceedings. They may sit at the designated media tables or in the audience. The media can cover your hearing without even being in the room. Reporters (and other members) can get the audio feed of public committee proceedings and listen for anything newsworthy.

So *always* assume that the media are either in the audience or are plugging into the proceedings.

The media spread your message. Newspaper articles on the hearing could be "clipped" and reproduced in the internal clippings package delivered to all members the next day.

Don't flatter yourself; hearings can get covered simply because there is little else going on around town. The flip side: a hearing can get bumped by a competing news story, such as a ministerial announcement. Media interest in a hearing can be unpredictable.

 **WHAT TO DO**

• Smile, you may be on camera.

> "It's amazing the number of smart witnesses who feel like deer caught in the headlights when reporters' microphones are thrust under their noses outside the committee room. Be ready to drive your messages again. This is part of the performance. It's like being called back for an encore."
>
> – Laura Peck, Vice-President, Barry McLoughlin Associates Inc.,
> Interview, September 22, 1997

- An hour of testimony can be displaced by a 10-second clip in a media interview following the hearing (and this becomes the "story"!). Your media and committee messages should be consistent. Make a conscious decision about what key message you are delivering inside and outside the committee.
- Media like numbers: survey results offer a crisp indication of a situation that they can quote.
- Get media relations training.
- Tape-record interviews (particularly if the issue is highly controversial).
- Have a spokesperson to handle interviews in both official languages.
- Make yourself accessible. One association president even encourages its spokespeople to make their home telephone numbers available following a hearing.
- Post your opening remarks and/or your submission on your webpage the moment you appear. Reporters can access it without having to chase down your employees for it.
- But don't look to the Internet to do your work for you. One reporter complained that downloading and printing information take up valuable time. Telephone and e-mail key reporters to alert them to your messages.
- Reporters might appreciate getting your submission in advance or, at least, an indication of your key arguments. (They may also be interested in getting a telephone call from you informing them about the time and date of your appearance.) Getting information to reporters may involve a pre-meeting. It's in your best interest to have reporters understand your key messages and the nuances. A columnist may even want to cover your issue even before you appear. But make sure that committee members do not think that the media are receiving preferential treatment.

Your Press Release
- A press release should be snappy. What is your "headline"? Echo your main points to be delivered at committee that day.
- Release your press statement only when you know that the hearing is actually proceeding. It would look a little funny trumpeting what you told parliamentarians when the committee meeting was postponed.

> ✅ **TIP** Some witnesses use media coverage to publicize a relevant toll-free telephone number or webpage address to a national audience, but don't abuse the opportunity. You're there to address parliamentarians, not advertise.

FOR YOUR EYES ONLY—ARE YOU SURE?

> "[The chair is] not a particularly dynamic or engaging character… Do not look to him for guidance or assistance with pressure situations."
> – "Tips help airline's boss avoid political turbulence," Mark MacKinnon, *The Globe and Mail,* May 10, 2001, A5

This is not likely the sort of media coverage you want.

 **WHAT TO DO**

- While at committee, just assume that the person sitting beside or behind you is not on your side. (In the quote above, this reporter apparently managed to scan these notes in plain view as they were passed back and forth to an aide behind the witness table.) Even better, don't bring such candid crib notes to committee.
- Also don't throw out any notes you took in wastebaskets in or around the committee room—they can be "retrieved." It's happened.

SECTION SIX Final Steps and a Follow-Up Checklist

YOUR HEARING IS OVER

There are a few things to keep in mind as you wrap up your testimony.

WHAT TO DO

- Thank the chair and the committee for the opportunity to have presented your case.
- Before leaving the committee table, ensure you have all your briefing binders and private notes.
- When you are in the last minutes of your testimony, be thinking of possible media interviews to follow.

FORGETTING THE FOLLOW-UP IS FATAL

"We believe the work of your predecessors was excellent and if it had been acted upon we wouldn't be here today. We don't want to grow cynical ... so I appeal to you that your work receive the appropriate attention and follow-up so that we may continue to have faith in our parliamentary system."

— Marie Smallface-Marule, President, Red Crow Community College,
Subcommittee on Aboriginal Education,
October 17, 1995

The hearing is over. But the game is not finished.

The media's take on the day has yet to be seen, heard, or read. Other witnesses may have their turn. The report has yet to be hammered out. The bill has yet to pass.

You can't just go to committee, drop your key messages, and leave. There is more to be done.

Despite all your efforts, recognize that, at the end of the day, perhaps only small victories are possible.

"The parliamentary process is not about making major changes. Focus on the small victories. The government doesn't have a whole lot of room to manoeuvre on issues. If you focus on small things to change, then participating in committee hearings becomes palatable."

— Lynn Toupin, Executive Director, The National
Anti-Poverty Organization, Interview, June 4, 1997

WHAT TO DO
Your Follow-Up Checklist

(a) Immediately following the hearing (within an hour or so), and depending on the situation, consider these points:

❑ Do you actively seek out the media to get your views aired?

❑ Before you forget, what information requests were made by committee members during your testimony?

❑ If a matter is controversial, is there a need to advise staff of the relevant minister about what transpired at the committee?

> ✓ **TIP** Retain copies of any media coverage of your hearing. Extracts can be reproduced in your group's newsletter or annual report to profile what you are doing in Ottawa.

(b) Within 24 hours:

❑ Prepare a synopsis of your appearance and send it to your association or group.

❑ What additional information/data are needed to send to the committee to reinforce your messages?

❑ Is a follow-up meeting with members necessary?

> "Unfortunately, I missed one presentation and part of another but I will catch up with the blues."
>
> – Francine Lalonde (BQ), Standing Committee on Foreign Affairs and International Trade, February 22, 2005

❑ You can review the transcript or unrevised floor text of your committee testimony (known as the "blues") to check for any minor errors (e.g., on terminology). The blues may be available a day or two after the hearing, but that depends on the committee. Consult the committee clerk about electronically accessing the blues. Any "important" changes to the record can be made only with a motion adopted in the committee.[24]

❑ The next day, assess media coverage of your appearance, if any, and determine whether your messages got across to the media. If they misrepresent what was said, consider your options (e.g., sending a letter to the editor to correct the record).

❑ Would other witnesses, who are favourably disposed to your position, benefit from getting a debriefing from you on your experience at committee to help them prepare (e.g., key questions)?

(c) After 24 hours:

"I think the inability of committee members to be able to access written copy of witnesses' testimony within a short period of time is just unacceptable ... I want to be able to read what witnesses said at the committee that I wasn't at. They're about two weeks behind."

– Wayne Easter (L), Standing Committee on Fisheries and Oceans,
November 4, 1997

Often, assessing what happened at committee requires having an actual copy of the transcript. It is frustrating to wait for the on-line version, which is not generally available in timely fashion. This can curtail your follow-up.

❑ Depending on the urgency of the matter, a brief letter could be sent to the chair thanking the committee for the opportunity to appear. Few witnesses do so. By reinforcing your key points, a letter can also include any additional information that was not tabled at the hearing. Or it can address a question that may not have been adequately answered by you during your testimony. You might want to hold off sending a letter until other witnesses appear.

❑ Talk with a few committee members and get their feedback on your testimony.

> **TIP** Correspondence sent to the chair should be copied to the committee clerk. The clerk will then copy all members of the committee.

There are various courses to pursue after the hearing (depending on the stage of the bill or whether the matter is a subject inquiry). Some examples are given below.

If a bill:

Clause-by-Clause Review

"We naively expected that at least some of the concerns brought forward by the public-sector unions and other interest groups would be reflected in the proposed amendments to this piece of legislation. However, the report to the House of Commons contained absolutely no amendments and no reference to the submission."

> – Steve Hindle, President, Professional Institute of the Public
> Sector of Canada, Standing Senate Committee on National
> Finance, June 13, 1996

❑ For legislation, clause-by-clause review of a bill can occur on the heels of the last witness. (See "Word for Word ... Clause by Clause," and "In and out of Committee," Chapter Four.) Whenever it is scheduled, clause-by-clause stage is critical as members may change the wording of the bill. You don't want your points left out.

Report Stage

❑ At report stage, the committee reports the bill with or without amendments. Substantive changes can be made in either chamber prior to third reading. This may present additional opportunities to press for your case. (See "Report Stage," Chapter Four.)

❑ If the committee has reviewed the bill prior to second reading, your efforts should not cease simply because you have had your say at the hearing. (See "Reference to Committee before Second Reading," Chapter Four.)

❑ If the bill has originated in the House and has completed all stages there, attention now shifts to the Senate. (See "Three Down, Three to Go (Senate Phase)," Chapter Four.)

Proclamation
- ❏ There are implementation issues to consider once the bill is proclaimed. (See "Royal Assent and Proclamation," Chapter Four.)

Regulation-Writing Phase
"Once the act is proclaimed, if you are not happy with the regulations, you certainly have recourse to the minister and the government to make your dissatisfaction known. I would be the first one to encourage you to do just that."

> – Senator Eymard Corbin (L), Standing Senate Committee on
> National Finance, June 22, 1994

- ❏ Even after the bill has passed all stages, you might pay attention to the regulation-writing phase. (See "Regulations," Chapter Four.)

If a subject inquiry:
Report-Drafting Stage
- ❏ The committee may need your follow-up information promptly as it moves to report writing (if one is being written). (See "Their Report Options," Chapter Four.)
- ❏ After the inquiry, recommendations are chiselled from perhaps hundreds of pages of testimony and submissions. Additional meetings with members may be needed to ensure that members understand your messages and reflect these in the report (and recommendations).

Presenting the Report
- ❏ If the committee has presented a report, consider writing to the committee to express your views on its conclusions. Letting the committee have the last word, or leaving recommendations unchallenged, may not be in your best interest. Members and other interest groups may recycle the recommendations to bolster a point down the road; e.g., committee members may be lobbying their caucus colleagues and ministers to adopt their recommendations.

> ❑ The committee may hold a press conference after presenting its report. (See "Press Conferences and Publicity," Chapter Four.)
> ❑ Write directly to the appropriate minister. The government may be formally replying to the committee's report within 120 days. (See "120 Days to Respond," Chapter Four.) Include departmental officials in your correspondence.

Some groups conduct a more thorough post-mortem on the entire lobbying process (and not only of the committee appearance) once a bill has been proclaimed or an inquiry has ended. This allows for a more thoughtful scrutiny of what was done right and wrong in pursuing the group's objectives.

Your formal committee contact has come to an end. But the spiral of public policy making continues.

TAKING IT TO ANOTHER COMMITTEE

"Just as an aside before I go to the questions, the Senate Committee on Energy, the Environment and Natural Resources is currently conducting a study on sustainable development which you will find germane to what you have just said, and it might be that you will have some interesting evidence to bring before that committee. I suggest that you might contact the clerk of that committee... You will find a warm welcome."

– Senator David Angus (CPC), Deputy Chair, Standing Senate Committee on Banking, Trade and Commerce, December 8, 2004

There can be multiple opportunities to advance your issue. You may have completed only your first stop.

TAKING IT TO THE COURTS

"I don't find it unusual but I find it rather despicable that the tobacco industry would go on that route [to the Quebec Superior Court] after having the opportunity to present their views before committee."

– The Hon. David Dingwall (L), Minister of Health, "Tobacco Ccompanies Fighting Back," *The Globe and Mail,* April 22, 1997, A1

Of course, if you can't get what you want in the legislative forum, you can always consider taking your case to the courts in order to strike down legislation.

ENDNOTES

1. Author's survey of parliamentary researchers, June 1996. Anecdotal evidence since then suggests that the quality of written communication with committees is still an issue.
2. Members can "pair" off if there is a vote in the House in order to remain in the room to hear testimony from witnesses. Pairing allows members on opposite sides of the issue to remain absent from the House during a vote provided they have registered to do so. House of Commons, Table Research Branch, *Précis of Procedure*, 5th ed. (1996), 51.
3. One source states that "It is important to note that a committee is entitled to address any issue within its mandate at any meeting, regardless of the order of business projected for that meeting." House of Commons, *Committees: A Practical Guide*, 5th ed. (1997), 18.
4. *The Globe and Mail*, April 27, 1996, A1.
5. Appending material to the proceedings is no longer as prevalent because of printing costs, notes one source. See Senate of Canada and the Library of Parliament, Economics Research Division, *An Introduction to the Standing Senate Committee on Banking, Trade and Commerce* (January 1994), 16. Committees can, however, determine how they want to proceed with a witness's presentation, which may include appending the brief to the electronic evidence (the version that would then be available on the web); see House of Commons, *A Guide for Witnesses Appearing before Committees of the House of Commons*, House of Commons committee website.
6. For example, in 1994, the Standing Committee on Human Resources' review of social security and unemployment was interupted by some 400 protestors. Al Toulin, "Martin's man?," *The Financial Post*, June 6-8, 1998, 10.
7. Joseph Maingot, *Parliamentary Privilege in Canada* (Canada: Butterworths & Co. Ltd., 1982), 203.
8. Demonstrating the tenor of some hearings: during discussion on the expense claims of a former Canada Post president, one Conservative member charged that he was like a "common thief" in the absence of providing certain business expense receipts. See Daniel LeBlanc, "Ouellet defends expense claims at Canada Post," *The Globe and Mail*, May 18, 2005, A5.
9. Author's survey of parliamentary research officers, May 1996.
10. A. Beauchesne, *Beauchesne's Parliamentary Rules and Forms*, 6th ed. (Toronto: Carswell Co. Ltd., 1989), 239, para. 862.

11. Standing Order 117.

12. Katharine Dunkley and Bruce Carson, *Parliamentary Committees: The Protection of Witnesses, the Role of Counsel, and the Rules of Evidence: Backgrounder*, 14; reproduced quote from Ontario Legislative Assembly, Standing Committee on Procedural Affairs, *Report on Witnesses before Committees*, 4th session, 31st Parliament (1980), 24.

13. Beauchesne, *Parliamentary Rules and Forms*, 239, para. 863.

14. Dunkley and Carson, *Parliamentary Committees*, 2.

15. Beauchesne, *Parliamentary Rules and Forms*, 239, para. 863.

16. Deputy Minister of Justice, *Privileges and Parliamentary Committees*, memorandum no. 168 (April 28, 1995).

17. Dunkley and Carson, *Parliamentary Committees*, 10.

18. As noted in Chapter Three, as officials cannot defend policy decisions, they should not debate policy alternatives with members either. Department of Justice, *Appearances before Parliamentary Committees* (January 16, 1996), 20. Public servants should know when it is needed to have their minister come to committee and speak to policy for himself or herself. Standing Joint Committee for the Scrutiny of Regulations, November 16, 1994, 13.

19. Department of Justice, *Appearances before Parliamentary Committees* (January 16, 1996).

20. Officials should also consult the Privy Council Office document *Guidance for Deputy Ministers* (July 20, 2003), 15, reproduced at www.pco-bcp.gc.ca.

21. Department of Justice, *Appearances before Parliamentary Committees* (January 16, 1996), 15.

22. Senate Committees and Private Legislation Directorate, *Appearances by Public Servants before Senate Committees* (January 1995).

23. Comment made by Frank McKenna, the ambassador-designate to the U.S. following his hearing before the Standing Committee on Foreign Affairs. During the hearing, this declaration was not made. Aileen McCabe and Anne Dawson, *The Ottawa Citizen*, February 23, 2005, A1.

24. Beauchesne, *Parliamentary Rules and Forms*, 233, para. 828.

CHAPTER EIGHT

From Here to There

"From there to here, from here to there, funny things are everywhere."
– Dr. Seuss, *One Fish, Two Fish, Red Fish, Blue Fish*[1]

Ottawa is a flurry of standing committee activity, departmental consultations, caucus work, and private one-on-one meetings between Canadians and parliamentarians.

While there are many ways to channel concerns to government, this book makes one part of the public policy process more transparent: the role of House of Commons and Senate committees. The reason for doing so is clear. Parliamentary committees link Canadians to their parliamentarians. There is simply no other forum for Canadians to hook into the legislative and policy-making process on a regular, formal, and public basis. However, getting a good grasp on committees is no easy matter.

THE NATURE OF COMMITTEES

Parliamentary committees are unique (when compared to other consultative mechanisms). Committee performance is measurable. Did their recommendations or amendments get picked up or not? Committees are (somewhat) accountable. They are, at least, open to public scrutiny (in-camera meetings aside), and their evidence is published. Also, being bound by Standing Orders and conventions, they operate with a certain amount of due process and a level of openness (although a lot goes on behind the scenes).

Knowing procedure and process is helpful, but this may not reveal what can drive committee activity. With apologies to Dr. Seuss, politics *is* everywhere on Parliament Hill. The unseen hand of the whip, minister, or leader's office can shape what committees do or hope to accomplish. Members can coalesce along party lines for a vote (despite the merits of the case). Reports can get sidelined. *Funny things* happen on the Hill. Recognizing the political undercurrents buffeting committees completes the picture.

Things don't always go swimmingly for witnesses. Committees often do what is expedient. With the backing of the majority, a committee can basically do what it pleases, within certain limits. Questioning can take sudden turns from one subject to another. The ebb and flow of members, reporters, and interest groups at committee can alter the dynamic and tone of each meeting. Committee work can be sideswiped by political sniping. Witnesses have to navigate through all of this.

Witnesses, for their part, do not always maximize the opportunities presented at committee. Many expert witnesses are not expert communicators. Harried members need crisp information. This guide provides a shopping list of options and techniques to enhance witness performance.

But coping with or capitalizing on a committee visit requires more. At times, witnesses have to know how to ride out any rough moments and perservere persistent jabs, aggressive questioning, or a reporter's microphone. It's also all about grasping the procedural opportunities. It's about sharpening your key messages and knowing how to deliver them in an upredictable setting. This guide sets the foundation for prospective witnesses to take a series of tactical decisions in managing a parliamentary committee appearance.

Moreover, for many (especially national associations, larger organizations, and public servants), dealing with committees is about managing a long-term relationship. What you say today could have implications for a future visit.

As a rule of thumb, each committee appearance requires a tailored response.

THE ROAD AHEAD

Is the desire by members for more committee authority like raising a teenager's curfew by an hour? Nothing much happens under the new limit that didn't already occur under the old, but the emboldened teenager now presses for an even later curfew.

The recent history of parliamentary standing committees is that members want more: they want more respect, seek more independence, and desire a more relevant policy role. The pressure to want more is inevitable.

While this book is not about assessing committee performance, it is apparent, however, that committees have considerable scope to tackle just about any matter as it is. Their formal authorities assure it. Plus, a unified committee, dedicated to a common purpose with a determined chair, presents a formidable team. (The right issue pursued at the right time helps, too.)

Changes are enabling committees to tweak their performance, such as allowing Senate committees to seek a government response to its reports. Elections of House committee positions mark a progressive milestone. Televised proceedings and enhanced committee websites have improved committee visibility, accessibility, and the quality of information available to Canadians. (But virtual hearings via video-teleconferencing will not supplant physical hearings—members will still prefer to look across the table into the eyes of witnesses.)

Parliamentary committees are a work in progress. They also must continue to work with limitations. Committees are ultimately beholden to the House or Senate chamber. For House committees especially, partisanship often chips away at effectiveness. No committee can wiggle away from the constraints placed on all by the parliamentary calendar. Workloads can be overwhelming: too many public appointees to review, too many estimates to consider, too many public policy issues to engage. Finally, limited funding for research and travel, although improved, curtail, what committees could do.

Still, parliamentary committees will continue to bind Canadians directly to the legislative process, engage their views on the public record, and seize media and political attention on a national platform. The challenge for witnesses is customizing the appearance when so many variables are at work: the issue, the political context, the players, the timing.

A FINAL WORD

No matter what new authorities committees have gained recently—or could gain (or even lose) in the future—and despite the constraints that they work under, one point persists: the calibre of their work depends on the motivation of their members themselves and how they are prepared to take on an issue. For witnesses, this also explains why appearing before a committee is primarily a communications exercise. You have to do your part in making the most of the opportunity. Effective messaging is mission essential.

Testifying is more than reciting a predictable position and serving up polished answers. It is an opportunity to captivate the committee. This alone does not secure success, but it helps to advance your cause one member at a time.

When taking your issue to Parliament Hill involves a visit to a parliamentary committee, this guide marks the necessary steps to get you from here to there.

ENDNOTES

1. Theodore Seuss Geisel, *One Fish, Two Fish, Red Fish, Blue Fish* (Toronto: Random House of Canada, 1988), 9.

List of Standing Committees

House of Commons Standing Order 104(2), (3), and Senate Rule 86(1) dictate that there be the following standing committees:[1]

STANDING COMMITTEES OF THE HOUSE OF COMMONS (21)

Aboriginal Affairs and Northern Development
Access to Information, Privacy and Ethics
Agriculture and Agri-Food
Canadian Heritage
Citizenship and Immigration
Environment and Sustainable Development
Finance
Fisheries and Oceans
Foreign Affairs and International Trade
Government Operations and Estimates
Health
Human Resources, Skills Development, Social Development and the
    Status of Persons with Disabilities
Industry, Natural Resources, Science and Technology
Justice, Human Rights, Public Safety and Emergency Preparedness
Liaison
National Defence and Veterans Affairs
Official Languages

Procedure and House Affairs
Public Accounts
Status of Women
Transport

STANDING COMMITTEES OF THE SENATE (15)

Aboriginal Peoples
Agriculture and Forestry
Banking, Trade and Commerce
Energy, the Environment and Natural Resources
Fisheries and Oceans
Foreign Affairs
Human Rights
Internal Economy, Budgets and Administration
Legal and Constitutional Affairs
National Finance
National Security and Defence
Official Languages
Rules, Procedures and the Rights of Parliament
Social Affairs, Science and Technology
Transport and Communications

JOINT STANDING COMMITTEES (2)

Library of Parliament
Scrutiny of Regulations

ENDNOTES

1. Note that the list of standing committees can change from one Parliament to the next; also, the listing of committees (as portrayed on the committee websites) can include special and subcommittees, not listed here. Finally, also not listed are some obscure joint committees such as those relating to printing and the parliamentary restaurant.

SELECTED BIBLIOGRAPHY

I. PRIMARY SOURCES
A) Government of Canada

Auditor General of Canada. *2004 Report of the Auditor General of Canada, Matters of Special Importance.* News Release. Ottawa, 2004.

Department of Justice. *Appearances before Parliamentary Committees.* Ottawa, January 16, 1996.

———. *Privileges and Parliamentary Committees.* Memorandum No. 168. Deputy Minister of Justice. Ottawa, April 28, 1995.

———. *The Making of Federal Acts and Regulations.* Legislative Services Branch. Ottawa: Public Works and Government Services Canada, 1996.

Information Commissioner of Canada. *The Access to Information Act and Cabinet Confidences: A Discussion of New Approaches.* Ottawa, 1996.

Minister of Supply and Services Canada. *Lobbyist Registration Act: A Guide to Registration.* Ottawa: Industry Canada, January 31, 1996.

Office of the Ethics Counsellor. *Lobbyists' Code of Conduct.* Ottawa, n.d.

Office of the Prime Minister. *Amending Bills at Committee and Report Stage in the House of Commons.* Ottawa: Legislative Services, Parliament of Canada, October 2004.

———. *Democratic Reform.* Ottawa, December 22, 2003. http://www. pm.gc.ca/eng/dem_reform.asp.

————. *Martin Government Tables Democratic Reform Action Plan, Strategy Aims to Reconnect MPs and Canadians with the Political Process.* News Release. Ottawa, February 4, 2004.

Privy Council Office. *Notes on the Responsibilities of Public Servants in Relation to Parliamentary Committees.* Ottawa, December 1990.

————. *Ethics, Responsibility, Accountability, An Action Plan for Democratic Reform.* Ottawa, February 4, 2004. http://www.pco-bcp.gc.ca.

————. *Guidance for Deputy Ministers.* Ottawa, November 27, 2004. http://www.pco-bcp.gc.ca.

————. *Guidance for Deputy Ministers.* Ottawa, July 20, 2003. http://www.pco-bcp.gc.ca.

————. *Guidelines for Preparing Government Responses to Parliamentary Committee Reports.* Ottawa, February 4, 2004. http://www.pco-bcp.gc.ca.

Treasury Board of Canada Secretariat. *Regulatory Process.* Ottawa: Treasury Board of Canada Secretariat Website, July 1998.

I) HOUSE OF COMMONS

Amending Bills at Committee and Report Stages. Ottawa: Legislative Services, House of Commons, October 2004.

Committees and Legislative Services Directorate. *2003-04 Annual Report on Committees Activities and Expenditures.* Ottawa, 2004.

————. *Activities and Expenditures, Annual Report 1997-98.* Ottawa, June 1998.

————. *Activities and Expenditures, Annual Report 1996-97.* Ottawa, September 1997.

————. *Appearing as a Witness before a House of Commons Committee.* House of Commons Website. Ottawa, March 1998.

Committees: A Practical Guide. Seventh Edition. Published under the authority of the Clerk of the House of Commons. Ottawa, October 2004.

Committees Directorate. *So You're Going to Work for a Committee? A Booklet for Contract Staff of the House of Commons Standing Committees.* Ottawa, March 1989.

————. *A Guide for Witnesses Appearing before Committees of the House of Commons.* House of Commons, Ottawa. http://www.parl.gc.ca.

Davidson, Diane. "Presentation to the Standing Committee on Privileges and Elections on the Powers of Parliamentary Committees to Send for Documents." Ottawa: Legal Counsel Office, March 1991.

————. "Presentation of General Legal Counsel to the Standing Joint Committee for the Scrutiny of Regulations on the Powers of Parliamentary Committees." Ottawa: Legal Services, November 16, 1994.

House of Commons Administration. *Reports on Plans and Priorities 2004-05.* Ottawa, Spring 2004.

House of Commons. *House of Commons Procedure and Practice.* Edited by Robert Marleau and Camille Montpetit. Montréal: Chenelière/McGraw-Hill, 2000.

Précis of Procedure. Fifth Edition. Clerk of the House of Commons, Ottawa, 1996.

Robertson, James R. *House of Commons Procedure: Its Reform.* Ottawa: Law and Government Division, Library of Parliament, February 21, 2002.

Speaker of the House of Commons. Standing Orders of the House of Commons. (Consolidated version as of June 30, 2005.) Ottawa: Public Works and Government Services Canada, June 30, 2005. http://www.parl.gc.ca.

————. Standing Orders of the House of Commons. (Consolidated version as of September 1997). Ottawa: Public Works and Government Services Canada, September 1997.

Special Committee on Reform of the House of Commons. *Report of the Special Committee on Reform of the House of Commons.* Ottawa, June 1985.

Standing Committee on Procedure and House Affairs. *The Business of Supply: Completing the Circle of Control.* 64th Report. Ottawa, 1997.

Table Research Branch. *Committees: A Practical Guide.* Fifth Edition. Clerk of the House of Commons, Ottawa, 1997.

II) SENATE

Appearances by Public Servants before Senate Committees. Ottawa, January 1995.

Committees Directorate. *Activities and Expenditures, Annual Report 2003-04.* Ottawa, 2004.

———. *Fundamentals of Senate Committees.* Ottawa, October 2004.

Committees and Private Legislation Directorate. *Senate Committees Activities and Expenditures Annual Report 1996-97.* Ottawa, 1997.

———. *A Guide for Witnesses Appearing before Senate Committees.* Ottawa, January 1994.

Senate of Canada. *Overview of Senate Committees.* Senate Website. 36th Parliament. Ottawa, May 1997. http://www.parl.gc.ca.

———. *Rules of the Senate of Canada.* Ottawa, October 2004.

———. *Rules of the Senate of Canada.* Ottawa, March 1996.

Special Senate Committee on the Pearson Airport Agreements. "The Power to Send for Persons, Papers, and Records: Theory, Practice and Problems." *Report of the Chairman and the Deputy-Chairman, Special Senate Committee on the Pearson Airport Agreements.* Ottawa, 1995.

Standing Committee on Privileges, Standing Rules and Orders. *Companion to the Rules of the Senate of Canada: A Working Document.* Ottawa, 1994.

III) LIBRARY OF PARLIAMENT

Committees and Private Legislation Directorate and Economics Research Division, Library of Parliament. *An Introduction to the Standing Senate Committee on Banking, Trade and Commerce.* Ottawa, January 1994.

Dunkley, Katharine, and Bruce Carson. *Parliamentary Committees: The Protection of Witnesses, the Role of Counsel, and the Rules of Evidence: Backgrounder.* Ottawa: Library of Parliament Research Branch, February 1986.

Stillborn, Jack. "House of Commons Procedure: Its Reform." *Current Issue Review (Revised).* Ottawa: Research Branch, Library of Parliament, September 1992.

II. SECONDARY SOURCES

A) BOOKS

Beauchesne, A. *Beauchesne's Parliamentary Rules and Forms.* Edited by A. Fraser, W. F. Dawson, and J. A. Holtby. Sixth Edition. Toronto: The Carswell Company Limited, 1989.

Erskine May, Thomas. *Erskine May's Treatise on the Law, Privileges, Proceedings and Usage of Parliament.* Edited by C. J. Boulton. 21st Edition. London: Butterworths, 1989.

Lee, Derek. *Back Bench Exercises: Some Procedural Changes and Attitudes to Strengthen Our House.* Ottawa: Self-published, March 2002.

Maingot, Joseph. *Parliamentary Privilege in Canada.* Toronto: Butterworths & Co. (Canada) Ltd., 1982.

———. *Parliamentary Privilege in Canada.* Second Edition. House of Commons and McGill-Queen's University Press, 1997.

B) CHAPTERS/ARTICLES IN BOOKS

Butler, D. B. "The Adequacy of Committee Legislation: The Case of Bill C-83." Edited by J. P. Hurley. In *Canadian House of Commons Observed.* Ottawa: University of Ottawa Press, 1979.

Lindquist, Evert A. "Citizens, Experts and Budgets: Evaluating Ottawa's Emerging Budget Process." Edited by Susan D. Phillips. In *How Ottawa Spends 1994-95: Making Change.* Ottawa: Carleton University Press, 1994.

Seidle, Leslie F. "Interest Advocacy through Parliamentary Channels: Representation and Accommodation." Edited by Leslie F. Seidle. In *Equity & Community: The Charter, Interest Advocacy, and Representation.* Montreal: The Institute for Research on Public Policy, 1993.

Stewart, John. "Procedure in the Trudeau Era." Edited by John Courtney. In *The Canadian House of Commons: Essays in Honour of Norman Ward.* Calgary: University of Calgary Press, 1985.

Thordarson, Bruce. "Foreign Policy and the Committee System." In *Canadian House of Commons Observed.* Edited by J. P. Hurley. Ottawa: University of Ottawa Press, 1979.

C) PERIODICALS

Bryden, John. "The Primacy of Parliament and the Duty of a Parliamentarian." Edited by Gary Levy. *Canadian Parliamentary Review* 28, no. 1 (Spring 2005).

Carstairs, Sharon. "Some Reflections on the Role of Caucus." *Canadian Parliamentary Review* 21, no.1 (Spring 1998).

Charlton, Chris. "Obstruction in Ontario and the House of Commons." *Canadian Parliamentary Review* 20, no. 3 (Autumn 1997).

Dobell, Peter C. "Comments on the Survey of Attitudes to Committee Work." *Parliamentary Government* (Parliamentary Centre for Foreign Affairs and Foreign Trade) 44 (August 1993).

————. "What New MPs Think about the Commons." *Occasional Papers on Parliamentary Government*, no. 1 (September 1996).

————. "Televising Committees." *Occasional Papers on Parliamentary Government*, no. 6 (February 1998).

Franks, C. E. S. "Parliamentarians and the New Code of Ethics." Edited by Gary Levy. *Canadian Parliamentary Review* 28, no. 1 (Spring 2005).

Gauthier, John-Robert. "Accountability, Committees, and Parliament." Edited by Gary Levy. *Canadian Parliamentary Review* 16, no. 2 (Summer 1993).

Good, David. "Parliament and Public Money: Players and Police." Edited by Gary Levy. *Canadian Parliamentary Review* 28, no. 1 (Spring 2005).

Levy, Gary. "Special Senate Committee on Euthanasia and Assisted Suicide." Edited by Gary Levy. *Canadian Parliamentary Review* 19, no. 1 (Spring 1996).

————. "Summoning and Swearing of Witnesses: Experience of the Pearson Airport Committee." Edited by Gary Levy. *Canadian Parliamentary Review* 19, no. 1 (Spring 1996).

Parliamentary Centre. "Parliament and the Private Sector: A Guide to Effective Communications Strategies." Edited by Nicholas Swales. *Parliamentary Government*, nos. 46-47 (June 1994).

Parliamentary Centre for Foreign Affairs and Foreign Trade. "Report of the Liaison Committee of Committee Effectiveness." Edited by Nicholas Swales. *Parliamentary Government*, no. 43 (June 1993).

————. "Committee Effectiveness: Comments on the Report." Edited by

Nicholas Swales. *Parliamentary Government*, no. 44 (August 1993).

———. "Sharing Power?" Edited by Nicholas Swales. *Parliamentary Government*, no. 44 (August 1993).

———. "Effectiveness of Parliamentary Committees." Edited by Paul Thomas. *Parliamentary Government*, no. 44 (August 1993).

Skogstad, Grace. "Interest Groups, Representation, and Conflict Management in the Standing Committees of the House of Commons." *Canadian Journal of Political Science* 18, no. 4 (December 1985).

Steeves, Valerie. "A Town Hall Format for Committee Meetings." *Canadian Parliamentary Review* 20, no. 3 (Autumn 1997).

Strahl, Chuck. "Politics and Procedure in a Minority Government." Edited by Gary Levy. *Canadian Parliamentary Review* 27, no. 4 (Winter 2004).

INDEX

II. GOVERNMENT BACKGROUND & INTERACTION:

III. WITNESS PREPARATION AND INTERACTION: